EDUCATIONAL TECHN

EDUCATIONAL TECHNOLOGY

Ankan Sinha

KALPAZ

First Published 2015

Published by

Kalpaz Publications
C-30, Satyawati Nagar,
Delhi - 110052
E-mail: kalpaz@hotmail.com Ph.: 9212142040

Laser Typesetting : Rajender Vashist, Delhi
Printed at: G. Print Process, Delhi

Cataloguing in Publication Data--DK
Courtesy: D.K. Agencies (P) Ltd. <docinfo@dkagencies.com>

Sinha, Ankan.
Educational technology / Ankan Sinha.
p. cm.
Includes index.
ISBN 9789351280828 (HB)

1. Educational technology. I. Title.

DDC 371.33 23

Dedicated to

My Family

Contents

Foreword

It is great honour to write a foreword to the book written by very young and enthusiastic professional of Physical Education, Dr. Ankan Sinha. He put in very hard work in writing this valuable book on Educational Technology for the physical education under graduate B.P.Ed course as well as for teaching professionals.

The book has been written in a simple language and deals with all aspect of theory as well as practical syllabus of the course.

This book is organised into five units namely, Introduction to Educational Technology, Teaching Aids and Models of learning experience, Art of questioning and answering, Programmed learning and team teaching, New teaching techniques and innovations and System approach and Teaching machines in education respectively.

I congratulate the author of this book for the good work he has done. Professional students of physical education of the Lakshmibai National University of Physical Education, Gwalior, LNIPE Guwahati Regional Centre and the students of General Education will be immensely benefited.

I hope that this useful book will find place in all the libraries of the colleges and universities.

Dr. Sambhunath Rakshit
Principal, Government Degree College,
Dharmanagar, North Tripura

Preface

This book has been written for students and teachers of 'Physical and Health Education' and General Educations of different schools and colleges. The book contains all the quality and relevant education literature and information for the students pursuing courses in Physical education and B.Ed and even for budding teachers. So, an attempt has been made through this book to provide quality, user-friendly information to the professionals and the students. This book will guide the Physical Educationist and students in getting the theoretical as well as practical knowledge of the subject. One can train themselves by having the knowledge through this book. I would like to request my readers to send us their valuable suggestions and comments for further improvement of this book. Such useful suggestions will be incorporate in our next edition.

Keeping all the aspects in mind, this book is divided into five units as Introduction to Educational Technology, Teaching Aids and Models of learning experience, Art of questioning and answering, Programmed learning and Team teaching, New teaching techniques and innovations and System approach and Teaching machines in education respectively.

The book will help the Educationist/Physical Educationist and the students in understanding educational technology in detail. The book can be considered as a reference book for others. This book will definitely enhance the level of teaching and learning experience.

Ankan Sinha

Acknowledgements

I would like to express my gratitude and appreciation to my colleagues and professionals who contributed directly or indirectly to the completion of this book. Their ideas and valuable inputs helped me. I sincerely thanks to all of them.

I gratefully acknowledge my gratitude to Dr. L.W. Vaz, a renowned physical educationist, coach of an International athlete and author of many books for his valuable suggestions and guidance to write this book.

While writing this book I faced unavoidable ups and downs in my life, but my family encouraged me to continue with the book by giving their constant support.

I am thankful to Ph.D scholars of LNIPE, Gwalior namely, Shri. Pradip Yadav, Arun Singh Rathore, Dharmendra Narwariya and Prasenjit Biswas for providing technical supports.

This book would not have been completed without unconditional the help of Litan Paul, manager of Zoom net cyber, Dharmanagar North Tripura.

Finally, I would like to acknowledge appreciation to the Kalpaz Publications for publishing this book.

Ankan Sinha

1
Introduction

Education

Education is an integral part of everyone's life. It secures the future of nation through its outcome. The development of a country is judged by quality education of citizens. Education has wide scope which enables person to live his or her life to its fullest. It can be introduced in the following modes:

- Change in behaviour
- Modification of behaviour
- Reconstruction of experiences

The term education can be understood through this abbreviation:

E- Experience

D- Development

U- Understanding

C- Continuous process

A- Authentic

T- Teaching tactfully

I- Innovative technique/Information

O- Overall development

N- Nourishment

Etymological Meaning of Education

1. Education according to first observation, the word education is being derived from Latin word "educare", which mean to nourish or to bring up.
2. According to second observation, the word education is derived from Latin word "educare", which mean to "lead out" or "draw out" or "to bring forth."
3. According to the third observation, the word education has been derived from "educatum", which mean the "act of teaching".
4. There is yet another theory that the word "education" owes to Latin word "Education" which is composed of two words "e" and "duco" wherein "e" means "out of", i.e., a progress from inward to outward, and word "duco" means to lead out or "to extract out" i.e., to develop and take out the best in man.

The word education has been derived from the Latin word 'EDUCARE' which mean to bring up or nourish, education is as old as human being /race, and it is never ending process, it is a product of experience. Through education, man developed his thinking, reasoning, problem solving, and reactivity. It is never ending process of inner growth and development and it continues from cradle to grave. The school is not the only agency which imparts education, the other agencies being home, family, religion, TV, cinema, press, library, radio.

Meaning of Education

Education is synonymous with learning product of experience. It is the process by which the experience of the race, i.e., knowledge, skills and attitudes are being transmitted to the member of the community. John Dewey speaks of "education as that reconstruction or reorganisation of experience, which add to the meaning of experience and increases the ability to direct course of subsequent experiences." Education proceeds from birth to death and the school is not the only agency that imparts education.

Dictionary Meaning of Education

According to the illustrated Oxford Dictionary (2011), education is a noun which means "the process of teaching or learning, the theory and practice of teaching, and information about or training in a particular subject".

Technology

Technology is the way to flourish the whole education system very creatively and innovatively. In recent world technology make things easier, concrete and faster. It is the demand of time or we can say nothing can be moved forward without technology. These are the few terms which gives the worth meaning of technology—modern changes/ trends, thoughtful trend/innovation.

The term technology can be understood through this abbreviation:

T- Trend

E- Expertise equipment

C- Creative

H- Helpful method

N- Novel

O- Original

L- Lively learning

O- Outstanding/Outrank

G- Gifted

Y- Youthful technique.

Meaning of Technology

The technology does not involve with gadgets and instrument only, but also involve with the trends and the method.

Technology is a systematic study of technique and the method applied to achieve an objective, it can also be said that it is a branch of knowledge, which deals with industrial art, applied science, engineering. Machinery and equipment owe to scientific knowledge.

Dictionary Meaning of Technology

According to the illustrated Oxford Dictionary (2011), technology is a noun which means; (a) "The application of scientific knowledge for practical purposes"; (b) "The branch of knowledge concerned with applied science".

Meaning of Educational Technology

Educational technology may be considered as:

- The utilisation of modern machines and gadgets in the field of education (a) To increase the rate of learning; (b) To develop the innate inner capacities of learners ; (c) For effective and productive learning; (d) For time saving, by exerting its influence on the teaching-learning process through its vicious and progressive use, technology cannot be isolated by its gadgetry use, but should also be taken as the use of trends, methodologies and instructions for the betterment of educational system.
- Educational technology could be helpful in education innovation by considering new systems and materials along with inventing instrument and finding procedures and then thinking proper solution for educational challenges.
- Educational technology is concerned with the systematic application of science and technology in the field of education. It facilitates the task efficient by making available all possible scientific and modern support.
- The National Council for Educational Technology has defined educational technology as "the development,

application, and evaluation of system, techniques and aids to improve the process of human learning." Therefore, educational technology means not only the hardware or machine, but those processes which help in human learning.

Definitions of Education Technology

(a) Leith Observes

Educational technology is "the application of scientific knowledge about learning and conditions of learning, to improve the effectiveness and efficiency of teaching and learning. In absence of scientifically established principles, educational technology implements techniques of empirical testing to improve learning situation".

(b) Sakamoto Observes

"An applied or practical study which aims at maximum educational purpose, educational environment contents, teaching materials, methods, educational environment, conduct of students, and behaviour of instruction between student and instructor".

(c) Unwin Observes

"The application of modern skills and techniques to the requirements of education and training. This includes the facilitation of learning by manipulation of media and methods, and the control of environment so far as this reflects on learning".

The Educative Process

Herbert Spencer states that the aim of education is a preparation for complete living. Educative process is sometimes termed as bipolar.

Sir John Adams sees it as a bipolar process—the two poles being teacher and pupil in one personality acting on the other modifies the development of other. This process is deliberate and conscious in the bipolar process, two persons are involved—teacher and disciple. The teacher in the process is an inevitable element. Without teacher, this process become difficult to operate; at the same time without disciple, this process cannot be operated. In this, one speaks other listens, one teaches other learns and one directs other follows.

All their activity is interrelated and interdependent. To make this process more effective, the educator must and should come down to the level of disciple—that is why this is a conscious and deliberate process.

Ross advocates and believes that education is tri-polar process. It involves an interaction between the pupil, the teacher and the social environment. In this, the teacher tries to develop the personality of the pupil in the light of the need of the society. In this process, the child's needs, interest, capacities and talents are given psychological importance and recognition, but the greater stress is being given a sociological importance. He believes that society plays vital role in the process of education. Thus, education involves with the interplay of three elements.

1. Teacher or educator
2. Pupil or taught
3. Social environment.

Social elements of education

Teacher | Pupil | Social environment

Teacher and Educator: The teachers occupy unique place in the process of education. They try to modify the personality of the pupil in the light of needs of the society to which he belongs. Teachers direct the activities and experiences of children through which they learn. They are the persons, who are not only the part of pupil's environment but also the controller of that environment.

As a part of pupil's environment, the teacher teaches through the impact of his personality upon the personality of the pupil.

As a controller of the environment, teacher selects and gives those experiences which lead to the fulfillment of the individual needs, skills and experiences, enable them to live besides the optimum life so that they can contribute to the welfare of the society.

The impact of good teacher makes upon the personality of the pupil. It is very significant on the aims of education which is to form the character of an individual and in its realisation the teachers owning personality has vital role to play. The influence of good personality continues to inspire when they are grown up.

The Pupil or the Taught: This is the second pole in the process of education. This process is impossible without discipline. The modern psychology emphasises on the importance of disciple in the educative process. It stresses on the worth of the disciple and his need. In the light of this, the concept of pupil-centred education is now occupying an important place in educational theory. Educational thinkers are almost unanimous that education must be based upon the psychological insight into the child's need and interest. The education should be the process of drawing out from within rather than imposing anything from outside. Education must provide adequate opportunities to the child for his personality development, keeping in view of his interest, aptitude and instinctive tendencies.

Social Environment: The third pole in the process of education is the social environment. The personality of the individual is developed only in such social environment.

In the democratic society, education has an important role to play and that is why the programme of education must reflect the ideals and needs of democratic society. The democratic education aims at providing a balance in which the needs of individual and those in society are balanced. John Dewey remarks education proceeds by participation of the individual in social consciousness of the race. The social forces provided by the social environment or the society, supply the material to the teacher and are being taught in the form of curriculum. The curriculum is being framed in the light of needs and demands of the society or social environment.

We admit that education is tripolar or some triangular process. It is a process of learning all round development of personality.

(i) Education is a continuous process; we can say it as never ending process; because it continues from cradle to grave empowering after birth.

(ii) Education is not only deliberate but also conscious process.

(iii) It is individualised.

(iv) It is a social process.

(v) It is a bipolar process.

(vi) It is a tripolar process.

The Teacher of the Era

In olden days, children were being taught in rigidly formal and stereotyped way. The education was conceived as process of transmission of factual knowledge. The teacher usually adopted an authoritarian attitude. The children were made to sit at particular place as if they were being fastened with pins. The facts were learned and written by children and were being tested from time to time. Such tests were neither concerned with conceptual understanding nor have led to the effective performance.

The main emphasis was on testing memory. A long gestation period intervened between child's response and the teacher's reinforcement. Most often, the verbal method was used by the teaching community. The teacher hardly used any memory or audio-visual material to supplement teaching.

Knowledge given was factual but not conceptual. The teacher considers today the child and helps grow according to abilities and aptitude. He does not consider the child as some vessel waiting to be filled up. He realises "to teach is to nourish or cultivate the growing individual or give him intellectual exercise and train the student in the horizontal sense of directing and guiding growth.

Modern teacher observes—education as the process of interaction between the child and his environment. The efforts are being made by teacher to direct and motivate student for the experiment and search the facts out for them and to take the projects also in small groups. Children learn by doing and thinking individually. The communication and media influence on students owe to the teaching community. Teacher feels the need for instructional planning and evaluation of learning. The principles of individual differences, i.e., difference in the background, difference in the abilities of the student and difference in the interest are being realised and that is why the teachers realise today on the need for presenting different experiences which suit the individual differences among the pupil, students selecting the use of media and method, accordingly.

There is a paradigm shift in the emphasis from the teacher to the pupil as the central figure in the process of education. The term math tic has been derived from Greek root signifying the learner and math tic is the science of behaviour of the pupil undergoing process of learning.

Evaluation is being done to get the feedback, i.e., for the students as well as for teacher who has to play the variety of roles in teaching as educator, as motivator, as guide, as counselor, as coach, as facilitator, as communicator *per se*. In the world today, teachers are supposed to be competent and skilled, teaching the application of science and technology as emphasised.

Use of Sensory Organs

Learning Through Senses

We are all gifted to learn and absorb new bits-bytes of information through our ability in surprising ways. However, we seldom realise but struggle with ineffective methods leading to spectra of feelings of inadequacy and self-doubt.

If we have ever struggled to find the creative spark that would propel towards learning and understanding, then it could cognise our approach to learn has been somewhat ineffective, and has lead us down the path of frustration and procrastination.

Within this part, we will discover that the doors to learning are always accessible. There is some means and ways to learn any information or subject as long as we are aware, and utilise effective multi-sensory strategies that will help in accelerating our learning potential.

The Process of Remembering

What we choose to think at any given moment in time is as important as the way we choose the learning strategies.

Learning studies have consistently shown us that they involve in more than one of our sensory organs. We can profoundly enhance our retention and recall of information.

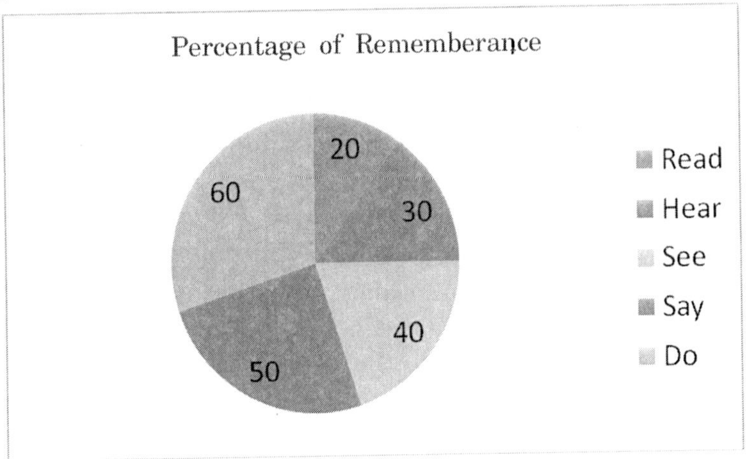

The studies have shown we remember some 20 per cent of what we read, 30 per cent of what we hear, 40 per cent of what we see, 50 per cent of what we say, and some 60 per cent of what we do. Of course, this will somewhat vary from person-to-person depending on their sensory preferences, howsoever, it is based on personal experience with learning; it seems to be pretty accurate.

What the results actually share that the more we interact with the information, we learn from greater volume of information we retain and hold them on to over an extended period of time.

Reading is on the bottom of this list, as it requires little involvement. However, *doing* is at the top of the list with **60 per cent** retention because it is multi-sensory activity that utilises many sensory cues to stimulate the brain in creative manner.

If we were to incorporate these methods (reading, listening, observing, saying and doing) into the learning process, we then find surprisingly our retention levels rise beyond 90 per cent.

Types of Learners

We exist through five physical senses with an opportunity to harness sixth sense for learning. The sense of *touch, smell, sight, hearing,* and *taste* are critical when it comes to improving methods of learning. The learning experience can be dramatically enhanced by each sensory cue from within which provides with extra support that will improve the memory and recall of information.

Science has shown time and again that we seldom forget anything that comes through our sensory organs. The memories are intrinsically ingrained into our psyche at deep unconscious level. In fact, this is why under hypnosis many people find sensory perceptions lying dormant for decades suddenly flash to the forefront as though they just replased yesterday. These types of memories are often very vivid, because they owe to multi-sensory vibrations, meaning the person with the memory can see, hear, feel, taste and smell the experience from variety of perspectives. And within this lies the key to the success as an accelerated learner.

For the purpose of discussion, we will look at the three most utilised senses that will help to improve study skills. However, please keep in mind that we will naturally have a preference for one sensory learning method over the other. Identify which one it is and approach the learning by focussing on this sensory organ to begin with. Only once we have a good grasp of the topic area, should we vary our approach and begin focussing on alternate methods, we should incorporate the other two primary sensory organs.

Here is a description of the three main sensory cues to get you started:

Kinesthetic Learners

Feelings are the medium to learn and remember pieces of information among these types of learners. They are *physically-oriented* individuals, thinking in shades of emotion through physical movement and involvement. They do enjoy contemplating and role play in the aspects of information they are learning.

Visual Learners

Eyes are the medium to learn and remember pieces of information among these types of learners. They are very *visually-oriented* individuals, thinking in terms of pictures, colours, and shapes. They enjoy visualising and using their imaginations to think about and recall the information they are learning.

Auditory Learners

Ears are the medium to learn and remember pieces of information in these types of learners. They are *listening-oriented* individuals, thinking in terms of sounds, music, and tones. They enjoy listening to audio recordings and utilising their voice to recall the information they are learning.

Multi-sensory Study Tactics

Advanced learning is very much a creative journey where we naturally identify our strengths and weaknesses that will assist us in selecting learning methods and strategies befitting our personality and learning style.

Within this, we will delve into the intricate specifics and details of the multi-sensory learning study process. The techniques and strategies presented here will compensate with variety of approaches when learning study materials.

Keep in mind that every method will not be ideal to the strategy, howsoever it is important to think flexibly and approach every subject and topic we learn with an open frame-of-mind—tackling every piece of material in new way, while incorporating as many of our learning sensory organs as possible.

Make Your Information Memorable

In order to get the most out of multi-sensory study time, it is absolutely critical to follow a few simple guidelines that will to expand focus, awareness and memory of the information we learn.

Here is a brief overview of guidelines as they pertain to three primary sensory learning styles:

Physical Suggestions

When learning through physical means and while incorporating kinesthetic learning strategies, ensure that physical learning experience has unique feelings associated with it, and is of a high emotional intensity.

As physical/kinesthetic learners, we naturally remember and recall information easily that comes across in memorable and vividly unique way.

As we are working through the physical learning strategies presented within this post, make sure to get all emotions involved within the process that seek unique and memorable feelings for enhanced thinking and awareness. This will not only improve each of the study strategies being chosen to pursue, but will also dramatically lynch the memory and recall of information.

As a final thought, while working through the physical study strategies, ponder over the following questions:

- How can one add greater amount of emotional intensity into the study time?

- How can one enhance the positive emotional tension of learning strategy that allow him/her better remember the information from studying?
- What unique experience and feeling one can drew from the strategy enhancing memory and recall?

Visual Suggestions

When learning through visual means incorporating visual learning strategies ensure that visual learning experience is *close, colourful, bright,* and *funny.*

The visual learners naturally remember and recall information easily that is designed in memorable and vividly imaginative way.

As we work through the visual learning strategies presented within this post, ensure that incorporate brightness, closeness, colour and humour into the study regime. This will not only improve each of the study strategies chosen to pursue, but will also dramatically enhance the memory and recall of information.

As a final thought, while working through the visual study strategies, ponder over the following questions:

- How can one make this information brighter influencing more readily in the mind?
- How can one bring this information closer so that he/she completely finds engrossed within its influence?
- How can one add more colour further enhancing the memory and recall?
- How can one create and build humour within making it stand out in the mind's-eye?

Auditory Suggestions

When learning through an auditory means incorporating auditory learning strategies ensure that auditory learning experience is funny, loud, and unique.

The auditory learners naturally remember and recall information easily that comes across in memorable and unique way.

As we work through auditory learning strategies presented within this post, ensure that incorporate volume, uniqueness of sound, and humour into the study regime. This will not only improve each of the study strategies which have chosen to pursue, but will also dramatically enhance the memory and recall of information.

As a final thought, while working through the auditory study strategies, ponder over the following questions:

- How one can add humorous sound effects, music and voices producing innovative information that he/she learn to remember more readily?
- In what creative mode, one increase the tone and volume of this strategy enhancing the memory and recall of this information?
- How one can make sound effects, music and voices unique enhancing automatically the thinking and awareness?

Communication

Communication is what we try to do, speak to others from within and afar. It is the exchange of information and ideas which flows from one person to another. It involves a sender transmitting an idea, information, or feeling to some receiver. An effective communication occurs only if the receiver understands the exact information or idea that the sender intends to transmit. Many of the problems that occur in an organisation are:

- the direct result of people failing to communicate;
- processes lead to confusion and failure of good plans.

Studying communication process is important because we counsel, coach, coordinate, supervise and evaluate throughout. It is the chain of understanding that integrates members of an organisation from top to bottom, bottom to top, and side to side.

Meaning of Communication

The word communication is derived from‘ Latin word ‘communis’ mean ‘*common*’. Hence, communication is having common experience with people. The word communication means variety of things about different people.

Definition of Communication

The following are some of the widely accepted definition for communication.

"Communication means *sharing of ideas and feelings* in a mood of mutuality".

"Communication involves *interaction* which encourages *give and take*" . This provides feedback to persons involved in exchanging ideas.

"Communication is a process of sharing of experiences till it becomes common possession".

"Effective communication is a two-way process including feedback and interaction".

Barriers to Communication

The thing that prevents understanding of the message as the barrier to communication is the message. Many physical and psychological barriers exist:

- **Background, culture, and bias:** The meaning of the messages change by our past experiences which are allowed by us. Our background, culture, and bias can be good as they allow our past experiences to understand something anew, it is when they change the meaning of a message that they interfere with the very process.
- **Ourselves:** Focusing on ourselves rather the other person can lead to confusion and conflict. The "Me

Generation" must be tossed aside for effective communication. Some of the factors are defensiveness (we feel someone is attacking us), superiority (we feel more about the other), and ego (we feel to be the centre of activity).

- **Perception:** When we feel the person talking fast, not fluently does not articulate clearly, we may dismiss such person. Our preconceived attitudes affect our ability to listen. We may listen uncritically to persons of high status and dismiss those of low status.
- **Noise:** Clear communication finds impeded by equipment or environmental noise. The sender and the receiver must concentrate on the messages being sent to each other.
- **Message:** Distractions do happen when we focus on the facts rather the idea being communicated. Our educational institutions reinforce this concept with periodic tests. Semantic distractions occur when some word is being used differently than our preference. For example, the word chairman instead of chairperson may cause focussing on the word rather the message.
- **Environmental:** Bright lights, an attractive person, unusual sights, or any stimulus provides a potential distraction.
- **Smothering:** We believe that the impulse to send useful information is automatic. It is not true. We believe too often that certain information seldom has no value to others or they are already aware of such facts.
- **Stress:** People do not see things in the same way under stress. What we see and believe at a given moment is being influenced by our psychological frames of references—our belief, values, knowledge, experiences, and goals.

These barriers can be thought of as filters, that is, the message leaves the sender, goes through above filters, and

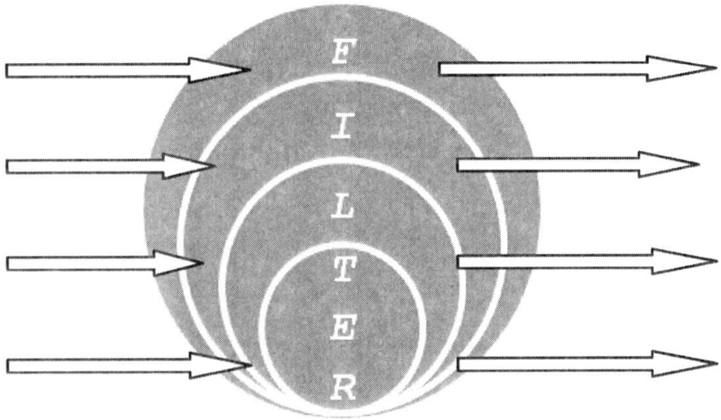

is being heard by the receiver. These filters may muffle the message, and the way to overcome filters is through active listening and feedback.

Types of Communication

We find three types of communication:

Speaking and Listening

In this type of communication, interaction remains face to face as in the case of listening some lecture. There are occasions when listener share the feeling of the source in the same way as in the case of eye-to-eye contact. An example for this type of communication is listening to radio programmers.

Visualising and Observing

The observer is physically separated from producers and yet feel the impact of ideas conveyed as in some motion film or television. Communication can take place more efficiently by face-to-face contact with source as in some case of dramatisation where facial expression and gestures produce greater impact.

Writing and Reading

In this type of experience, the 'decoder' is physically separated from the 'encoder', yet he is able to enjoy and appreciate the feelings.

Eather arrows in the three types of communication indicate that communication is nothing but interaction, sharing and circular or cyclic in the process.

Communication Cycle

We find four components in the process of communication.

They are:

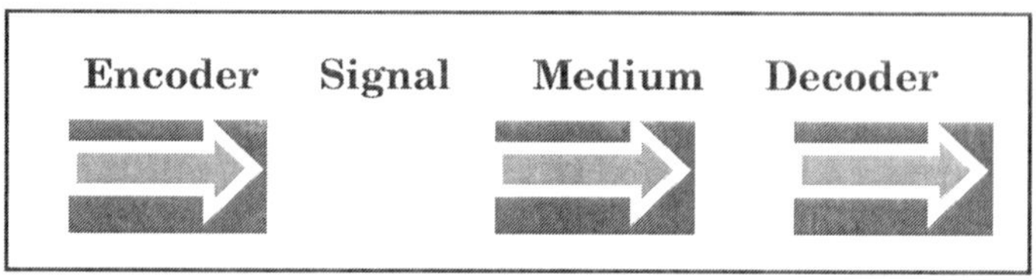

1. *Sender or Source*, technically called as 'encoder',
2. *Message or Signal*,
3. The *Medium or Channel* of Communication, and
4. The *Receiver or destination* or *'decoder'*.

In the process, the source must have correct information and transmit accurately at optimum speed. The message may be designed for single person or a group of people. It may be conveyed by expression, gesture, spoken or written symbols or by hand drawn or photographic picture. Every medium expertise its influence and peculiarities on the message and becomes part of the message. The receiver must understand the message or in other words, must decode or interpret and produce desired response, or react to be perceived by the sender. This is called the *feedback* channel.

The *Communication Cycle* can be represented by the following diagram.

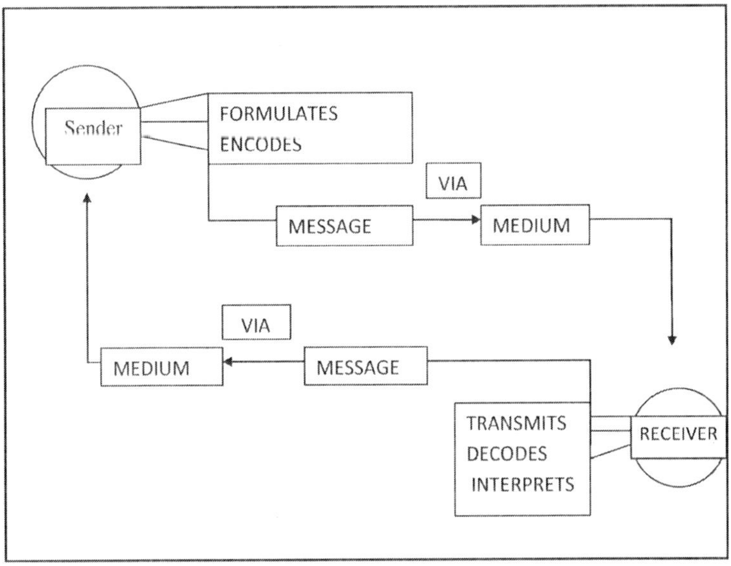

According to Wilbur Schramm there are four essential elements of communication:

1. Source
2. Message
3. Channel
4. Destination

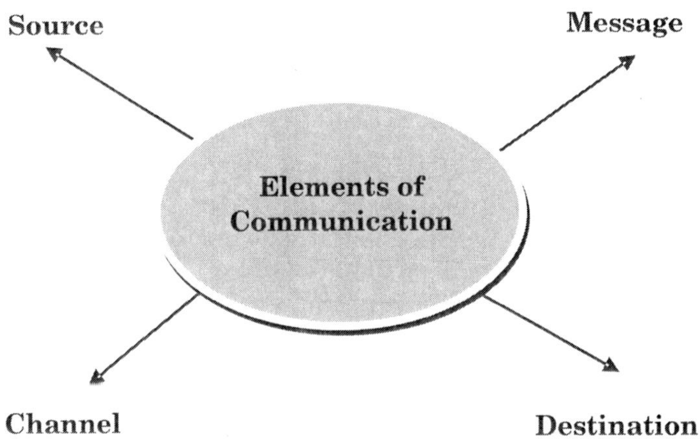

This system of communication may be divided as:

(a) Human

(b) Mechanical

When we say *Human*, it concerns with the personal or human communication. Here, the message is being transmitted or conveyed by expression, gesture, postures, spoken or written symbols or picture and figures. In *Mechanical,* Brown *et al.,* call the same as encoder, message as signal or sign channel as some medium and destination as the decoder. In some, the source is the sender, or one who initiates the process and destination is the receiver.

Communication in Classroom

For centuries, the typical communication in the classroom has been lecturing. One who possess the knowledge (the instructor) is supposed to convey to those who do not (the students), like someone pours liquid into empty glasses. This approach focusses on the activity of such instructor. Students are tested on their ability to regurgitate what the instructor has interpreted.

Learning, however, requires an active step on the part of students and is being measured by what students to do with the material (the so-called "learning outcome"). In this view, such activity of students is more important than that of the instructor. Learning results from interaction between the students and the material to be learned—an interaction the instructor could catalyse.

This will help you prepare for run and evaluate effective classroom session as part of the course. It will help you define learning outcome and design samilar activities, create classroom atmosphere conducive to student activity and encourage such activity in possible ways, reveal the structure of the course to students, and evaluate your performance as an instructor. It also provides valuable tips on managing large groups.

Communication in the classroom requires three things namely, words, body language and tonnes of voice

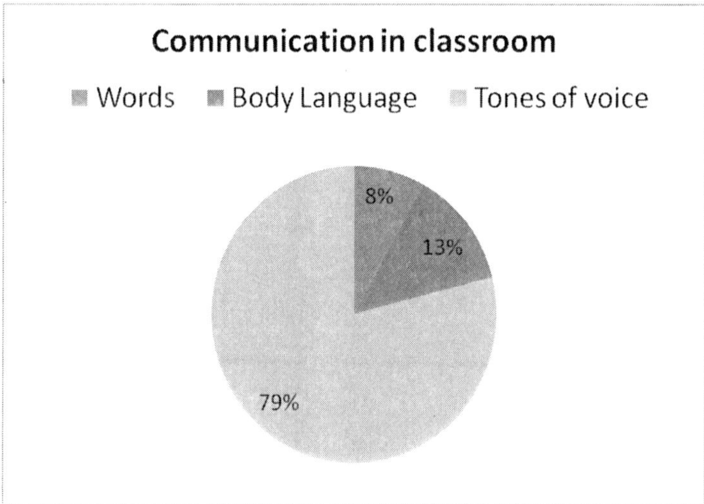

intonation. They have given 8, 13 and 79 per cent respectively to apportion in classroom communication.

Communication in class room is to some extent carried on through language spoken and written, with the former playing a relatively greater role. According to *Jean Piaget*, the early speech of children is *'ego-centric'*. They interpret words, use them in terms of limited personal experiences, yet not grasping the possibility that other children and adult who have had different experiences cashed in on different concepts. Only by 7-8 year does, 'socialise' speech developed. They have taken into account the ego-centricity of speech as due to the inability of the child think more about one thing at a time. These characteristic conditions of thinking enable children, use words and understand them in a different way from elder than in communicating in the classroom should never be ignored. *Jerome Bruner* believes similarly, when he speaks of three stages of 'intellectual development', 'enactive', 'icons' and 'symbolic' representation stage and states using language as an instrument of communication and thinking is clearly a designed in the symbolic stage.

In trying to communicate using language in the classroom, teachers may benefit by the concept of *David P. Ausuble* 'advance organiser' about learning and retention of meaningful verbal material. The advance organiser roughly correspond to broad categories within a unit of learning and permit thereupon.

2
Models of Learning Experience

Teaching Aids

As we know in the age of science and technology, learning programmes have been affected by teaching. The process however, depends upon different types of equipment available in the classroom. The aids help learners grasp things more accurately for longer duration.

Teaching aid is the combination of two words "teaching" and "aid". Teaching means the art of giving information about particular subject to a class or pupil or show someone how to do something. On the other hand, aid means help or that supports someone or something. So, teaching aid is an equipment which helps the teacher convey the information about particular subject to the student community or pupil.

The Need

(1) Every individual has some tendency to forget. The proper use of teaching aids obviously help him/her retain more concepts permanently.

(2) Students can learn better when they are being motivated properly through different teaching aids.

(3) Teaching aids develop proper image when the students *see*, *hear*, *taste* and *smell* properly.

(4) Provide complete example for conceptual thinking.

(5) Create the environment of interest for the students.

(6) Help to increase the vocabulary.

(7) Help the teacher to get some time and make learning fun.

(8) Provide somewhat direct experience.

The Importance

Teaching aids play a very important role in the overall teaching learning process:

(1) **Motivation:** Teaching aids motivate students for better learning.

(2) **Clarification:** The teacher clarifies the subject matter more easily.

(3) **Discourage Cramming:** These facilitate in proper understanding students discouraging the act of cramming.

(4) **Increase Vocabulary:** These help in increasing student vocabulary more effectively.

(5) **Saves Time and Money:** These help the teacher save time and money, so that he can harness them in other parts of teaching.

(6) **Vibrant Classroom:** The aids make the classroom live and active.

(7) **Avoids Dullness:** The aids should not be practised monotonously.

(8) **Direct Experience:** The aids provide direct experience to students.

Criteria for Selection

Adequate teaching aids should be made available to

accomplish effective teaching in geography. To be effective, aids should be used to achieve definite objective and should be well constructed to gain the learners' attention and sustain his interest. It follows therefore that teaching aids must be carefully selected and used. When selecting teaching aids, teachers should apply similar guidelines when choosing-learning activities. These are:

(i) The aids should be used to achieve specific objectives;

(ii) The aids should be suited to the maturity level of students;

(iii) The aids must be used with skill and understanding. The choices of aids are therefore guided by various considerations or factors. In more specific terms, the following factors should be borne in mind:

- Appropriateness—i.e., whether relevant to the topic being discussed?
- Level of sophistication of the students—i.e. this refers to the age or level of maturity of students;
- Cost Effectiveness—i.e., it could produce appropriate software rather depending on commercially produced stuff;
- Availability;
- Technical quality—clear, bold and produced through appropriate conventional logos.

Types of Teaching Aids

Many aids are available these days. We may classify them as:

- Visual Aids
- Audio Aids
- Audio-visual Aids

Visual Aids

The aids which use sense of vision are called Visual aids. For example Actual Objects, Models, Pictures, Charts, Maps, Flash Cards, Flannel Board, Bulletin Board, Chalkboard, Overhead Projector, Slides. Out of these, black board and chalk are the commonest ones.

Audio Aids

The aids that involve the sense of hearing are called Audio aids. For example Radio, Tape Recorder, Gramophone.

Audio-Visual Aids

The aids which involve the sense of vision as well as hearing are called Audio-Visual aids. For example—Television, Film Projector, Film Strips.

Visual and Audio Aids

Many visual and audio aids are available to ensure your meeting effective. Each has advantages and disadvantages. It is important to remember that these are just aids, rather than end in them, so that you do not subsist in meeting your requirements. Avoid talking to the visual aid instead of the group. This is a common mistake, and obviously takes your focus away from the group. Here are some common aids with their features:

1. **Chalkboard or Chart Pad:** These are the most commonly used, because they are portable and readily available. They offer some sense of spontaneity and can provide group involvement. They are most appropriate for small groups, for recording simple, unsophisticated information, e.g., ideas generated in information-taking or problem-solving meeting. They keep information in front of the group, though chart pads are better for they offer much space. Each sheet can simply be removed from the pad and taped on to the wall.

Furthermore, chart pad notes can be kept or given to the note-taker, so that the information can be incorporated

into minutes. Use coloured chalk or brightly coloured pens when you want to emphasise. Use no more than seven words per line and seven lines per chart. Beware of common mistakes. Do not downcast anyone by excluding their contribution from the board. Do not write illegibly or use tiny letters that are too small to read.

2. **Prepared Charts (Overhead Transparencies):** These emphasise points and draw the attention group to specific point or group of ideas. They are good for larger groups. Over-use can detract from discussion. Stand aside when presenting any material on boards, screens, or charts. Be prepared for equipment needs (test the equipment ahead of time) and check the availability of outlets or extension cords; ensure over spare projector bulbs on being burn out often so be sure you have an extra.

When using charts or overheads, place most of the information across the top two-thirds of the sheet, and make sure to proofread. If you use an overhead projector,

adjust the angle and focus before presentation. Make sure the projector doesn't block anyone's view. Keep the light off until you actually use it. For *Power Point slides*, match the image size on the screen to the size of your group. Never stand in front of the slide or in the light. Don't turn the lights completely off in the room.

3. **Handouts:** Handouts can be discussion points, case studies, summaries or statistics. They should be as short as possible. These should be carefully timed with discussion, or used when you want the participants leave with specific pieces (e.g., in some data base meeting). Distribute handouts either before or after but not during. Advice the group over a referenced handout during discussion. Instruct participants when to put away handouts during discussion, to minimise distraction. If some handout covers the

discussed material, inform the group so they avoid taking notes unnecessarily.

Be sure to prepare enough handouts in advance that every member finds one, or you will distract and foster small discussions. Ensure the handout is not so involved that participants are drawn into reading that instead of partaking in the meeting. Number the pages of your handouts and label them clearly. Make sure they are clearly typed and always check for types.

4. **Demonstrations:** These are used mostly in instructional situations where the leader or a participant explains some operation or particular function, and the real thing is the best way to demonstrate it. This tool usually involves objects, models or other physical equipments. In using this technique, be sure that:

- The demonstration is in full view of the group, but kept out of sight (if possible) until needed.
- Let that not too long or cumbersome for the time and facilities you have.
- Let that be properly integrated with the session material. Questions and points to be raised following the demonstration should be planned in advance.
- If the model is small enough to be passed around, don't do it. It will distract the participants from the meeting.

5. **Video and Film:** We are in a TV/Video generation, this can be a powerful aid. Use it when:

- The participants need to see the operation of something complex.
- Expert testimony is required from someone in absentia.
- You want to model or teach some skill or behaviour. If you use any sort of films (slides, videotapes), tell the participants how long the material is when you introduce and discuss its relation for the purpose. Adjust the volume prior to meeting, and try not to

turn lights completely off so that participants can take notes. Stay in the room during presentation; the projector or VCR could break down voluntarily without notice.

6. **Sound:** Tape recordings, records, sound effects, or sound with film are very useful as teaching aids. Tape recording is an useful device for preserving meeting sessions for review or "make-up" sessions, but it requires appropriateness, clarity and fidelity, and skilled design.

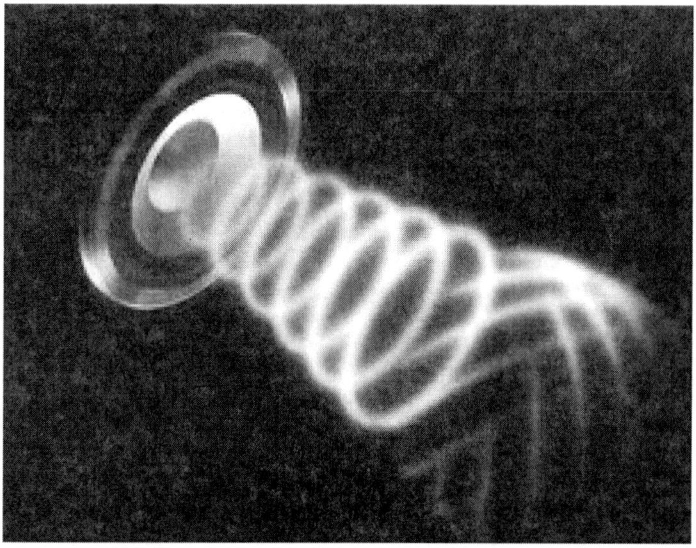

How to Use Audio and Visual Aids

Source: Work presentation image by Rido from Fotolia.com Visual aids have been in use since the first cave drawings, when stock figures illustrated hunt and herd migrations. They were so effective that scientists can still understand them today. This is still relevant in business, school, and personal presentations. Audio and visual aids can be created from variety of sources, and using them aids some listener through visual stimulation, and illustrating concepts makes them easier to understand and follow, thus improving the communication of thoughts and ideas.

Audio and visual aids are still used when they were originally created. An example is the stained glass windows

of the large European Cathedrals, such as Notre Dame in France, where biblical stories are still communicated through the art. Classroom teachers utilise audio and visual aids to enrich lecture and classroom instructor, as do people leading business conferences or meetings, military commanders who present information to other officers or troops, or even a person who simply draws a map for someone to give them directions. Audio and visual aids are appropriate anywhere that communication finds enhanced and understanding deepen through their use.

Instruction to Use Audio-Visual Aids

Regardless of the overall quality, audio-visual aids are

of little use, if operators do not know how to incorporate them effectively into presentation. Introducing audio-visual

Source: Lecture hall image by GeoM from Fotolia.com

aids at the wrong time or using them inexpertly can disrupt the flow of some presentation and make you nervous to forget what you say. Keep certain techniques in mind and you can use audio-visual aids professionally and incorporate them effectively and smoothly into your presentations.

- Display audio-visual aids where they are visible to everyone. According to Rudolph Verderber and Kathleen Verderber, co-authors of "The Challenge of Effective Speaking," when holding an aid (for example, an object or model) one should "position it away from the body and point it at the various parts of the audience" Such positioning allows everyone to see what we are holding. When discussing something on a chart, graph or slide, we should use a pointer (perhaps a pencil or ruler) since this allows us to stand farther away from the aid and decreases the chances of our blocking anyone's observation view.

- Talk to the audience, not the audio-visual aids. Although, we need to glance at the aid occasionally and the audience's will naturally focus upon maintain theeye contact with the audience. Therefore, says Stephen E. Lucas, author of "The Art of Public Speaking," when pointing something about the aid, we should use the arm nearest the aid. This positioning enables us to continue facing our audience. Using the opposing arm would necessitate turning our back and losing eye contact.
- Display audio-visual aids only while discussing about them. When incorporating aids into some presentation, say Verderber and Verderber, we should "use this basic rule of thumb: When the visual aid is no longer the focus of attention, remove it, turn it off, or get rid of it". After all, people are naturally curious; they like to look at things. Whenever an audio-visual aid is in sight, some listeners will be focused upon it, not upon us, so do not display aids until we are ready to discuss about them. Once we have discussed, remove them from view.
- Explain audio-visual aids clearly and concisely. Never assume that the audience knows the purpose of presentation aids. In reality, people won't know unless we tell them. As Lucas points out, "Visual aids don't explain themselves. Like statistics, they need to be translated and related to the audience." Therefore, we should describe their main features; explaining the significance of charts, graphs or images; discussing the relevance of bulleted points; and interpreting statistics, percentages or numbers.
- Distribute audio-visual aids after the presentation. We might share copies of materials with our listeners. However, as Lucas says, "Once visual aids get into

the hands of our listeners, we are in trouble, because we have just lost the attention of at least three people: The person who just had it, the person who has it now, and the person waiting to get it next." If we wish to share materials with the audience, distribute them after the presentation, but not during session.

Good Audio-visual Aids: One of the basic functions expected to perform is to help students visualise the phenomena with geographic data. In order to achieve this function, any audio-visual aid must possess the following characteristics:

(i) It must be clear, clean, interesting and in good condition;

(ii) It should be of a suitable size, i.e., it must be large enough (bold) for the whole class or small for group work;

(iii) It must be adequate, accurate, giving up-to-date information;

(iv) Must be relevant to the topic being discussed;

(v) It must not be over-crowded with details;

(vi) It must illustrate the specific point being taught;vii. Any audio-visual aid must be realistic in terms of the pupils' ability to interpret aids; andviii. It should be related to pupils' experience.

Importance of Audio-visual Aids

Audio-visual aids or technological media are additional devices that help the teacher to clarify, establish, correlate and co-ordinate accurate concepts, interpretations and appreciations with enabling his/her learning more concrete, effective, interesting, inspirational, meaningful and vivid. They help in completing the triangular process of learning, viz., motivation-clarification-stimulation. The aim of teaching with technological media is 'clearing the channel between the learner and the things that are worth learning'.

The basic assumption underlying Audio-Visual Aids is that learning (clear understanding) stems from sense experience. The teacher must 'show' as well as 'tell'. Audio-visual aids provide significant gains in informational learning, retention and recall, thinking and reasoning, activity, interest, imagination, better assimilation and personal growth and development. The aids are the stimuli for learning 'why', 'how', 'when' and 'where'. The 'hard to understand principles' are usually made clear by the intelligent use of skillfully designed instructional aids. Therefore, the need and importance of teaching aids can never be overstated. In the words of Edgar Dale, "Because audio-visual materials supply concrete basis for conceptual thinking, they give rise to meaningful concepts enriched by meaningful association, hence they offer the best antidote for the disease of verbalism." Now let us look at some advantages of the audio-visual aids that make them an important in the teaching-learning process.

Good Motivators: Teaching aids are good motivators. They make students work with more interest and zeal as well as to become more attentive.

Supplement Verbal Instruction: Teaching aids help in reducing verbalism. They help in giving clear concepts and bring accuracy in learning. As observed by Raymond Wyinaii (1957) "We (teachers) tell students, and we provide them with written materials so much of the time. Words are wonderful. They are easily produced, reproduced, stored and transported. But the overuse or excessive use of words can result in serious problems, chiefly, the problem of verbalism (using or adopting words or phrases without considering what they mean) and forgetting."

Clear Images: Clear images are formed when we see, *hear, touch, taste* and *smell,* as our experiences are direct, concrete and more or less permanent. Learning through senses becomes the most natural and consequently the easiest.

Vicarious Experience: It is beyond doubt that the first-hand experience is the best type of educative experience. It is neither practicable nor desirable to provide similar experience to pupils all the time and for everything. Substituted experiences may be provided under similar conditions. There are many inaccessible objects and phenomena. For example, it is not possible for the pupils living in Africa to see the Eskimo. Similarly, it is not possible for any average person to climb the Mount Everest. There are innumerable things to which it is not possible to have direct access. So, in all such cases, teaching aids help us.

Variety: 'Mere chalk and talk' do not help. Audio-visual aids give variety and provide different tools in the hands of the teacher.

Freedom: When audio-visual aids are employed, there is great scope for children to move about, talk, laugh and air their comments. Under such atmosphere, the students work; because they like to work and not because the teacher wants them to work.

Opportunities to Manipulate: Many visual aids offer opportunities to students to handle and manipulate things.

Categories of Technology-based Aids

A Power Point presentation (PPT) is standard aid for many businesses, teachers, and the US military. The slides are easily created on any computer with the installed software and bullet points of key pieces of information, show pictures, load audio clips, and even create interactive presentation. A knowledgeable hand can create PowerPoints with animation, automatic slide progression, and special effects that can be mastered through a little exploration of the program. Another technological innovation that aids audio and visual communication is the smart board. A smart board is an innovative and interactive white board that can be used to effectively communicate lessons, ideas, and presentations to prospective audience. The smart board is often compared to an interactive computer tablet where it can scroll and save notes made upon. Programs such as Power Point and Auto Cad can be loaded on to the smart board, making it an interactive tool similar to super computer that the audience could monitor.

Interactive Aids

Models provide three-dimensional visual aid that participants examine and follow with lecture. For example, if a science teacher present the anatomy of human intestines, a model comprising pieces replicate inner organs, assemble to show students how they fit together and relate with each other. An art historian might bring in models of historic pottery, or an architect might have some scale model of proposed building to show potential investors. Allowing the audience to walk around and interact with the model improves the communication of plans and ideas, as well as the very presentation concerned.

Paper-based Aids

A large easel pad is an ideal paper-based aid for interactive engagement of the audience. For example, if some presenter wishes to have the audience provide commentary on different ideas, all they must do is post large sheets with the marker around the room. These remarks can then be used for further brainstorming discussion. Participants can be grouped and asked to make their own visual aid on the given topic in such presentation, thus adding new level of engagement to the presentation. Flip charts are preferred for presentation because of their ability in an organic method as the presentation unfolds. The presenter needs to use the flip chart marker. The presenter can write down key with the points of information, draw charts, note questions from the audience, and even draw illustrations. Flip chart prevents the presentation, from becoming too formulaic and allows the audience some control and investment in the presentation.

Designing Visuals

We have discussed about the uses of visuals and importance of visuals. Good message design is also important. Over the years, educators have found several design principles we adapt to enhance visuals. The principle components are:

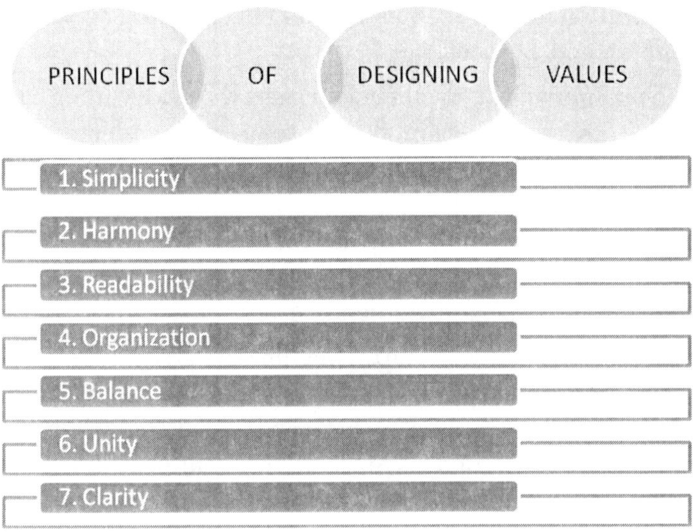

Simplicity. You should ask yourself this question: Are there any unnecessary words, symbols, or ideas within the presentation? The number of points to be made should be limited; key words should be shown instead of complete sentences. As a general rule, a visual should have: one idea;

- no more than eight items; about six words per line;
- mixed upper and lower case letters;
- simple, clean typefaces; and
- Large enough type to be read easily. Avoid useless decoration, eliminate fancy borders and backgrounds, and use artwork selectively, with white space unaccustormed in calligraphy.

Harmony. The elements of visual should fit together in some harmonious relationship. Distracting visual elements might include colour, layout, type style, visual symbols, or background. Associating pictures with names sometimes help relationship becoming more concrete. Only one or two type styles should be used during such presentation unless used for special effects. Simple lettering styles should be used.

Emphasis: The use of colour, arrows, underlining, and bolding are ways to emphasise some major elements in specific visual. To attract attention, extreme colours of red and blue may be used. Visuals that vary in size, colouring, brightness, and shape attract more interest than those that remain the same for an entire presentation. Novel visuals also help gain audience attention.

Readability. The lettering on the visual must be legible. When the content suggests some list, use numbers or bullets. The visual list is better retained than the same information presented as part of the sentence. Legibility can be improved by mixing upper- and lower-case letters.

Organisation. The visual should be arranged in some comprehensible pattern for the viewer. Visuals should use arrows, numbers, underlining, and other cues to organise how the audience perceive the content.

Balance: The elements of visual should be arranged in an interesting manner but not distracting.

Unity: Are the elements of visual arranged to form single unit?

Clarity: Is the purpose of the visual obvious to the audience for whom the message is intended? You should logically organise the visuals; divide complex information into smaller units, and present important information more than once.

Effective Use of Teaching Aids

Concept Maps

Concept maps graphically illustrate the relationship among the data base. In a concept map, two or more concepts are being linked by words that describe the relation. These encourage understanding by helping students organise and enhance their knowledge on any specific topic. They help students learn new information by integrating each new idea.

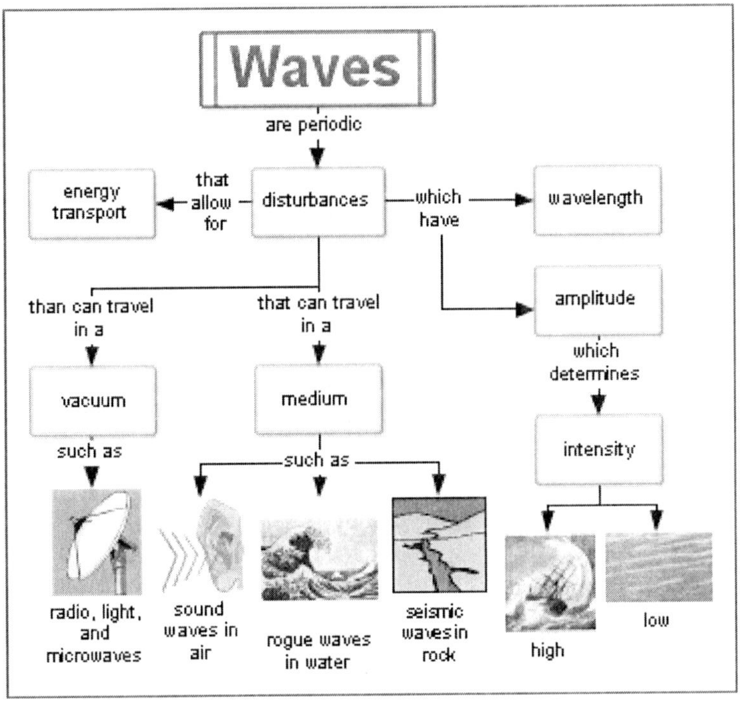

Posters and Flipcharts

You can prepare posters or flipcharts for the classroom. Keep them large, simple and clear, without much information. The following posters can be useful: classroom instructions; classroom requests; language tables. Posters and flip charts are very effective for information tips.

Care should be taken to ensure that graphs and charts are as simple as possible and larger enough to see.

Flip Charts/Posters

Advantages

- Easy and inexpensive to draw and update.
- Portable and transportable.
- Left in view of the audience.
- Good for interaction with the audience.

Disadvantages

- Unsuitable for large groups.
- Anxiety provoking the facilitator with poor handwriting or spelling.

Guidelines for Charts

A few guidelines are suffice.

Text Charts

- Keep titles and subtitles to single line.
- Present only one main idea.
- Keep simple, follow brevity mode
- Use key words.

- Mingle upper and lower case letters.
- Maximum of 25 letters per line.
- Maximum of eight lines per chart.
- Leave some blank space in between statements.
- Maximum of eight words per line.
- Ensure bullet types seldom clash with other graphics.
- Show the audience one line at a time.

Computer-generated Slides/Graphics

Computer-generated slides are similar to overhead transparencies through textual information using computer (usually the laptop) and computer projector. However, computer-generated slides incorporate scanned-in photographs and slides, clip art, audio clips, and video segments. Interactive World Wide Web pages can also be included in such slide contents.

Advantages

- Professional in appearance.
- Good for large groups.

Disadvantages

- Formal and impersonal.
- Shown in the dark.
- Not good for discussion and interaction.
- More difficult to update than other visual aids.
- Require special equipment.

Videos

Advantages

- Professional in appearance.
- Good for large or small groups.

Disadvantages

- More expensive than other visual aids.

- Requires special equipment.
- Not good for discussion and interaction.
- require accurate cueing.

Overhead Transparencies

Advantages

- Good for large groups.
- Easy to create.
- Easy to transport.
- Provide an informal atmosphere.
- Open to interaction with groups.
- Easy to update.

Disadvantages

- Impermanent; they yellow with age.
- Require less common equipment.

Computer Projections (e.g., Power Point)

Advantages

- Professional in appearance.
- Evidence of preparation.

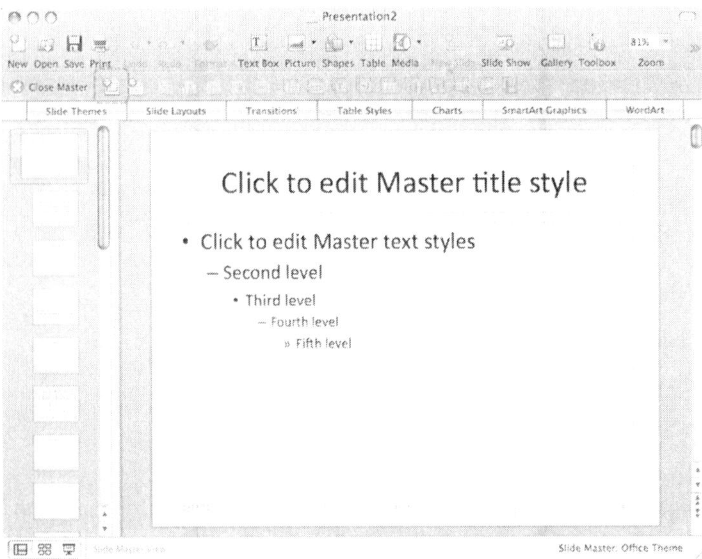

- Good for large or small group.
- Easy to integrate with classroom discussion.
- Animated.
- Up-to-date technology.
- Easy to update.

Disadvantages

- Require special equipment/facilities.
- Require initial training to create.
- Require significant time to create.
- Require basic graphics/composition skills.

Pictures, Photos and Postcards

Using one large picture

Two types of picture:

1. A scene with lots of happening;
2. One simple picture of a street; room; house.

Periodicals and Brochures

Apart from providing you with plenty of images to make into flashcards and small cards, periodicals replete advertisements which can be used in contrast with each other.

Examples could be: four or five advertisements for perfume, jeans, teenage accessories or vacations; two photos to exploit (can be fashion make-over); two teenage rooms and two lifestyles.

Personal Computer Projector

These tools have the features and uses of a board and more. They can be used without reverting to the class, and the sheets can be prepared in advance, which saves time and helps to be better organised. We can control how much we disclose students and when. We can re-use overhead transparencies with other classes, or copies of our slide can be given as handouts. Presentation programmes such as Microsoft PowerPoint allow us to modify the slides to suit each class.

The Whiteboard

This is the main piece of equipment in most schools and it is vital that we use it well. Not every school provides unlimited access to photocopiers. However, the amount of English acquired by students is not linked to the amount of equipment at the teacher's disposal. So don't despair if we have little more than a blackboard to work with.

Black Board

Tips for Optimum Use

- Underline important features or use different coloured chalk/pens. We can highlight points which might be difficult for students, such as, auxiliaries, irregular endings, use of pronouns or contracted forms.
- Use tables for prompting. We can build these up with students and can use for controlled practice.
- Use diagrams, mind maps and time-lines to clarify abstract concepts such as time, space, quantity.

Models of Objects

When certain characteristics of physical objects, such as their size or complexity, make their use inappropriate, then models of such objects might serve the purpose. A cutaway model of the diesel engine would probably better serve most presentations than the actual engine, since the engine's interior could be studied in detail.

Motion Picture

Motion picture or film, also called a movie, is a story conveyed with moving images. It is produced by recording photographic images with cameras, or by creating images using animation techniques or visual effects. The process of film-making finds developed into an art form and industry.

Series of still photographs on film could be projected in rapid succession onto a screen. Motion pictures are filmed with movie camera, which makes rapid exposures of people or objects in motion, and shown with a movie projector, which reproduces sound synchronised with the images. The principal inventors of motion-picture machines were Thomas Alva Edison (US) and the Lumière brothers in (France).

Films are cultural artifacts created by specific cultures,

which reflect those cultures, and, in turn, affect them. Film is considered to be an important art form, the source of popular entertainment and powerful method for educating or indoctrinating citizens. The visual elements give motion pictures the universal power of communication. Some films became popular worldwide attraction through dubbing or subtitles translating the dialogue into the language of the viewer.

Difference amongst Methods, Techniques and Aids

Teaching methods: These reflect the strategies to go through some specific topic or subject.

Techniques: These are the "ways" to present or deliver the "methods".

Aids: These are the documentations and equipments meant for training.

Method is the way the teacher approaches the students. It is the manner in which we use tools for teaching. In the teaching method, how teacher deliver the content material for brainstorming discussion. The technique refers to skills in handling teaching tools such as OHP, gesture of explaining things... method....whole class, small group, one to one and technique, how we use visual aids or other materials to teach/inspire those pupils.

Models of Learning

Cone of Experience—Dale

The Cone of Experience is a visual model meant to summarise Dale's classification system for mediated learning experience.

The original labels for Dale's ten categories are: Direct, Purposeful Experiences; Contrived Experiences; Dramatic Participation; Demonstrations; Field Trips; Exhibits; Motion Pictures; Radio; Recordings; Still Pictures; Visual Symbols; and Verbal Symbols.

When Dale researched learning and teaching methods, he found that much of what we found about were true about direct and indirect (and of concrete and abstract) experience that could be summarised in a pyramid or 'pictorial device' Dales called 'the Cone of Experience'.

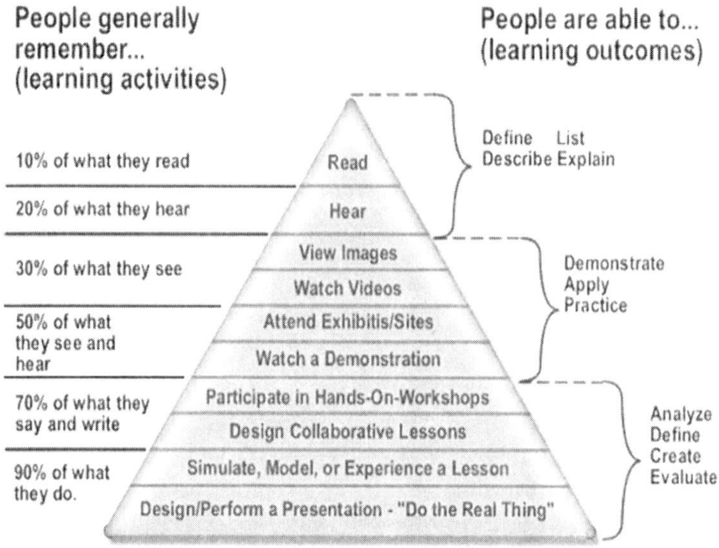

In his book *'Audio Visual Methods in Teaching'* - 1957, explained that the cone was not offered as the perfect or mechanically flawless picture to be taken absolutely literally. It was merely designed as visual aid to help explain the inter-relationships of some various audio-visual materials, as well as individual 'positions' in the learning process.

Dale points out that it would be a dangerous mistake to regard the bands on the cone as rigid, inflexible divisions.

He said, *"The cone device is a visual metaphor of learning experiences, in which the various types of audio-visual materials are arranged in the order of increasing abstractness as one proceeds from direct experiences"*

People Remember

It is said that people remember:

- 10 per cent of what they read;
- 20 per cent of what they hear;
- 30 per cent of what they see;
- 50 per cent of what they see and hear;
- 70 per cent of what they write and say;
- 90 per cent of what they say as they do;

The percentages beyond 10 per cent of what they read, 20 per cent of what they hear, 30 per cent of what they see, 50 per cent of what they head and see 70 per cent of what they say or write, 90 per cent of what they say as they do a thing. The bogus percentages appear to have been first published by an employee of Mobil Oil Company in 1967, writing in the magazine "Film and Audio-Visual Communications". These percentages have since been discredited.

Old Chinese Proverb

"What I hear, I forget;

What I see, I remember;

What I do, I understand."

Stands true but only again as a saying, and NOT as statistical fact.

The Learning Pyramid

In a similar vein, Dale's Cone of experience is the 'Learning Pyramid' from "National Training Laboratories in Bethel Maine", where retention rates are shown as percentage rates against delivery techniques. There is a lot of similarity between the two models—the difference is that this appears to be a complete hoax.

Where these numbers come from is a mystery to many, and indeed difficult to understand what 90 per cent retention actually means? 90 per cent of what for how long? As a model, it looks and on first thought appears to be credible, however as many of us know some people have almost 100 per cent retention for a considerable period of time, if they read something, teach others from some structure or procedure which they seldom understand.

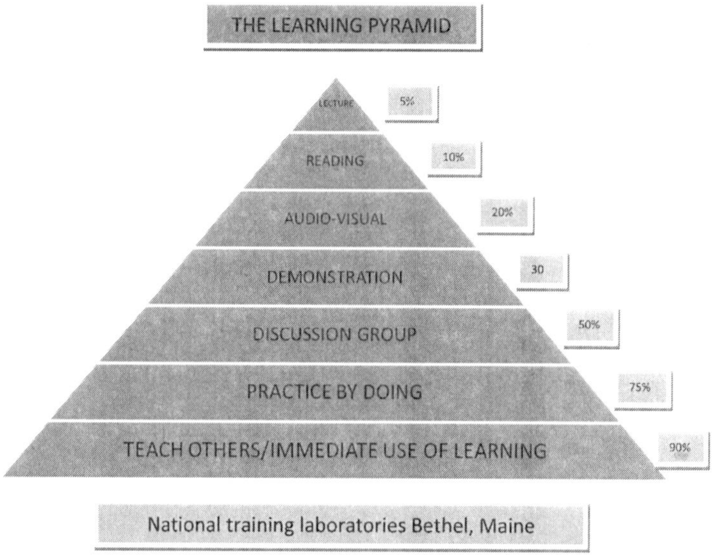

90% - 75% - 50% - 30% - 10% - 5%

Remember

The Numbers on Dale's Cone of experience and the learning pyramid are models without demonstrable research and should not be used as evidential fact.

3
Art of Questioning— Programmed Learning

Art of Questioning?

Questioning is the most important devices of teaching. The success of teaching to a great extent depends upon the skill of art with which we put questions. According to Thring, "Teaching means skillful questioning to force the mind to see, to arrange, to act". Parker says, "Questioning is the key to all educative activity." In the words of Colvin, "No teacher of elementary or secondary subject can succeed in his instruction that has not a fair mastery of the art of questioning."

Art of Answering

A teacher must address on a daily basis, the most frequent would undoubtedly be the task of answering questions out of countless duties and responsibilities. This is, after all, an extension of the basic role of a teacher; to pass knowledge, to relay information, and to resolve uncertainty. In fact, the volume of queries proposed to a teacher on any given day can be remarkably overwhelming. There have been occasions in which the teacher felt as though he/she had to consciously strain to keep their own eyes from crossing by the end of a class, simply because of the barrage of questions. As teachers, we must be incredibly cautious in endeavouring to address requests. In fact, it is because of the task of answering questions, the sequence ought to must be handled with a certain degree of delicacy and thoughtfulness. We must constantly remain intentional about how we answer mindful of the fact that there is an art to answer questions.

The way most of the questions answered by us not only speak volumes to a student about how we regard the content of our class, but it will also greatly inspire their own perception of the subject and their motivation for the remainder of the course. We must be careful to answer questions promoting thought in the mind of student instead of preventing it. When teachers simply dole out direct answers and advice upon request, students become less capable of developing their own sophisticated ideas and become squarely dependent on the teacher. The best way to avoid this is to, whenever possible, reciprocate questions. By doing so, we redirect the responsibility for creative thinking back, between the ears of the student. It develops a tendency among students to internalise their questions and finding answers for themselves when this is done consistently. This should, of course, be the goal of every teacher, to create independent thinkers, who no longer need our constant advice and direction.

The Purpose

1. **To test knowledge:** Questions are being asked to test the previous knowledge of students, i.e., to find out what the students already know.

2. **To locate difficulties:** Questions can be used for locating difficulties so that these may be resolved.

3. **To arouse motivation:** Questions are being asked to arouse motivation in them. They aim at simulating curiosity, focusing attention and awakening interests of the students.

4. **To secure active participation:** Questions are being asked for co-operation and active participation of the students. If the teacher asks questions, students are

compelled to respond to what is being said and are forced to remember.

5. **To apply knowledge:** Another purpose of asking questioning is to allow pupils to apply basic knowledge. In answering those, the pupil ought to make use of the acquired information. This helps him in retaining the memory.

6. **To recapitulate:** Questions are also being asked to recapitulate the lesson learnt and to fix it securely and clearly in the minds of pupils.

7. **To promote original thinking:** Sometimes, questions are being deliberately framed so that their answers cannot be found directly in teacher's lecture or in any text book. Such questions encourage independent thinking and originality of ideas.

8. **To increase self-confidence:** When students answer questions successfully, they feel to have understood and learnt the concerned lesson, gaining self-confidence.

9. **To maintain discipline:** Oral questions have some disciplinary value in class in keeping up attention and preventing misbehaviour. A student who appears to be inattentive or creates mischief can be questioned.

10. **To promote intellectual development:** Questions are being used for maintaining and creating intellectual atmosphere in the class. Asking question can be the means of intellectual and social development of the child. It increases mutual contact of pupils enabling their development.

Prof. Frank A. Butlar emphasises on the purpose of questions:

(i) To change view-points.

(ii) To bring out cause effect relationships.

(iii) To develop new ideas.

(iv) To promote understanding.

(v) To apply information.

(vi) To stimulate thinking.

(vii) To develop appreciation.

(viii) To discover the status of group or individual learning.

(ix) To create mind set.

(x) To test for objectives taught.

Classification of Questioning

1. **Natural Questions:** Natural questions are those which the questioner spontaneously asks . He does not know the information about which he enquires, except to know the information. Children's spontaneous questions belong to this type.

2. **Formal Questions:** Formal questions are those where the questioner knows about the answer. The teacher questions this category. They are usually asked by him to stimulate some response on his response on the part of pupil. The formal questions can be classified into three types:

(a) **Introductory or Preliminary questions:** These questions are being asked at the beginning of each lesson. The purpose of introductory questions are:

(i) To test the previous knowledge.

(ii) To know on how and where to start.

(iii) To bring the knowledge of students in the forefront for knowledge anew.

Precautions: The precautions in introductory questions are:

(i) Questions should be a few in number.

(ii) Only relevant questions should be asked.

(iii) They should help in revision of the previous lesson.

(b) **Developing Questions:** These questions are being asked by the teacher in the course of his lesson. He develops his lessons with the help of such questions. The purpose of asking such developing questions are:

(i) To stimulate the mental activity among pupils.

(ii) To discover new facts, to formulate new generalisation.

(iii) To direct attention on important facts.

(iv) To proceed along by step.

Precautions: The precautions in developing questions are:

(i) These questions should lead the students discover new facts with solution.

(ii) Questions for the sake of questions should not be asked.

(iii) While narrating a story or incident, questions should not be asked in between. However, questions may be asked in the end.

(iv) If a paragraph is being read, questions should not be asked till it is finished.

(c) **Recapitulatory Questions:** These questions are being asked at the end of the lesson as well at the end of the each section in its progression. They are being asked for the following purpose:

(i) To revise the lesson.

(ii) To make the teacher ensure students on being properly learnt the subject matter.

(iii) To fix up the knowledge learnt in their minds.

Precautions: The precautions in recapitulatory questions are:

(i) Black-board writing should be rubbed off.

(ii) Pupils may be allowed to think for a while.

(iii) The questions may be in detail preferably topical.

Characteristics of Good Questions

Questions direct critical learning of the taught and in

order to be of worth, following are some characteristics of good questions:

1. *These must be brief and direct:* To the point of clarity, the question should be brief and direct. It should be reasonable and simply short so that the thought can be easily grasped by pupils. It saves time and makes the understanding very easy.

2. *The rapport of pupils must be encouraged:* Profitable reflection and thinking depend upon good questions. The learners should comprehened the significance of questions according to the aim and nature.

3. *Carefully planned questions help the sequence:* Advance homework is needed in every stage of learning. It should be formulated with reference to the objective and *selected* care.

4. *Thinking and reasoning:*Accomplishment of objective, stimulation and encouragement of favourable expression develop through provoking. There should not be any direct questions vetoeing the answer. The exercise will be a failure without stimulation.

5. *Question must be definite:* When required, definite reliable, objective and valid questions should be asked. In this way, assured thoughts constructively find conveyed when found susceptible.

6. *Allocated in logical order:* To understand the comprehensiveness or entirety of the lesson, the questions must be arranged in logical order to avoid confusion among the pupil, who falls short of the teacher's purpose.

7. *Good questions must be interrelated:* The consequences relate to one another on specific relationship between facts or points.

8. *Certain Aims:* Questions must follow certain aims which have direct relation to the objectives of the lesson. There should be an obvious and clear reason for each narration, presentation and recitation amongst the pupil,

even each and every question so asked to the class shall have conceived purpose.

9. *Avoid textbook language*: Effective questions must be free from the textbook to facilitate thought-provoking initiative, thinking, opinion, accepted wisdom, judgement, analysis, interpretation, logic and reasoning power of pupils. textbook questions can be used.

10. *Questions reflect variance:* The degree of difficulty of question must progress from easy to difficult level. Simple questions must begin to encourage and develop interest in the pupil but with the progression more difficult question should be posed.

Techniques of Asking Questions

A. When to ask questions

1. **In the beginning:** Questions may be asked in the beginning to test about the previous knowledge in antcipation about what and where to start.

2. **In the course of lesson:** Questions may be asked in the course to discover new facts and proceed step by step.

3. **During exposition:** Questions may be asked during exposition to stimulate mental activity and direct attention points.

4. **During recapitulation:** Questions may be asked at the end of the lesson as well as at the end of the each section in progression to revise the lesson and fix up the learnt knowledge of students.

B. How to ask questions?

1. **Address to the whole class:** Questions should be addressed to the whole class rather on the individual pupil. it has two merits:

- Secure attention for everybody all: It secures attention of all students awakening their interest.
- Avail equal opportunity: It provides opportunity to

the members of the class attentive answer. If a particular student had been called in by name, the rest of the class will beecome inattentive.

2. **Apportion the questions:** Questions should be well distributed over the whole class. These should not be confined to a few bright students or front benchers. The teacher should not ignore any pupil nor questions asked in rotation. Pupil should not know beforehand who ought to answer ahead.

3. **Space sufficient time:** The teacher should give sufficient time to think and formulate the answer. However, the time so allowed depends upon the difficulty of question and the capacity of pupils. Allowing much time makes the brighter students impatient.

4. **Avoid repetition:** Teacher should not repeat the questions unnecessarily. Habitual repetition leads to inattention, as pupils think to hang on indefinitely.

5. **Avoid change in structure:** Change in structure discourages response and hinders the mental activity of students. The question should be put in the very first instance in the best possible mode.

6. **Ask only relevant questions:** Only relevant questions should be asked. There should be some logical sequence for unifying learning.

7. **Ask well-graded questions:** Questions should neither too easy nor too difficult. Easier questions may cause inattention or indifference and difficult questions will certainly discourage the children. The standard of difficulty should be according to the intelligence and achievement of individual pupils.

8. **Back benchers shoudn't be ignored:** Teacher should occasionally ask questions to back-benchers and inattentive pupils. The back-benchers should not be ignored simply because they are seated at a distance.

9. **Ask questions without suggestion:** The teacher

should frame the question without pootraying answer.

10. **Show some adaptability:** The teacher should show some adaptability in questioning. He cannot guess fully the class room situation. He should leave well planned questions aside and formulate new questions on demamd.

11. **Audible to all:** Questions should be audible even to those sitting on the back-benches.

12. **Be jovial and cheerful:** Questions should be asked in pleasing and affectionate manner. The teacher should make the pupil confident. This has some healthy psychological effect.

Avoid elliptical questions: Teacher should avoid elliptical as well as echo and double—barreled questions.

Programmed Learning

Concept of Programmed Learning

1. **Susan Markle's view:** According to Dr. Susan Markle, "Programmed learning is a method of designing a reproducible sequence of instructional events to produce a measurable and consistent effect on behaviour of each and every acceptable student.

2. **Harold W. Bernard's view:** Programmed learning refers to the arrangement of instructional material in progressive sequences.

3. **Michael J. Apter's view:** "Programmed instruction is a method of instruction in which the information to be taught is broken down into small units which are to be presented to the student (usually in a written form) in a carefully planned sequence. Each unit, or 'frame', contains not only information but is also terminated with a question.

In the light of above concepts, programmed learning is a method of individualised instructions where the student receives input relating to personal needs in progressive sequence, but in small units. He remains active and proceeds at his own rate. He knows immediately whether he is right or wrong. In a sense, programmed learning makes effective use of programmed books, language laboratory, teaching machines, films, radios, television, tape-recorder and responsible teacher.

Fundamental Principles

1. **Small steps:** A programme is made up of a large number of small and easy steps. We learn better in small steps, on the likelihood of errors reduced.

2. **Active response:** Programmed learning is based on the principle of active response. A student learns better if he actively participates in the lesson. In programmed learning, the student learns best, if he responds actively while learning.

3. **Immediate confirmation:** The student learns best if his answer finds immediately confirmed. This will serve as a kind of motivation or reinforcement.

4. **Self-pacing:** In programmed learning, each student can proceed at his own rate (pace). Some students learn more rapidly or more slowly than others. The student can learn very effectively, if he learns at his own pace. The principle is based on the individual differences in the process of teaching and learning.

5. **Evaluation:** Constant evaluation is another fundamental principle of programmed learning. It helps students learn and grasp the material tailored in each frame. The purpose of this arrangement is not to test the student but to improve the quality of programmed materials through checking the number of errors in each step.

The Steps Involved

Dr. K.P. Pandey enlisted the following steps in preparation of such programme:

1. **Selection of Unit:** The first step in preparation of programme is selection of a unit to be programmed. As far

as possible, the programme should begin with small unit. The programmer need not have tendency to select a very wide and general topic. If he does so, he will commit mistakes, ending up frustrated. Lysaught and Williams have suggested six criteria for selection of a unit to be programmed:

(i) **Programmer's Own Field of Study:** The topic selected should belong directly to programmer's own field of study.

(ii) **Ease:** Ease in the handling of material is another criterion.

(iii) **Length:** Length of the unit should be determined according to the desired objective for the subject matter. Instead of programming a full course in mathematics or grammar, it is better to take a unit of the course.

(iv) **Depressed Level of Learning:** Notorious stumbling blocks of learners must be programmed.

(v) **Logical Order of Material:** Logical order of material needs be followed in such selection.

(vi) **Special Student Needs:** Special student needs in selecting a topic for programme are also an important criterion.

2. **Writing Assumptions:** Characteristics of learners or the audience for whom the programme is being prepared should be written fully and accurately. Programmer should assume about their age, interests, abilities or skills, ambitions and background. It should be written in objective, concrete and specific terms. Cumulative records, achievement tests, intelligence tests, aptitude tests, case history and above all, the personal experiences of the programme as a teacher or learner may prove useful in portrayal of learners.

3. **Defining Instructional Objective:** Instructional objectives should be defined in behavioural terms on the following points:

(i) **Subject matter and teaching method:** Statement of instructional objective guides selection of the subject matter, the teaching methods, and the material to be used.

(ii) **Evaluation of instruments:** Statement of instructional objectives should provide a guide for constructing tests and other equipments for evaluation.

(iii) **Student performance:** State each objective in terms of student performance rather on the learning product.

(iv) **Learning process:** State each objective in terms of learning process rather on learning the product.

(v) **Terminal behaviour:** State each objective on terminal behaviour rather on the subject-matter to be covered.

(vi) **General outcome:** State each objective incorporating general learning outcome rather on the combination of several results.

4. **Define pre-requisite knowledge:** Pre-requisite knowledge and skills should be defined in behavioural terms. It demarcates the mastery or terminal behaviour the programmer ought to develop. A careful study is essential in effective learning and teaching. The list should be prepared in terms of an empirical study on representative sample of learner for whom the programme is being prepared.

5. **Criterion test:** A criterion test shows the range of terminal behaviour ought to be developed. It determines the success or failure of the programme. Think carefully about the unpleasant situations evoking desired behaviour. The whole structure should be reviewed by an expert on the subject matter as well as the techniques involved following the entire test administered on representative group of subjects. The choice of words, the use of language and relevance of each test item should be properly analysed. In the words of Dr. K.P. Pandey, "A good criterion test is

one which reflects representative elements of the universe of behaviour which have been considered as the terminal behaviour."

6. **Developing contents:** Specific outline of content to be programmed ought to be developed. At this stage, the programmer writes the complete information. He lists relevant examples, concepts, illustrations, i.e., diagrams, maps, charts be included in the content. Ensure the authenticity of the subject matter. Decide on which instructional matter need to be presented. Subject matter should be presented according to the level and needs of students.

Team Teaching

Definitions

1. **J.T. Shplin's view:** "Team teaching is a type of instructional organisation, involving teaching personnel and the students assigned to them, in which two or more teachers are given the responsibility, working together, for all or a significant part of instruction of some group of students."

2. **M.B. Naik's view:** "In a team teaching method, two or more teachers make a plan of the subjects co-operatively, carry it out, and always evaluate its effects on the students periodically".

3. **Michael J. Apter's view:** In his book "The New Technology of Education", Apter remarks. "Team teaching involves bringing together a number of classes whose teaching is then the joint responsibility of the teachers of these who now constitute a team."

In the light of listed definitions, it can be believed that team teaching involves some group of teachers jointly responsible for planning and instruction at an elementary, secondary or college level. The group may be as few as two or as many as five or six depending upon the nature and objectives of the course, the size of the class, and the facilities to be used. The teachers cooperatively develop the programme of instruction and share in expert teaching, evaluation and course improvement.

Operational Definitions

A group of two or more teachers work together to plan, conduct and evaluate about the learning activities for the same group of learners.

Quinn and Kanter (1984) define team teaching as "simply team work between two qualified instructors who, together, make presentations to an audience."

Here two broad categories of team teaching appear:

- **Category A: Teachers plan and execute together:** Two or more teachers are planning together for teaching at the same time to the same students in the same classroom;
- **Category B: Teachers plan together and execute Separately:** The teachers plan together but do not compulsorily teach at the same time to the same groups of students.

In Category A, the team teachers might perform a number of different roles. This type of teaching generally involves two associates for economic reasons. **Maroney (1995) and Robinson and Schaible (1995)** have identified some six models of team teaching.

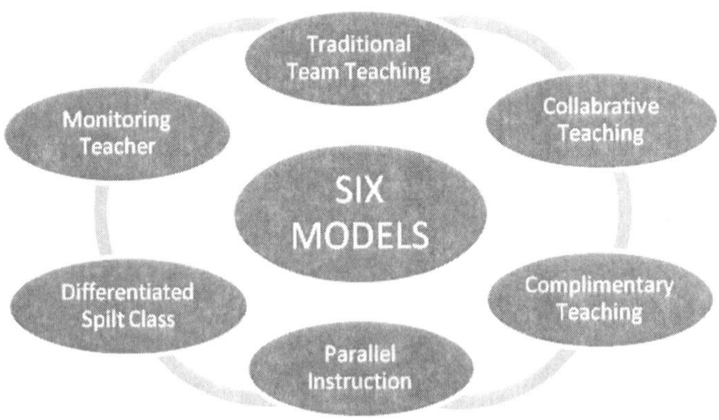

Combination of those models by and large involves in Category A team teaching according to the personalities and strengths of learners and the personalities, philosophies or strengths of team teachers.

- **Collaborative teaching**: The description of traditional team teaching situation depends upon the academic experience, where the team teachers work together in designing the course and teach the material not by usual monologue, but rather by exchanging and discussing ideas and theories in front of learners. Not only do they work together, but the course adopt group learning techniques for learners, such as small-group work, student-led discussion and joint test.
- **Traditional team teaching**: The instruction of content and skills to students are being shared by teachers. For example, one teacher may present the new material to students, while the other constructs a concept map on the overhead projector as students listen to the presenter.
- **Monitoring teacher**: A teacher assumes the responsibility for instructing the entire class during particular situation, while the other circulates the room and monitors student understanding and behaviour.
- **Differentiated split class**: Dividing the class into smaller groups according to learning needs remain the features of this type of teaching. Each educator provides the respective group with the instruction material for their learning needs. For example, a class may be divided into learners grasping adding fractions and those in need of more practice. One teacher would challenge the learners who grasped the concept more quickly, while the second teacher would likely review or re-teach those requiring further instruction.
- **Complimentary/Supportive Team:** A teacher is

responsible for teaching the content during particular situation, while the other takes charge of providing follow-up on the related topics or study skills.

- **Parallel instruction**: In this setting, the class is divided and each teacher finds responsible for teaching same material to her/his smaller group. This model is used in conjunction with other forms ideally suited to the situation when students are involved in projects or problem-solving activities, as the instructor could roam and extend individualised support.

Category B team teaching consists of a variety of team teaching models, where the instructors work together but necessarily not teach same groups of students, they do not teach simultaneously. This category of team teaching can take many forms:

- **Sharing ideas and resources independently:** An example arose during the Master of Teaching (MT) lecture series on November 9th, 1999, when five recent MT graduates shared their experience after 50 days on job. Although, these teachers were not teaching in the same class, they participated in daily meetings, ongoing discussions and planned curriculum together. A recent article in *Mathematics Teacher* (Rumsey, 1999) describes *cooperative teaching* wherein instructors share ideas and resources but otherwise teach independently. This version of cooperative teaching entails weekly meetings and teaching-resource notebook. The goals of the meetings discuss the concepts to be covered during the following week about the ways of teaching for ideas anew. The resource notebook is a comprehensive collection of teachers' best ideas for ready use.
- **A common resource centre:** In this form, teachers instruct classes independently, but share resource materials such as lesson plans, supplementary textbooks and exercise problems. Teams, wherein

members share a common group of students, share the planning for instruction but **teach different sub-groups within the whole group**. This resembles the Master of Teaching program where the professors share a common group, or cadre, but teach sub-groups separately.

- **Individual plans:** This model does not take full advantage of the team concept as an individual's ideas are being incorporated. Sometimes, due to time or financial constraints, there woft be no alternative for designing the entire program.
- **The team members share planning, but each instructor teaches his/her own specialised skills area to the whole group of students**. An example could be some seven instructors teaching seven different topics in Mathematics 30 to seven different classes, rotating the duration throughout the course.

Guiding Principles

Kenneth has the following guiding principles:

1. **Appropriate size and composition:** It may be convenient and most effective to assemble two or more classes and pupils. Much smaller groups are desirable for others. Individual tutoring and private study are essential. Streaming and setting may be the best solution. Fixed ability groupings may be preferred. Reduction in the size of classes seldom act as panacea, whether it be 40, 35, or 20. The number may be 200, 20 or suit the needs of learning. The concept of the fixed size class is obsolete.

2. **Allotted time must be appropriate:** A fairly fluid time table is essential. Since the pupils' interests cannot be switched on and off. All lessons should be dissimilar in length.

3. **Appropriate environment:** For 'straight' lessons, the conventional class room may still have laboratories, libraries, workshops, listening and viewing rooms, with

individual study cartels. The physical layout of the typical school rarely provides such things.

4. **Supervision depends upon the purpose:** The arrangement where one teacher takes charge of the class works tolerably well. Many situations seldom expect the teacher carry on single-handed. He needs the assistance of his colleagues, either as consultants or as fellow workers.

5. **Teachers should discharge on qualifications and interests:** A teacher who is a first rate lecturer may not necessarily be good leader for discussion group or remedial work take backward pupils his métier. Some have a flair for expounding subject to larger audience, others for sympathetic attention to individual pupil. Ideally every teacher should assume the role for which he is best fitted.

6. **Matching of style of instruction with learner:** Attention should be duly paid to individual differences.

Advantages of Team Teaching

- *Better planning:* In traditional system, two teachers spend time in planning separately the same unit for different classes in different rooms. In team teaching, each teacher devote more time to plan and prepare his unit since he has more time for that purpose.
- Improvement in teaching technique.
- Lecture-style instruction is being eliminated in favour of a dynamic style:

Interplay of personalities

Lectures require students to act as passive receptors of communicated information, but team teaching involves the student in the physical and mental stimulation created by viewing individuals at work.

- Teaching staff act as role models for discussion and disagreement.

Teaching staff members demonstrate on disagreed modes exposing students to the course content.

- Team teaching makes effective use of existing human resources.

  Acquisition of additional resources or equipment is not required except reorganisation.

- Team teaching has the potential for revitalising instructional capabilities through dialogue.

  Team teaching begins with the recognition that the instructor/student link is critical and offers an approach enriching student understanding.

- Interest in traditional courses can be stimulated since students share the enthusiasm and intellectual discourse that the lecturers communicate.

  Team teaching is not boring. Students are drawn into the situation from the first moment.

- The effective use of facilities is possible.

  The impersonal nature of large lecture halls can be enlivered through an interactive and dynamic situation.

- Team teaching provides opportunities for interaction with the audience.

Working as part of team has a multitude of advantages. It gives the participating teacher supportive environment, allows for development of new teaching approaches, aids in overcoming academic isolation, increases the likelihood of sound solutions regarding the discipline of problematic students besides augmenting the opportunity for intellectual growth.

Team members are part of supportive environment in where they are exposed to different styles of planning, organisation, and class presentation. This avails the team members an opportunity to develop and enhance self-styled teaching approaches and methods. Another benefit of team teaching is that working closely with one or more colleagues enables teachers to overcome the inherent isolation.

When an instructor teaches solo, she rarely has the time or the opportunity for interacting with her fellow teachers, though she is surrounded by educational colleagues. By working together, team teachers can discuss issues relating to students, such as behavioural expectations, student motivation and teaching policies, and end up with improved solutions.

Robinson and Schaible (1995) describe each team member as a sounding board for sharing the joys and the disappointments of particular class sessions. When team teaching involves interdisciplinary subjects, each member could enlighten about lesser-known fields, and grow intellectually.

Students seldom learn at the same pace. Periods of equal duration are not appropriate for learning situations. Educators are no longer dealing primarily with top-down transmission of the tried and true approach by the mature and experienced teacher to the young, immature, and inexperienced pupil in the single-subject classroom. Schools are moving toward the inclusion of another whole dimension of learning: the lateral transmission to every sentient member of society of what has just been discovered, invented, created, manufactured, or marketed. For this, team members with different areas of expertise are invaluable.

Of course, team teaching is not the only answer to problems plaguing teachers, students, and administrators. It requires adequate planning, skilled management, willingness to risk change and even failure, humility, open-mindedness, imagination, and creativity, but the results are worth valuable.

4

Teaching, Techniques and Innovations

Micro-level Teaching

Concept and Features

Micro-level teaching is a feedback device used for the modification of teachers behaviour. It is a skill-based approach modifying teacher's behaviour, according to specified objectives.

It has been considered an effective technique for development of teaching skills-level. The technique has been refined over a period of 3 decades. Micro-level teaching is like a simulation technique for developing teaching skills and is used to shape the teacher's behaviour based on effective feedback.

Micro-level teaching is a scaled down teaching wherein the teacher teaches short lesson to a small group of students for a short period. One teaching skill finds practiced at a time. It is a miniature form of teaching wherein the teaching is being scaled-down in terms of :

- Class size;
- Time;
- Complexity;
- Activities focus on developing specific teaching skill.

Micro-level teaching is carried under controlled

laboratory or clinical situation. It provides opportunities to the teacher trainee to teach specific skills and get immediate feedback on his performance. Thus the trainee first teaches and then analyses what he has done in terms of acquiring teaching skills. The cycle of micro-level teaching continues till the necessary skills required by the profession are acquired entirely. The provision of getting feedback about performance immediately after completion of lesson is a boost to trainee teacher. Micro-level teaching provides excellent opportunity to investigate variables which effect human learning in general and learning of teaching skills in particular. In micro-level teaching, the scheme provides an opportunity for a teacher trainee or experienced teacher to acquire new skills and to refine the old ones. It involves the following operations:

- The analysis of teaching skills in behavioural terms.
- Demonstrations of teaching skills on video tape or film or in normal classroom.
- The trainee plans a short lesson in the subject of his interest wherein he can use teaching skills.
- The trainee teaches the lesson to smaller group of student (5 to 10) which is videotaped or audio-taped.
- Feedback is provided to the student teachers, who observe and analyse his lesson with the help of a supervisor.

Features of Micro-level Teaching

According to Allen and Ryan (1969), there are five important characteristics of micro-level teaching. They are as follows:

(i) It is a genuine teaching work. Although, its teaching situation is constructed one, the real teaching does take place.

(ii) It reduces the complexities of normal class-room teaching in terms of class size, scope of content and duration.

(iii) It emphasises the acquisition of competency in specific teaching skills. Training for accomplishing particular tasks and the practice of teaching techniques are laid stress.

(iv) It aims at increased control of practice. The variables like time from methods of feed-back from and supervision can, however, be manipulated according to needs and circumstances.

(v) It provides immediate feedback of the trainee's performance and gives wider scope for getting knowledge of results without delay.

Micro-level Teaching Procedure (Steps in Micro-Teaching)

The micro-level teaching procedures involve the following steps:

1. **Defining the Skill:** A particular skill is defined to trainee in terms of teaching behaviours to provide the knowledge and awareness of teaching skills.

2. **Demonstrating the Skills:** The specific skill is demonstrated by the experts or shown through video tape or film to the teachers, trainee.

3. **Planning the Lesson:** The student teacher plans a short (micro) lesson with the help of his supervisor, in which he can practice on a particular skill.

4. **Teaching a Lesson:** The pupil-teacher teaches the lesson to a small group of pupils (i.e., 5–10 pupils). The lesson is observed by supervisor (teacher) or peers or video-taped or audio-taped or televised on close circuit television (C.C.T.V.).

5. **Discussion:** The teaching is followed by discussion for feedback (suggested improvement) to the trainee. The awareness of his own teaching performance provides the re-enforcement to the pupil-teacher.

6. **Re-planning:** In the light of discussion and

suggestions, the pupil-teacher replans the lesson in order to practice the small skill effectively.

7. **Re-teaching:** The revised lesson is re-taught to another small group of students of same class for the same duration to practice the same skill.

8. **Re-discussion:** The re-teaching is followed again by discussions, suggestion and encouraging the teaching performance. Thus, the trainee fetches the feedback again.

9. **Repeating the Cycle:** The 'teach-re-teach' cycle is repeated till desired level of skill is being achieved.

Difference between Micro-level and Traditional Teaching

1. **Simple versus Complex Teaching:** Micro-level teaching is a simple and non-threatening. Traditional teaching is relatively complex and threatening.

2. **Objectives:** In micro-level teaching, objectives are specified in behavioural terms. In traditional teaching objectives are not specified in behavioural terms.

3. **Providing Feedback:** In micro-level teaching, immediate feedback is provided, but not in traditional teaching.

4. **Size of Class:** In micro-level teaching class is divided into small group of five to ten pupil-teachers. In traditional teaching, the class consists of some fifty to hundred pupil-teachers.

5. **Duration:** In micro-level teaching, the duration runs between five and ten minutes. In traditional teaching, the duration hangs on for forty to sixty minutes.

6. **Interaction Pattern:** In micro-level teaching, patterns of classroom interaction can be objectively studied, but not in traditional teaching.

7. **Practising Skills:** In micro-level teaching, the pupil-teacher practices only one skill selected for practice. In traditional teaching, the pupil-teacher practices the whole complex teaching behaviour.

8. **Role of Supervisor:** In micro-level teaching, the role of supervisor is specific and well-defined to improve teaching. In traditional teaching the role of supervisor is vague and not useful to improve teaching.

9. **Awareness:** Micro-level teaching develops more awareness among student–teachers with regard to professional training.

10. **Score:** Micro-level teaching results better score in university examination than their counterparts in conventional teaching.

Principles Underlying Micro-level Teaching

1. **Principle of Practice:** 'Practice makes a man perfect' is a well known proverb. If any activity is repeated again it could be learned effectively. Micro-level teaching provides practice in each small task or skill. Hence, the pupil teacher gains mastery.

2. **Principle of Reinforcement:** Psychologists have been aware of the value of reinforcement in the learning process. The reinforcement involves teacher encouraging pupils' responses using verbal praise accepting their responses or non-verbal ones like a smile. In micro-level teaching lesson, (reinforcement) encouragement is given to the pupil–teacher from time to time for his better performance with feedback. Consequently, he attains satisfaction and his performance finds damn improved. Reinforcement and feedback stimulate him for better learning and better teaching.

3. **Principle of Experimentation:** Micro-level teaching was born from an experiment. Experimentation consists of objective observation of action performed under controlled conditions. Controlled conditions are being provided in micro-level teaching. The pupil-teacher and supervisor conduct experiment on teaching skill under controlled conditions. Variables such as time, content, students, and teaching techniques can easily be manipulated or controlled. From its very beginning, micro-level teaching has been used as means of research. Many aspects of micro-level

teaching that render valuable training technique also render valuable research tool.

4. **Principle of Evaluation:** A proper evaluation of pupil-teacher work can become an effective motivation for better learning and better teaching. In micro-level teaching, the supervisor supervises and evaluates each micro-level lesson. Self-evaluation is possible. With the help of video-tape recorder, the teacher-trainee will be in a position to evaluate their own performance. On the basis of self-evaluation, improvement can be made.

5. **Principle of Precise Supervision:** The supervision that accompanies micro-level teaching is highly specific and precise. The supervisor pays full attention to one point at a time. The supervisor and the teacher duo are clear about the aim of the micro-level lesson ahead of time. The supervisor possesses an 'observation schedule' which he fills up while supervising. He makes an assessment on a rating scale. Rating is a method wherein we systematise the expression or opinion concerning particular trait.

6. **Principle of Continuity:** Micro-level teaching implies continuity. The teacher learns and relearns the skills of teaching continuously.

Note: Planning→Teaching→Feedback→Replanning→Reteaching→Refeedback till mastery is attained in its unique feature.

Micro-level Teaching Skills

The concept underlying micro-level teaching assumes that teaching consists of various skills. Teaching practice becomes effective only on acquisition of specific skills. It is found by experiment that the behaviour of the teacher and pupil through micro-level teaching gets modified and the teaching-learning process is being made more effective by the skill training.

The researchers in Centre of Advanced Study in Education, M.S. University of Baroda have developed thirteen skills favouring Indian conditions. These are skills in writing instructional objectives introducing a lesson, fluency in questioning, explaining, illustrating with examples, stimulus variations, silence and non-verbal cues, reinforcement, increasing pupil participation, using black-board, achieving closure and recognising attending behaviour. These are different according to the subject area, class level and other varieties.

For micro-level teaching, one skill is selected by a teacher according to his need. The various characteristics of that skill are being identified and practiced according to the micro-level teaching setting.

The concept underlying micro-level teaching assumes that teaching consists of various skills. Teaching practice becomes effective only on acquisition of specific skills. It is found by experiment that the behaviour of the teacher and pupil gets modified through micro-level teaching and the teaching-learning process is being made more effective by the skill training.

The different micro-level teaching skills are as follows:

1. **Skills in Introducing a Lesson:** This skill involves writing objectives that are:

(a) Well-stated,

(b) Adequate with respect to learning outcome;

(c) Relevant to the content;

(d) Adequate with content outline.

2. **Fluency in questioning:** This is a skill in asking questions by the teacher in a given period of time keeping in view of its effectiveness.

3. **Skill explaining:** An explanation is a set of inter-related statements made by the teacher for increasing the understanding among pupils. In order to become an effective explainer in the classroom, the teacher should adopt desirable behaviours like using explaining links, using beginning and concluding statements and testing understanding behaviours like making irrelevant statements, lacking in continuity, using inappropriate vocabulary, lacking in fluency, and using vague words and phrases as far as possible, by the student.

4. **Illustrating with examples:** The use of examples is basic to teaching. Examples are necessary to clarify, verify, or substantiate concepts. An effective use of examples includes:

(i) Starting with simple examples and progressing to more complex ones.

(ii) Starting with examples relevant to students' experience and knowledge.

(iii) Relating the examples to the principles or ideas being taught.

5. **Stimulus variations:** This skill is related to class-room attention. It is based on the principle that changes in the stimuli in one's perception capture his attention. This skill includes the teacher's movements, gestures, change in speech patterns, focusing, changing interaction, styles, shifting sensory channels, pausing and such others.

6. **Silence and non-verbal cues:** The use of silence

and non-verbal cues is a powerful tool in the class-room. During silence deliberately introduced by the teacher, he uses some non-verbal cues like gestures, body movements, to encourage the participation of pupil.

7. **Reinforcement:** Reinforcing desired pupil behaviour through the use of positive reinforcing behaviours is an integral part of learning process. This skill involves teacher encouraging pupils' responses or any desirable behaviour using verbal statements like 'good', 'continue', or non-verbal cues like a smile, nodding the head.

8. **Using black-board:** This skill involves:

(i) Writing legibly on the blackboard using distinctly different letters which are large enough to be read by pupils.

(ii) Neatness in the black-board work can be achieved by retaining only the relevant matter under focus and by seeing that there is no over-writing.

(iii) Appropriateness of written work on the black-board, meaning, brevity, simplicity and continuity in the points being presented, underlining the important facts with coloured chalks, developing the necessary and proportionate diagrams along with the lesson, etc.

9. **Recognising attending behaviour:** Teachers can be trained to become more sensitive to the class-room behaviour of the pupils. The successful teacher, through visual cues, quickly notes indications of interest or boredom, comprehension or bewilderment. Facial expressions, directions of the eyes, the tilt of the head, and bodily posture, offer commonly recurrent cues which make it possible for the skilled teacher to evaluate his class-room performance according to the pupil's reactions.

10. **Increasing pupil participation:** It involves integrating the four components namely, creating set, questioning, encouraging pupil's participation, and pausing in such a way that pupil's participation is maximised.

11. **Class management:** The management dimensions of teaching consist of number of functions or activities that teachers perform as an integral part of the teaching job, i.e., creating conditions within the class-room, group as well as in the class-room environment which enables the students to behave in socially approved ways, and makes learning, challenging and appealing, for

Dr. L.C. Singh described some important skills apart from the above mentioned. These are as follows:

1. Set induction
2. Closure
3. Probing questions
4. Skill of using audio-visual aids
5. Skill of giving assignment
6. Skill of pacing the lesson
7. The use of higher order questions
8. Divergent questions
9. Lecturing
10. Planned repetition
11. Completeness of communication.

For micro-level teaching, one skill is being selected by a teacher according to his need. The various characteristics of that skill are identified and practiced according to the micro-level teaching setting.

Advantages of Micro-level Teaching

1. **Modification of Teacher Behaviour:** Micro-level teaching is an effective feedback device for the modification of teacher's behaviour.

2. **Knowledge of Teaching Skills:** The knowledge and practice of teaching skill can be given by the use of micro-level teaching.

3. **Developing Teaching Skill:** The specific teaching skills are developed by micro-level teaching experiences e.g., reinforcement skill, explaining skill, skill of using blackboard, skill for using audio-visual aids, skill for classroom management, etc.

4. **Developing Teaching Efficiency:** Micro-level teaching is useful for developing teaching efficiency in pre-service and in-service teacher education programmes.

5. **Improving Teaching Practice:** Micro-level teaching is a training device for improving teaching practice and prepares better and effective teachers.

6. **Individual Training:** The training of teachers becomes individualised, each trainee makes progress in developing teaching skills at his own rate depending on his ability.

7. **Regulating Teaching Practice:** Micro-level teaching permits increased, controlled and regulated teaching practice.

8. **Real Teaching:** Micro-level teaching is real teaching. It can be done either in real classroom or simulated conditions.

9. **Reducing Complexities:** Micro-level teaching, as we have stated earlier, reduces the complexities of normal classroom teaching by skilled down teaching. Class size, scope content and time are all reduced.

10. **Focus on Teaching:** It focusses attention on the teaching behaviour to modify and improve in the desired direction.

11. **Self-evaluation:** Micro-level teaching is an economical device and the use of video tape enables the trainee to analyse his own teaching performance.

12. **Extended Reinforcement:** The mechanism of feedback device can be combined with other devise such as simulated social skill training and interaction analysis device, which provide extended reinforcement to the trainee performance.

13. **Research Tool:** Micro-level teaching is a useful research tool which can be used by teacher-candidates to study teaching even during training.

Limitations of Micro-level Teaching

1. **Expensive:** Micro-level teaching is expensive for Indian schools, as an effective micro-level teaching system requires tape records, video tapes and close circuit television.
2. **Narrow scope:** Micro-level teaching provides opportunities for developing only a few skills (say 20 to 25). But, in reality the teaching requires more skills.
3. **Disturbs existing timetable:** Micro-level teaching disturb the existing timetable of practicing schools by calling small group for few minutes (say five or ten).
4. **Presentation in parts:** In five or ten minutes a very small content is being presented which separates or breaks the limbo of lesson.
5. **Difficulties in practice:** In a class of five to ten pupils, the pupil-teacher may gain a lot of confidence, whereas in the class of fifty or more, the teacher fails to teach.

Simulation Teaching

Simulated teaching is one of the best techniques being used currently in India and elsewhere for modification of teacher's behaviour. Under this approach, the classroom rules are simulated. Behavioural problems and classroom managements are better handled through simulated teaching. Cruickshank in 1968 developed a system which is denoted by several terms such as Role playing, Artificial teaching, Pilot training, Laboratory method, Clinical method and Inductive scientific method.

Simulation teaching technique is also employed for bringing modifications about teacher's behaviour. Here the student teacher tries to develop an important skill of communication in a simulated situation by identifying it with the actual classroom environment. This approach of training is known by various names such as role playing, artificial teaching, pilot training, and clinical method. As the term indicates simulation, the technique is an artificial method to develop certain psychomotor behaviour in the trainees. The teacher trainee ought to play zone role related to teaching. The various principles on which simulation is based are:

(a) Learning by doing.

(b) Providing immediate feedback and reinforcement.

(c) Providing a safe platform for practice and

(d) Rehearsal before facing real classroom teaching.

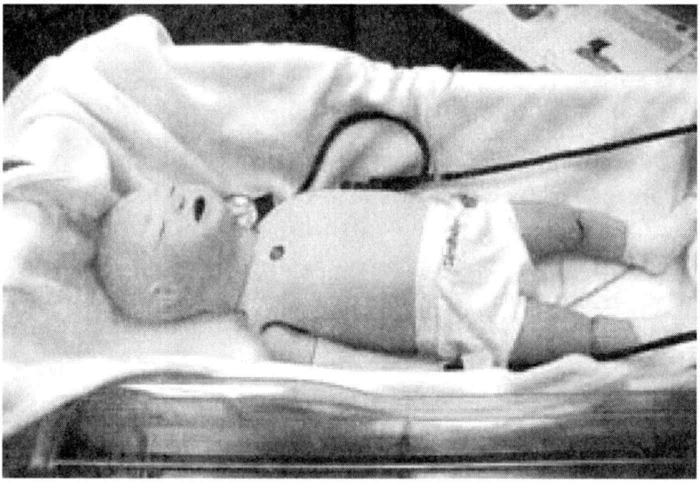

Meaning of Simulation

(i) View of **Thomas** and **Deemer**: "To simulate is to obtain the essence of, without the reality".

(ii) **Harman's** view: "Simulations contain the important parts of, but not all of, reality. Simulations do not have to look like the real-life counterpart, but they do have to 'act' like the real thing."

From this definition, it is clear that when a simulation includes important aspects of reality, it omits other elements of real life situation. When simulations are designed, unimportant elements from real life are subtracted. In the case of simulated displays, there is a reduction of information from the real life source, information that is in some sense unnecessary for the learning of the task. Simulation might be thought of in the following terms.

Simulation = Real life – Task irrelevant elements.

iii. **Webster's** dictionary: Webster's New International Dictionary defines simulation as, "Giving the appearance or affect of; to have characteristics of."

iv. **Tansey'e** View: Simulation is the all-inclusive term which contains those activities–which produce artificial environments or which provide artificial experiences for the participants in the activity.

Simulation can best be defined as a role playing wherein the process of teaching is enacted artificially and an effort is made to practice some important communication skill. Under this, the pupil-teacher and the students simulate a particular role and try to develop and identify with the actual class-room environment. Thus, the whole simulated teaching program becomes training in role perception and role playing. Simulation is the basis of sensitivity training, socio-drama, role-playing and psycho-drama.

Types of Activities

Simulation embraces three types of activities:

1. **Role playing:** Role playing is the simplest of all activities included in 'simulation'. It is essentially either of two types of activities:

(i) It is the act of being someone else, or

(ii) It is the act of acquiring experience in a set of activities wherein the actor seeks to acquire or increase his competence.

The role assumed in role playing is one wherein the

actor portrays either a fictitious role or an actual role, but performs that role in an artificial environment. The use of role playing enables the participant acquire understanding of some situation or relation among real life participants a social process, or the role playing may be used to assist the participants to gain some perception of actions, attitudes, and/or situation of another person.

The role played by the participant may also be one wherein the actor desires to acquire competence, or the actor has previously acquired some familiarity, but desires to improve his level of competence.

2. **Socio-drama:** Socio-drama is the use of role playing as a means of enabling the players seek solution to the social problem being posed. The problem may be one extracted from the real world, or designed for solution. Regardless of this employed situation, the role players (or actors) are required to devise an acceptable solution.

Socio-drama differs from role playing only in objective which is being sought. Role playing seeks to provide competence or understanding in the particular role for the person playing that role. Socio-drama, on the other hand, seeks to utilise the role playing as the means of devising solution to problem situation, prescribed for role players. The problem may be an abstraction from real life.

3. **Gaming:** Gaming is some addition to the technique of socio-drama of an element which demands the development and choice of strategies (or decision making) and some type of pay-of-rewards of deprivations dictated either by chance or by the choice of strategies. The decisions and the rewards are subject to the structures of rules known to set of players. By definition, the situations employed involve outcome which are affected by conditions made by one or more decisions. The game may be designed in the manner which enables some chance to affect the outcome, or chance may be prohibited.

Steps in Simulation

Flanders recommends the following steps:

(i) Selecting pupil-teachers: A small group of pupil-teachers is selected. Letters A, B, C, D, etc., are assigned to each person in the group. Role assignments are rotated by letters so that each individual has a chance to be an actor or observer.

(ii) Selecting and discussing skills: The skills to be practiced are selected and discussed. Topics of conversation befitting skills are also being suggested.

(iii) Deciding on consideration: Consideration as to who will start the conversation, who will intervene, who will stop the interaction and when it will be stopped are decided.

(iv) Evaluation: The procedure of evaluation, kind of data to be recorded and the method of recording, etc., are decided.

(v) Practice session: First practice session is conducted and the actor is provided with feedback on his performance. If necessary, the procedure of the second session is changed in order to improve the training procedure.

(vi) Change in procedure: If need arises, one should be prepared to change the procedure and the topic and move on to the next skill so as to present meaningful challenge to each actor to keep his interest as high as possible.

Advantages of Simulated Teaching

1. **Device for motivating students:** Simulated teaching is a device for motivating students in the words of Cruickshank, "The technique provides reinforcement to students to develop teaching skills and avoid the risk of actual class-room encounter".

2. **Analysis of teaching problems:** Simulated teaching provides opportunities to student-teachers study and analyse critical teaching problems.

3. **Insight into behavioural problems:** A simulated teaching helps students in understanding behavioural problems of class-room and develops insight to encounter them.

4. **Acquisition of class-room manners:** Simulated teaching helps students in acquiring class-room manners. It enables the students to improve social skills and gain confidence in their ability to use such skills.

5. **Link between theory and practice:** The major advantage of using simulated teaching is that we forge close links between theory and practice.

6. **Factual and conceptual knowledge:** Simulated teaching is a means of enabling students acquire factual and conceptual knowledge and retain the knowledge acquired.

7. **Laboratory experiences:** Simulated teaching serves as a social laboratory. It avails opportunities to students exercising social skills acquired, utilise knowledge previously acquired in an artificial environment, and gain some comprehension about the complexities of selected social processes.

8. **Interesting and enjoyable:** Simulated teaching is interesting and enjoyable to students.

Limitations of Simulation

1. **Difficulty for beginners:** The beginner participants may face some difficulties in posing different kinds of questions. A simple task such as "open" and "closed" questions may provide an introductory challenge.

2. **Incorrect recording:** It is quite possible that the observer may record incorrectly during an exercise.

3. **Misconception:** The most common error in serious skill training is the misconception that adults could play in the role of pupils.

5
The System Approach

The System Approach

Its Meaning

System Approach is an innovative and rational problem-solving method of analysing the very educational system and making it more effective. It views the process as a whole with various dimensions and components like:

- Pupils
- Teachers
- Curriculum
- Teaching media and materials instructional strategies
- Physical environment
- Evaluation of instructional objectives

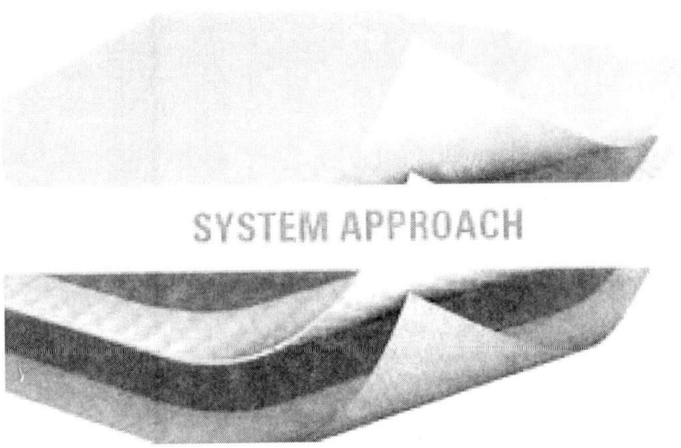

According to the systems approach, the entire teaching-learning process is taken as cybernetic or organic, which is self-generating as well as self-controlling. As the general health of an individual depends upon working conditions of different sub-systems like respiratory, digestive, circulatory, etc., so also the educational achievement and progress at particular stage is proportional to the functional efficiency of various sub-systems like:

- Teacher
- Supervisor
- Administrator
- Librarian
- Evaluator

And so on.....

Integration and interaction among these agencies ought to be promoted for overall efficiency.

The following steps are adopted in the systems approach in education:

1. Definition of instructional goals, behavioural objectives and stating them in operational terms
2. Determination of function for achieving these objectives through the use of various media and materials.
3. Identification of learners' needs and characteristics.
4. Selection of suitable methods for effective learning of the topic.
5. Selection of appropriate learning experiences.
6. Choice of relevant materials, media and resources for such experiences.
7. Assignment of appropriate personnel roles as teachers students, AV personnel, librarian etc.
8. Implementation of the programme starting with a try out under typical conditions.

9. Evaluation of the learning outcome in the light of instrument/instructional and behavioural objectives.
10. Re-definition and revision of goals, objectives, content methods, strategies, for improving learning experiences.

With a view to improving the teaching-learning (input-output) process at the outset, the instructional objectives should be formulated and the operational behavioural objectives be decided in the light of instructional objectives. Adequate linkages should be established between the inputs and outputs and a feedback system be developed for bringing about necessary changes in the teaching-learning process. As Bloom has pointed out, this process is not merely cognitive. It operates in a social, emotional and effective environment. According to Pande, motivational and affective considerations have occupied significant place in the learning process and outcome.

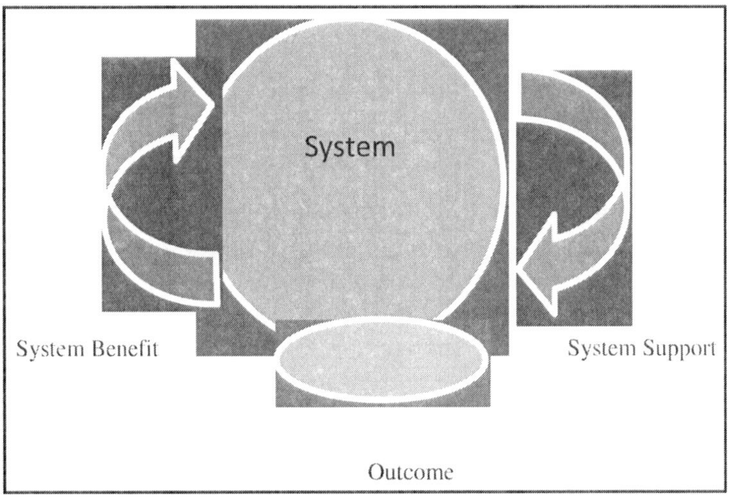

Definition of System

The Webster's dictionary defines a system as "a regularly interacting or independent group of items forming a unified whole". A system is "a group of objects related or interacting so as to form a unity". It also defines a system as "organised or established procedure, or a methodically arranged set of ideas, principles, methods or procedure". System analysis essentially is a systematic way of identifying goals of any system and scientifically working out different steps to move towards these goals, suggesting 'models' for application.

The approach in general includes the following steps:

1. An analysis of the existing situation,
2. Setting up of goals for the desired situation,
3. Defining mechanisms to evaluate the achievements or goals,
4. Generating alternative solutions,
5. Choosing the best possible solution through cost-benefit analysis,
6. Detailing out the design of the system,
7. Outlining the monitoring mechanism for the system, and
8. Working out for introducing the solution.

Systems approach is a rational, problem-solving method of analysing the educational process and making it more effective. System is the process taken as a whole incorporating its aspects and parts, namely pupils, teachers, curriculum content, instructional materials, instructional strategy, physical environment and the evaluation of instructional objectives. Hence, it may be seen that the purpose of the systems analysis is to get the "best equipment in the best place for the best people at the best time and at the best price". The systems approach in instruction is an integrated, programmed complex of instructional media, hardware and personnel whose components are structured as single unit with schedule of time and sequential phasing".

The Components

System approach is a systematic attempt to coordinate the aspects of a problem toward specific objectives. In education, this means planned, organised use of available learning resources, including audio-visual media, to achieve desirable learning objectives by the most efficient possible means. The systems approach focuses first upon the learner and his performances. Only then, it makes decisions about the course content, learning experiences and the most effective media and instructional strategies. Such system incorporates within the capability of providing continuous self-correction and improvement. It is concerned with elements of instruction including media. Its purpose is to ensure the components of organic whole available with proper characteristics at proper time to contribute to the total system fulfilling objectives.

The procedural steps in the system approach in education are:

1. Defining instructional goals, behavioural objectives and stating them in operational measurable terms.
2. Determining functions related to the achievements of goals by proper aids like films, recordings, videotapes, etc.
3. Defining learner characteristics and requirements.
4. Choosing appropriate methods suitable for effective learning of the topic.
5. Selecting appropriate learning experiences from many alternatives available.
6. Selecting appropriate materials, facilities, equipments, resources, environment, and tools required for students experiences.
7. Defining and assigning appropriate personal roles—teachers—team teaching members—supporting personnel—students.

8. Implementing the programme—try with a few pupils in typical and appropriate condition.
9. Testing and evaluating the outcome in terms of original objectives measured in student performance.
10. Refining and revising if necessary to improve production and efficiency of the system to improve student learning.

The Flow Diagram

Planning is fundamental for systematising. System can be easily represented by drawing a map called a flow diagram. The relationship between the input (pupils), instructional strategy (process) and the output can be shown by means of the following simple flow diagram.

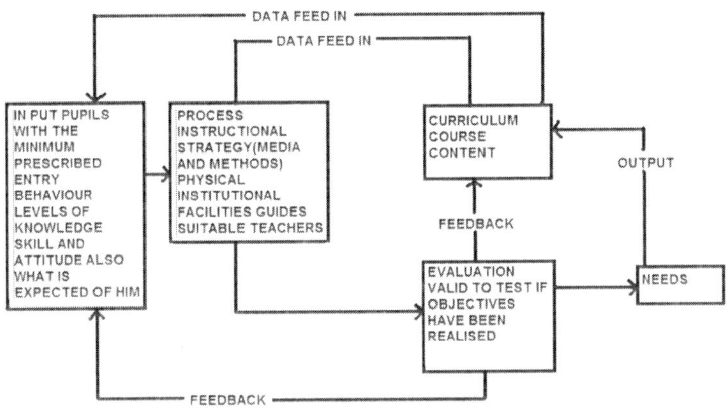

A more extended simple showing in detail the path followed in general at the macro-institutional level can also be illustrated in the form of a flow diagram. Suppose we wish to develop a new course or instructional unit according to the systems concept. We should begin with a survey and analysis of subject matter identifying the skills to be learnt and the characteristics of learners. The specific objectives, learning outcome and performance criteria should then be formulated. An inventory of human, technological and financial resources must be made besides considering the limitations or constraints like time, money, facilities, etc. This is the stage at which we are concerned with media along with other materials. No doubt, course construction and software production can begin only after completion of content, method and media strategies, available materials must be reviewed and examined. Where no suitable materials are available, we must prepare a 'package' in the form of good kits. Field testing and validation provide opportunities to try out newly developed instructional package with a representative sample of students. While full scale try out is underway, we must observe closely all aspects and note further adjustment that may be needed. Implementation is the final step of putting the validate materials into full-scale operation. Continuous feedback should be obtained from learners at every stage leading to further cycle of updating and modification. The least effective methods are recycled out and better materials are incorporated.

Advantages

Sampath *et al.*, have enumerated the following merits in the system approach:

1. It provides a conceptual framework building plans for implementing change in education.
2. It helps to identify the suitability of otherwise of resources material achieving the specific goal.
3. It helps to assess the resource needs, their sources and facilities in relation to quantities, time and other factors.
4. Technologies in advance could be harnessed to provide integration.
5. It permits an orderly introduction of components required for system's success in terms of students.
6. Rigidity in plan of action is avoided as continuous elevation affords desired beneficial changes to be made.

Teaching Machines

Learning usually involves—students and a teacher. However, in the recent tooling up of educational system, the teacher need not be physically present. Of late, both the teacher and student are vitally concerned with the question of acquiring information most rapidly and effectively. Various teaching techniques have been developed and tested. Some have proved their efficiency in this respect. Teaching machines and programmed instruction represent this development and have attracted considerable amount of interest. "Teaching machines and programmed materials are not monsters designed to enslave thought and turn teachers and students into Robots." On the contrary, these methods act as liberating devices that allow for individual differences. Teaching machines and programmed instructions provide not only better education for better costs and savings in time, but also ensure maximum student achievement, the pioneering work in the field of teaching was done by **Sydney L. Plessey** of the Ohio State University, but the peak period of development came after *World War II*. The research and writing of **B.F. Skinner** was chiefly responsible for this remarkable development.

Its Meaning

A Teaching machine is a piece of device designed to be operat by an individual student. It can interact with the student to a remarkable degree. The essential characteristics of various teaching machines are as follows:

1. The student is presented with a question or problem by some form of display on the machine.
2. The student is required to respond overtly. He must do something about the problem, either to write an answer or to push a button to indicate the correct answer.
3. The student is informed as to whether his answer is right or wrong. This is being done either by showing the correct answer or by moving forward to the next frame when a question has been answered correctly.
4. An account is kept on the responses made by the student not for the purpose of testing the acquisition of knowledge, but for teaching purposes.

Programming is done by presenting the subject matter in small discrete interlocking steps, each depending upon the preceding step. Only after the student is committed himself by writing the response to the problem, he operates a lever or button, which exposes the correct answer moved under the piece of glass. The student can only check whether the response is right or wrong but there is no scope for making corrections.

Most teaching machines present the linear programme through a few function as branching type. In some of the complex electronic machines, branching of the complex short is possible.

Like other "Visual aids" mechanical or electronic devices, teaching machines offer much scope as instructional aid, but with marked difference. While other means of communication are primarily aid at teaching masses, teaching machines are intended for individual to proceed at his own pace and continually interact with students. There are machines allowing the student to question, for further information, review and demanding, review and explanation. They are completely individualised in every respect.

Types of Machines

Auto-instructional devices exist in a wide range of technological sophistication. They can be broadly classified under two categories namely constructed response devices and multiple choice machines.

1. Constructed response devices

Constructed response device are based on Skinner's principle namely emission of a response is considered more effective in learning than simple recognition.

(a) The glider machine;

(b) The disc type machine;

(c) The typewriter-input computing machine;

or adopt one of our lovingly restored and converted machines

(d) Audio-visual combination.

2. Multiple Choice Machines

In multiple choice machines, it is responsible to prepare branches for every reply to give question.

(a) Plessey's machines;

(b) Audio-visual machines;

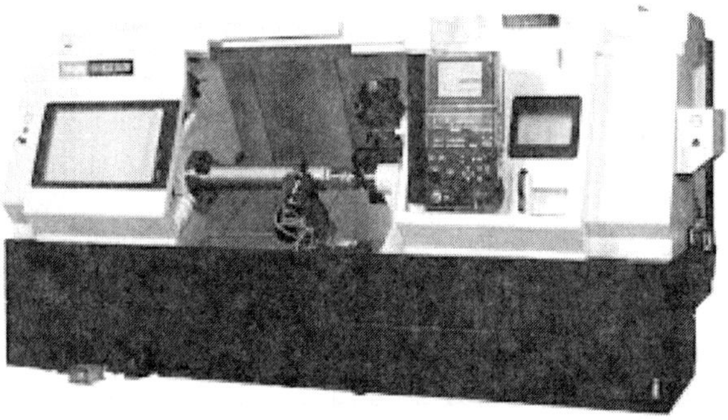

(c) Electronic Computers and Multiple choice Programmes;

(d) Non-mechanical Multiple choice Devices.

Its Values

Programmed Instruction and Teaching machines provide technological solution to the problem of individual differences. Any number of students taught with machines extend teaching experiences. In the present set up, no teacher can be a tutor to each individual, but auto-instruction can be tutorial instructions.

Teaching machines are helpful from the student's point of view. Every student can proceed at his own rate of learning. If he is fast, he goes ahead; if slow, the programmer is not tired to teach him as long as it is required. Sometimes, it will encourage/motivate the students to learn in faster pace.

Machine vs. Teacher

Owing to the advent of teaching machines, teacher's role in a classroom will be changed. Under no circumstances, the teaching machine can replace the teacher. For the overworked teacher burdened with large classes, teaching machines are helpful. The need of the teacher is to inspire and motivate' to guide and correct is in no way diminished by the development of these machines.

Teaching machines are primarily due to the work of research and psychologists. The machines may appear cured as they are today, but painstaking research is still going on. It will definitely improve the technique so that teaching will became the most humane profession.

The greatest value of such mechanical devices and the programmed material used make individualisation of instruction possible. Programmer catering to individual differences among pupil should account not only speed of learning but other physical and psychological variables found in classes. Individual instructions are not just paying personal attention to each pupil, but it consists of designing specifically tailored learning experiences for each pupil on the basis of his or her needs and interests as well as strength and weaknesses. In such a task, planned use of the tools and techniques of educational technology is indispensable.

Computer-assisted Instruction

Today, computers are widely used in business and research. Its applications are enormous. They help in guiding astronauts and space capsules. It counsels students, controls betting at race tracks and chooses the ideal mate for cautious bachelors. It grades the university students, diagnoses football strategy, and plays chess and war games. The efficiency of human beings as data-processing organisms is also being challenged by the computer. The computer can do million calculations within a second. Almost in every field of human activity, computers can stretch its arms and make it perfect. A computer is the most important invention man has found out since the invention of printing machine. While printing has amplified the process of information transmission, the computer has amplified the possibility of information processing.

With these developments, computerisation is still in its infancy. What lies ahead may be beyond the reach of our imagination.

The most exciting innovation in the educational technology is the Computer Assisted Instruction (CAI). Though, it is still in the experimental stage, the day is not far when it will revolutionise the whole process of instruction.

Computer assisted instruction is therefore not merely a sophisticated type of programmed instruction, but a different kind of instruction altogether. No doubt, it uses programmed instruction, but also uses electronic data processing, data communication, concept of audio-visual and media theory, communication theory, systems theory and learning theory.

Advantages of CAI

Computer assisted instruction proves better than other aids in several respects. There is not only saving of time in learning, but it also performs miracles in processing the performance data. This latter characteristic helps determining subsequent activities in the learning situation.

The large amount of information stored in the computer in made available to the learner more rapidly than any medium. The dynamic interaction between the student and instructional programme is not possible in any other media. With CAI, we would completely individualise materials.

Before computers can be of any use, they must be carefully programmed to perform desired functions. This requires thorough planning of every step and prior thinking.

The Limitations

1. It is very expensive.
2. Computers may inject a non-human quality into education programme.

Terminology

Aids : Help or support someone or something - Origin - Old French *aide*.

Analysis : A detailed examination of the element or structure of something.

Answering : Act of something said or written in reaction to a question or statement.

Brochures : A periodical containing information about a product or service.

Collaborative : Persons work jointly on an activity or project.

Communication : The action of communicating, a letter or message, and means of sending message.

Computer : An electronic device capable of storing and processing information in accordance with a set of instructions.

Constructive : Building something usefully and helpfully.

Curriculum : The subjects included in a course of study in a school or college.

Decoder : Convert a coded message into understandable language, convert audio or video signals from analogue to digital.

Demonstration : The action of showing and explaining how something works or is done.

Education : The process of teaching or learning, the theory and practice of teaching, information about or training in a particular subject.

Encoder : Convert into a coded form.

Evaluator : A person who form an idea of the amount or value of.

Experimentation : Process wherein a scientific test is being undertaken to make a discovery, investigate a theory, or demonstrate a known fact.

Feedback : Comments about a product or a person's performance, used as a basis for improvement.

Flow diagram : A diagram showing a sequence of stages making up a complex process or computer program.

Gaming : The situations employed involve the outcome, affected by decisions arrived at by one or more decisions.

Handout : An amount of money or other aid given to a needy person, a piece of printed information provided free for charge.

Harmony : A pleasing quality when things are well arranged, agreement, the combination of musical notes sounded at the same time to produce chords with a pleasing effect. Origin — Latin *harmonia* 'joining'

Illustration : A picture in a book or periodical, the action of illustrating, an example that proves something or helps to explain.

Interactive : Influencing each other, (of a computer or other electronic device) allowing a two-way flow of information between it and a user.

Interpretation : The action of explaining the meaning of something.

Kinesthetic : The sensation by which bodily position, weight, muscle tension, and movement are being perceived.

Learning : Knowledge or skills being gained through study or by the taught.

Machine : A device using mechanical power and having several parts, for performing a particular task, an efficient group of influential people, make or work on something with a device using mechanical power. Origin—Greek *mçkhanç*.

Micro-level Teaching: Micro-level teaching is a scaled down teaching, wherein the teacher teaches a short lesson to a small group of students for a short interval of time.

Modification : The action of partially changing something, a change made.

Monitoring : A person or device that monitors something.

Motivators : Stimulate someone's interest in something; provide someone with some motive for doing something.

Non-verbal : Not using words or speech.

Objective : Not influenced by personal feelings or opinions.

Operational : Being used or ready for use.

Originality : The ability to think independently or creatively, the quality of being new or inventive.

Perception : The ability to see, hear, or become aware of something through senses, a way of understanding or interpreting something, the ability to understand true nature of something; insight. Origin—Latin.

Preliminary : Happening before or preparing for a main action or event.

Presentation : The action of presenting something or the way wherein it is presented.

Programmed : Cause to behave in a particular way, arrange according to a plan. Origin—Greek *programme*.

Projection : A forecast based on present trends, the projecting of an image or sound, a thing that sticks out.

Questioning : It is an act of rising of a doubt or objection.

Recapitulate : Give a summary of what has just been said.

Recorder : A device for recording sound, picture, etc.

Reflection : The throwing back by a body or surface of light, heat, or sound without absorption.

Reinforcement : The action of strengthening something.

Reliable : Able to be depended on or trusted.

Remembering : Have in or bring to your mind someone or something from the past, keep something necessary in mind.

Self-confidence : Trust in your abilities, qualities, and judgments.

Sensory : Relating to sensation or the senses.

Simulation : Use of computer to create conditions that reflect those in real life.

Socio-drama : The use of role playing as a means of enabling the role players seeking solution to social problem which is posed for them.

Stimulus : Something that causes response or that promotes activity, interest, etc.

Supervisor : The person who watches and directs the performance of some task or the work of some person.

System : A set of things working together as the mechanism or network.

Teacher : A person who teaches in a school.

Teaching : Give information about particular subject to a class or pupil, show someone how to do something, make someone realise, understand, or be less likely to do something. Origin — Old English, *show.*

Technique : A particular way of doing something, especially something requiring special skills.

Technology : The application of scientific knowledge for practical purposes, the branch of knowledge concerned with applied sciences, machinery and equipment developed from such scientific knowledge.

Traditional : Relating to or following tradition.

Transparency : The condition of being transparent.

Valid : Legally binding or officially acceptable.

Vicarious : Experienced in the imagination after watching or reading about another person's actions or feelings.

Vocabulary : All the words used in a particular language or activity, all the words known to an individual person, a list of words and their meanings, accompanying a piece of specialist or foreign writing. Origin—Latin *vocabularius.*

Index

THE MAKING OF MODERN INDIA

Rammohun Roy to Gandhi and Nehru

Dr. G.N.S. RAGHAVAN

GIAN PUBLISHING HOUSE
DELHI – 110007

THE MAKING OF MODERN INDIA

ISBN : 9788121201209

Published in 2016 in India by
Gyan Publishing House
5, Ansari Road, Daryaganj,
New Delhi - 110002

e-mail : books@gyanbooks.com
website : gyanbooks.com

PREFACE

Jawaharlal Nehru wrote about history even while he was engaged in making history. He demonstrated, through the *Letters from a Father to his Daughter*[1] and the *Glimpses of World History*,[2] that the subject need not be tedious.

The secret of his success as an amateur (in the sense of non-professional) historian was his perception that history is not something pertaining to the dead past but has relevance to the living present and to the shaping of the future. Inaugurating the Asian History, Congress in New Delhi in December 1961, Jawaharlal Nehru said that he approached history not as a catalogue of kings and dates but as "an exciting story, a developing drama leading up to the present and making me wonder where it will lead to in the future."[3] There is no better cue for the narrator of a tale from the history of any branch of the human family.

The present book tells the story of the regeneration of Indian society which began in the early part of the 19th century with Raja Rammohun Roy and culminated in the freedom struggle. The success of this struggle was marred by the partition of the sub-continent and the blood-bath which accompanied it. These events can be properly understood only

1. Children's Book Trust, New Delhi, 1985 ; first published in 1929.
2. Jawaharlal Nehru Memorial Fund, 1982 ; first published in two volumes in 1934-35.
3. *Jawahrlal Nehru's Speeches* Vol. IV (p. 177), Publications Division, New Delhi.

in the context of India's long history. The first chapter therefore attempts to present a panorama of this background, stretching over nearly 5000 years. The quick look at the past shows both integrative and disruptive forces at work. The latter made India's society and polity vulnerable to penetration by European colonial powers during the 18th century. The British had become the *de facto* rulers of a great part of India when the first Governor-General was appointed in 1774.

The national awakening which began in the 19th century was characterised by assimilation of the good features of the science and philosophy of the West, to which access was provided by English education, alongside pride in India's own heritage and readiness to purge it of the accretions of superstitious practice. This constractive response, unaffected by the abortive Uprising of 1857, led on to the formation of the Indian National Congress, the heightened political consciousness reflected in the agitation against the partition of Bengal and finally to the nonviolent mass movement for independence under the leadership of Mahatma Gandhi.

India' s freedom struggle had several dimensions besides the political. It brought about social and economic changes even as it proceeded. And it had the vision of greater changes to follow after independence. The freedom movement stimulated and in turn drew inspiration from a flowering of literature in the languages of India. It was a movement of ideas and ideals, some of them mutually reinforcing and others conflicting. The major conflict was between a pan-Indian consciousness transcending differences of religion, caste or language, and the sense of separate identity among certain communities which the British sedulously encouraged in order to divide Indian from Indian so as to consolidate their own rule. The national movement stood for unity amidst diverstity based on equality of citizenship rights in a free India. But the forces of separatism fostered by the imperialists triumphed because many Indians, instead of settling their differences among themselves, rose to the bait of the favours held out by the British to members of this religion here and that caste there.

After World War II when the British, economically

enfeebled and faced with disaffection in the ranks of the Indian armed forces, realised that they could no longer hold on to their Indian empire, they followed the tactic of scorching the earth—not their own—while retreating. Britain divided India while quitting. In a passage that sounds prophetic in retrospect Subhas Chandra Bose had said in his presidential address at the Haripura Congress on 19 February 1938 (two years before the Muslim League formulated the demand for partition and the creation of Pakistan) : "Every empire is based on the policy of divide and rule. But I doubt if any empire in the world has practised this policy so skilfully, systematically and ruthlessly as Great Britain. In accordance with this policy, before power was handed over to the Irish people. Ulster was separated from the rest of Ireland. Similarly, before any power is handed over to the Palestinians, the Jews will be separated from the Arabs. An internal partition is necessary in order to neutralise the transference of power. The same principle of partition appears in a different form in the new Indian Constitution.[4] Here we find an attempt to separate the different communities and put them into water-tight compartments. And in the Federal Scheme there is juxtaposition of autocratic Princes and democratically elected reparesentatives from British India. If the new Constitution is finally rejected, I have no doubt that British ingenuity will seek some other constitutional device for partitioning India and thereby neutralising the transference of power to the Indian people."

Many of todays' problems of— and between— India, Pakistan and Bangladesh are the bitter legacy of the imperialist policy of divide and rule, ending in the parting kick of partition. How this diabolical policy was systematically pursued is vividly brought out in this book, through extracts from historical documents (including correspondence between-successive Viceroys and Secretaries of State for India) know-ledge of which has been confined so far to a small circle of

4. The reference is to the Government of India Act of 1935 which retained separate electorates for Muslims and Sikhs and made special provision for the Depressed Classes (now referred to as the Scheduled Castes.)

scholars. Wider awareness of the damage caused by a section of Indians playing into the hands of colonialists in the past can today help all concerned to realise the need to resolve peacefully the problems which threaten the country's, unity.

In various parts of the world, colonial powers other than Britain adopted the same policy of keeping their victims divided. The straight lines which mark the boundaries of many African States are a striking example of arbitrarily imposed division when the imperialist powers parcelled out the contenent among themselves. The Indian experience will be of interest to the many countries in Asia and Africa which have become independent in recent decades and which, like India, need to remain on guard against neo-colonialist pressures and antignes in any shape or form.

The book also examines the two faces of the religious traditions of India : one humanist and beautiful, and the other fanatical and ugly—a dualism which is by no means peculiar to India. The Hindu-Muslim problem, aggravated by British imperialist policy, brought about the sub-continent's partition but the problem did not disappear with the partition. Tensions continue to break out from time to time because they are incited not only by religious fanatics but also, and to a greater extent, by power-seeking politicians. These unscrupulous politicians, who practise internally the divide-and-rule tactics of the erstwhile colonial rulers, are of two varieties : those within a religious community who appeal for votes in the name of religion ; and those outside that religious group who make promises of protection and favours in return for votes. In coping with these present ills, it is useful to remember the lesson of history that internal division weakens the country and invites external interference. The Indian experience in this respect will be of interest to other, specially the newly independent, countries with plural societies who face a similar challenge of bringing about emotional integration.

The major events of the freedom struggle are narrated largely in terms of the principal actors—the men and women from different parts of the country who brought to the action the individuality and colour of their personality. Not all the important figures in India's freedom struggle could be discussed

in a volume of this size. However, illustrative examples from all regions of the country have been included. Also noticed is the valuable contribution made by British friends of Indian freedom, all the more admirable for their being exceptions to the rule.

The arrangement of the chapters is broadly chronological but the discussion of a theme covers, in appropriate cases, events and personalities of a later stage in the freedom movement. Also, there are references at a few places to major post-1947 developments which have their roots in the pre-independence period.

Given at the end of the book, for ready reference, are select documents pertaining to the major landmarks in the struggle for India's independence : the movement against the partition of Bengal ; the first civil disobedience movement launched in 1920 ; adoption of complete independence as the national objective ; definition of the social and economic content of freedom ; the Congress resolution demanding that the British 'Quit India' ; the dawn of Independence Day ; and the proclamation of the Republic.

G.N.S. Raghavan

New Delhi
10 March, 1987

CONTENTS

CHAPTER ONE

BACKGROUND TO THE BRITISH CONQUEST

INDIA is so known because it is the land of the river Indus. Sindhu is the Sanskrit name of this mighty river which rises in the Himalayas and flows westward into the Arabian Sea. The names Indus (for the river), India (for the country), Hindu (for the people of the land of the Sindhu as well as for their religion), Hindi (for the language spoken by many of them), Hindustan (another name for the country), and Sind (the province of present-day Pakistan where the river meets the sea)—all these are Persianised or Anglicised forms of Sindhu.

When we speak of India, it refers till the year 1947 to the whole sub-continent, including present-day Pakistan and Bangladesh. There was in this large peninsula a mingling of many races and interaction of many religions over nearly 5000 years. This process often resulted in the fusion of different cultural elements into something distinctively Indian. It also sometimes added a racial or religious dimension to power struggles between Indian rulers. These divisions were taken advantage of by the British to extend and consolidate their empire in India during the 18th and 19th centuries. The roots of these two tendencies—integrative and disruptive—which have been at work throughout India's social history are surveyed rapidly below.

THE MAKING OF INDIAN SOCIETY

Some of India's earliest inhabitants are represented to this day by the tribal people of central, southern and western India. Known as Adivasis, or original dwellers, they exhibit the physical features, mixed in different proportions of the Negroid, Austric and Dravidian races.

An Urban Civilisation of 3000 B.C.

Archaeological excavations in the early part of the 20th century brought to light a very early but well developed urban civilisation which flourished in and around the Indus river basin. These excavations were in delayed follow-up of the discovery in 1865, by John and William Brunton, who were engaged in building the East Indian Railway from Karachi to Lahore, of huge dusty mounds under which they found burnt bricks which were very useful as ballast. John Brunton wrote in his memoirs about one of the dead cities he had stumbled on : "I had been much exercised in my mind how we were to get ballast for the line of the Railway. If all I heard were true, this ruined city, built of bricks, would form a grand quarry for ballast".[1]

Carbon-dating tests on the archaeological finds have shown that the Indus Valley civilization endured for over a thousand years from about 3000 B.C. It was thus one of the earliest civilisations of man, like those which developed along the Nile river in Africa, the Tigris and the Euphrates in Mesopotamia, and the Yellow River in China.

The first sites of the civilisation were uncovered by Sir John Marshall and his colleague R.D. Banerji, of the Archaeological Survey of India, at Harappa and Mohenjodaro (both now in Pakistan) in the Indus Valley. Subsequently, however, many more sites of the civilisation have been discovered over a much wider area—in Gujarat, Rajasthan, Haryana, Punjab and Jammu.

The high level of development of the civilisation is indicated by the remains of a dockyard found at Lothal (on the Gujarat coast) and by the evidence here as well as at other sites like Kalibanga (Rajasthan), Harappa (West Punjab) and Mohen-

jodaro (Sind) of excellent town planning with well-laid streets, an elaborate drainage system, granaries and public baths. Ornaments of gold, silver and precious stones, copper vessels, and metal implements and weapons have been collected from the ruins.

There are depictions of pregnant females suggesting a mother goddess or earth goddess cult, and of a male god resembling Siva, prominent in the Hindu pantheon to this day. Religious significance seems to have been attached to the humped bull and to certain trees. Some scholars find significant similarities between the people of this early civilisation and the Dravidian races and culture of south India. Though the civilisation was urban and literate, the script used for its language has not yet been deciphered. We do not therefore know to what name the people of this civilisation answered.

Archaeological excavations in Mesopotamia have shown that there were extensive economic and cultural contacts between the Indus Valley and the contemporary civilisation of Sumer in West Asia. Historians offer different explanations for the similarity between the toilet sets, seals and other artifacts found in the Sumerian and Indus Valley sites. Some believe that the civilisation spread westwards from the Indus basin till it reached the banks of the Euphrates and the Tigris. Others are of the view that it travelled to India from Sumer.

Whatever be the case, the Indus Valley civilisation came to an end in circumstances which are not fully known. Perhaps it was due to a catastrophic flood, or a climatic change resulting in the drying up of cultivated land and the encroachment of the desert. Or perhaps the urban civilisation, weakened by over-refinement, was over-run by a less sophisticated but more hardy people.

The last explanation is the most widely held, since the disappearance of the Indus Valley civilisation was approximately at the same time as the entry of Aryan tribes into the sub-continent. The Aryan influx is placed by scholars variously between 2000 and 1500 B.C. The Aryaus are believed to have come from Bactria, through the passes of the Hindu Kush mountains, into Afghanistan and from there to the land of the Sindhu and its tributaries.

Aryan-Dravidian Encounter

A vigorous people who ate meat and drank a fermented liquor called Soma, the Aryans (literally, 'the noble ones') were nomadic pastoralists to begin with. They gradually took to agriculture, and the cow became their most precious animal. The northern plains were at that time thickly forested and agriculture required the clearing of the forests as a first step.

The Aryans were gifted with a poetic sensibility. They also thought deeply on the universe and the meaning of human life. The language of their literature, beginning with the Vedas and Upanishads, is an old form of Sanskrit. It is allied to Persian, Greek, Latin and to the Celtic and Slavonic languages. There is a striking phonetic relationship between such key words as 'Pita' of Sanskrit, 'pater' of Latin and 'father' of modern English, as of 'Mata', 'mater' and 'mother'. It strongly suggests the derivation of these languages from a common parent speech, which scholars describe as Indo-European.

The Aryans brought with them religious ideas connected with naturalistic or functional deities. Such are Agni, god of fire ; heaven and earth as the divine parents ; Varuna, god of rain ; Ushas, the goddess of dawn ; and Indra, god of the atmosphere wielding the thunderbolt. All these have their mythological counterparts in the traditions of Iran, Greece and Rome. Aryan ritual involved the offering of sacrifices to the gods through the medium of fire.

The Aryans migrated eastward and southward in search of new lands for settlement, under pressure from fresh waves of entrants through the north-west. In this process they gradually took over many of the religious beliefs and practices of the people whom they subjugated. The Aryan-Dravidian encounter was thus a case of conflict being followed by synthesis. Though there was no suggestion of idol-worship in the Vedas, it became part of the religious amalgam which now emerged. It was this amalgam of Aryan and Dravidian practices which the Persians and others who came to India in a later age designated as the 'Hindu' religion, or the religion of the people of the land of the Sindhu.

The Caste System

The fusion on the plane of religion was a counterpart of large-scale racial mixing. This mixing took place despite the prohibition of intercaste marriage—specially of Sudras with the supposed higher castes—under the caste system developed by the Indo-Aryans.

This system reflected, and was intended to preserve, the pattern of political, economic and social dominance in the Indo-Aryan order. There were three Aryan castes, differentiated by occupation : the Brahmanas (now Brahmins in popular usage), who were the priests and scholars ; Kshatriyas, denoting kings and warriors ; and the Vaisyas who owned land and carried on trade. Members of these three castes were known as Dwijas, or the twice-born, because the Aryan boy, on being initiated into learning, was endowed with a sacred thread marking his 'second birth'.

The Dravidians, who were the main element of the local population, were classified as Sudras and assigned to manual work as artisans and agricultural labourers. Some of the Aryan tribes defeated by other Aryans were also reduced to the status of Sudras. They were denied access to learning by being prohibited from studying the Vedas which were a compendium of the then existing knowledge. The most lowly were the Mlechhas, consisting of aboriginal groups. They were outside the pale of the four-caste society. They were also known as 'Panchama' or the fifth caste. For them were reserved the most menial and dirty of occupations such as scavenging and the skinning of animals. Doubtless because of their association with dirt and stench, the Mlechhas came to be regarded as untouchables and unfit to approach members of the four-castes. Over time, each of the castes split into innumerable regional sub-castes.

The colour dimension of the caste system was as important as the economic. Indeed, the Sanskrit word for caste, Varna, stands for colour. The Aryans were light-skinned and proud of the fact. The Sudras and Mlechhas were of a skin colour ranging from brown to black. The prohibition of intercaste marriage was based on racial pride and prejudice.

The prohibition notwithstanding, there was an extensive

mixing of the races. It is noteworthy that, according to tradition, Vyasa, who compiled the four Vedas and wrote the Mahabharata epic was three-quarters non-Aryan.

Krishna, the semi-divine mentor and friend of the Pandava heroes of the epic, is dark-hued : *neela varna* (blue in colour) is how he is unfailingly described in literature and depicted by artists. That an indigenous tribal chief came to be deified and to rank with the Aryan king Rama, of the Ramayana epic, is a measure of the integration that took place between the Aryans and non-Aryans.

Though the caste system was in principle hereditary, the Kshatriya group was exceptionally flexible and accommodative. Anyone who succeeded in seizing power in a kingdom or republic would declare himself a Kshatriya in order to legitimise his position. Similarly, leaders and camp-followers of invading tribes who settled in India got incorporated into the social order in appropriate castes. Influxes of Scythians, Turks, Persians and Afghans and others, over the centuries, were thus absorbed. The caste system may be said therefore to have served to integrate in a common Indian polity diverse ethnic elements, indigenous and from outside.

This integrative role notwithstanding, the system was essentially inequitous. The fixation of caste by birth greatly inhibited the mobility essential for social health. The injustice of the system bore heavily on the so-called lower castes and on the untouchables. They were ruthlessly exploited economically and despised socially. With its pretension to religious sanction, the caste system came to be used to rationalise the treatment of the labouring classes as if they were less than human. This was bound to weaken Hindu society. The vulnerability became apparent when, in later periods of history, Islam and Christianity were able to recruit large numbers of converts from the exploited and oppressed castes, though conversions were not confined to them. During the freedom movement, the British rulers were to encourage separatism among the non-Brahmins of south India as against the Brahmins, and among the Depressed Classes all over the country as against the Caste Hindus, as part of the policy of divide-and-rule.

Hindu-Jain-Buddhist Interaction

The caste hierarchy of Brahmanism (another name for Hinduism) was challenged by Vardhamana Mahavira (599-527 B.C.) and Siddhartha Gautama (563-483 B.C.)—both born to non-Brahmin chieftains—who preached new systems of values. These protestant faiths came to be known as Jainism and Buddhism.

They gained a large following. There were Jain monks on the banks of the Sindhu at the time of Alexander's invasion in 326 B.C. The most notable among the adherents of Buddhism was the Mauryan emperor Ashoka of the 3rd century B.C. In the South, the two Tamil epics *Silappadiharam* and *Manimehalai* reflect the Jain and Buddhist faiths respectively. There were conflicts between the new religions and Hinduism, as well as within Hinduism between the Vaishnavite and Saivite cults. Zealous votaries often converted kings from one faith to another. Sometimes there was persecution of non-conformists.

By and large, however, the three religions co-existed peacefully. The Chinese traveller Fa Huien, who visited India early in the 5th century, noted that Buddhist monasteries flourished side by side with Hindu temples. However, Buddhism eventually declined in the land of its birth though it spread far and wide outside India. Jainism also declined. Hinduism became established as the sub-continent's dominant religion with its host of gods and goddesses of popular worship, the social system of *Chatur Varna* or four-castes, and the value system of *Dharma* (ethical norms) governing the pursuit of *Artha* (power and prosperity) and *Kama* (pleasure).

Despite the differences of language in a country of continental size, Hindus were held together by a shared religious and cultural heritage : the Ramayana and Mahabharata epics ; household rituals connected with birth, marriage and death ; and the institution of pilgrimages to holy places in far corners of the country. On the last, Mahatma Gandhi commented : "What do you think could have been the intention of those far-seeing ancestors of ours who established Setubandha (Rameswaram) in the south, Jagannath in the east

and Hardwar in the north as places of pilgrimage? You will admit they were no fools. They knew that worship of God could have been performed just as well at home. They taught us that those whose hearts were aglow with righteousness had the Ganga in their own homes. But they saw that India was one undivided land, so made by nature. They, therefore, argued that it must be one nation. Arguing thus, they established holy places in various parts of India, and fired the people with an idea of nationality in a manner unknown in other parts of the world."[2]

Coming of Islam : Conflict and Synthesis

Mutual strife among the north Indian kingdoms facilitated raids from Afghanistan around 1000 A.D. by Sultan Mahmud, who was a Turk of central Asian origin. During the preceding three centuries Islam had come peacefully and taken its place among the many religions of India—the indigenous faiths of Hinduism, Buddhism and Jainism ; Judaism, which was brought by the first batch of Jews who, fleeing from Jerusalem where they were persecuted by the Romans, sailed in the 2nd century A.D. to Cranganore on the Kerala coast ; Christianity which, according to one tradition, St. Thomas introduced in South India around 50 A.D. and was definitely prevalent by the 5th century ; and Zoroastrianism which was brought by the Parsis who fled from Iran when Islam swept their country in the 7th century.

Now Islam came with the sword, and caused much bitterness. Particularly offensive was the destruction of shrines, the most notorious example of which was the sack of the Somnath temple in Gujarat. As remarked by Jawaharlal Nehru, "Mahmud was more a warrior than a man of faith and, like many other conquerors, he used and exploited the name of religion for his conquests. To Mahmud India was just a place from which he could carry off treasure to his homeland. He enrolled an army in India and placed it under one of his noted generals, Tilak by name, who was an Indian and a Hindu. This army he used against his own co-religionists in central Asia...It is therefore misleading to speak of a 'Muslim period' of Indian history. It is as if we should refer

to the years of British rule over India as the 'Christian period."[3]

Punjab passed under Turkish rule following the raids of Mahmud of Ghazni. Though there was a respite of a century and a half before the next invasion, by Muhammad Ghori from Afghanistan, the Rajput princes who ruled Delhi and its environs had not learnt the lesson of history. Their disunity enabled Ghori, at the second attempt, to take Delhi in 1192. Over the next 150 years the Delhi Sultanate established its control over north India and the greater part of the south.

Though the Turks and Afghans who came with and in the wake of Muhammad Ghori behaved in the beginning as conquerors, and some of them brought about forcible conversions, they settled down in the sub-continent unlike the earlier raiders. The domicile and Indianisation of the Sultans of Delhi is illustrated by the fact that one of them, Allauddin Khilji, married a Hindu lady and so did his son. India became their home and Delhi the capital, not far-off Ghazni. Another example of assimilation is the emergence of the Bahmani (variant of Brahmani) kingdom in the south, so named by its Afghan Muslim founder in grateful memory of an early Hindu patron of his called Gangu Brahman. When the Bahmani kingdom broke up, one of the new units was Ahmadnagar, founded by Ahmad Nizam Shah, son of Nizam-ul-Mulk Bhairi—the father bearing the name of his Brahmin sire, an accountant named Bhairu. This shows the extent of Indianisation of the Muslim states in the south.

A remarkable example of the interaction and mutual enrichment of the Persian culture of the Afghan newcomers and the indigenous languages and arts is provided by Amir Khusrau, of the 14th century. A Turk whose family had been settled in north India for two or three generations, Khusrau was versatile. Adept in poetry and music, he knew Sanskrit and wrote both in Persian and in Hindi, the language of the common people. He is said to have invented the Sitar, which became a widely popular stringed instrument of India.

The process of assimilation reached its climax in the 16th

century during the Mughal empire. It was founded in 1526, when the throne of Delhi was taken by Babar, a Turko-Mongol from central Asia where the influence of the arts and culture of Persia was strong. His grandson Akbar, the greatest of the Mughals, was a conscious integrator. In the words of Jawaharlal Nehru, "As a warrior he conquered large parts of India, but his eyes were set on another and more enduring conquest, the conquest of the minds and hearts of the people. In him the old dream of a united India again took shape, united not only politically in one state but organically fused into one people. Throughout his long reign of nearly fifty years from 1556 onwards he laboured to this end. Many a proud Rajput chief, who would not have submitted to any other person, he won over to his side. He married a Rajput princess, and his son and successor, Jehangir, was thus half Mughal and half Rajput Hindu. Jehangir's son Shah Jehan, was also the son of a Rajput mother. Thus racially this Turko-Mongol dynasty became far more Indian than Turk or Mongol."[4]

Akbar relied as much on his Hindu advisers, Raja Man Singh and Birbal, as on Abdul Fazl and Abul Rahim Khan-khana. His court was a meeting place for learned men of all faiths. Indeed his toleration was so wide that it angered the more orthodox among Muslims. They disapproved of his effort to promote a new faith, *Din-i-Ilahi* (Divine Faith), a synthesis of Hindusim and Islam. His eclectic search for religious truth led him to arrange for abridged translations in Persian of the Atharvaveda, the Ramayana and the Maha-bharata. Dara Shikoh, great-grandson of Akbar, studied Hindu Philosophy and translated several verses from the Upanishads.

The Indo-Afghan and Indo-Mughal period brought about significant changes in the way of life of the common people. A totally new language, Urdu, evolved from the combination of Hindi syntax with Persian and Arabic vocabulary. It marked the fusion of the two cultures. Since the majority of the Muslim population were converted Hindus, the pattern of living of Hindus and Muslims—including marriage within a caste, even after conversion—was basically similar. The synthe-

sis promoted by Akbar was sustained by the coincidental waves of Hindu Bhakti (devotionalism) and of Sufi mysticism, both of which preached a common religion of human brotherhood. The humanism of the Bhakti cult, which originated in and spread from the south, attracted the artisans and cultivators who were ranked low in the Brahmanical hierarchy. The devotional movement attached little importance to idol worship and ritual, and proclaimed the possibility of every individual, irrespective of the accident of origin, attaining union with the divine. These preachers of human brotherhood spoke and wrote in the regional languages of the common people, not in the Sanskrit of Brahamanic scholarship.

The accents in which the Muslim Sufis spoke were similar to those of Bhakti. According to the Sufis, the Ulema learned from books while the mystics learned from God. Al-Ghazali (1059-1111), the great theologian and mystic, asked : "In what do discussions on divorce and on buying and selling prepare the believer for the beyond ?"

Abu Said Abdul Khair, the Persion mystic, wrote "Whosoever you be—an infidel, idolater, Jew or anyone besides-Come! You are welcome in our company, in the lane of love of the Beloved." Kabir, born in a low weaver caste in Banaras in 1440, was claimed on his death in 1518 by Hindus and Muslims as one of their own. His teaching is summed up in the follwing verse :

> "Hari is in the East ; Allah is in the West. Look within your heart, for there you will find both Karim and Ram. All the men and women of the world are His living forms. Kabir is the child of Allah and of Ram."[5]

Four centuries later, Mahatma Gandhi was to invoke the same Bahkti-Sufi strain in the Indian ethos when he popularised the verse. "Iswar and Allah are both Your names. Grant us all good mind."

Emergence of Sikhism

This syncretist movement, in which the mystics and good men of Hinduism and Islam reached out towards each other,

culminated in the emergence of a new religion, Sikhism, based on the teachings of Nanak (1469-1538). Born in a Punjabi Hindu family, Nanak left the service of the Muslim governor of the province and abandoned his home to teach all over the country the unity of God, whom all could approach through service and devotion. Nanak was accompanied during his wanderings by a Muslim disciple, the singer Mardana. Nanak rejected idol worship, stressed the importance of good conduct, and deprecated the distractions of wealth and family ties.

The teachings of Nanak were compiled by his third successor, Guru Ram Das, in the last quarter of the 16th century. This compilation known as the 'Adi Granth' or 'First Book' includes a large selection from Kabir and other Bhaktas and Sufis.

It is characteristic of Akbar that he admired the saintly lives of the Sikh Gurus of his time. There was no conflict between the new religion, which was gathering recruits from both Hindus and Muslims, and Islam or the state.

The tradition of Akbar's statesmanship and benevolent interest in all religions (he invited a group of Jesuits from Goa to expound their faith at his court) was continued, by and large, by his successors Jehangir and Shah Jahan. In the result, the Mughal empire became stable and successful.

Aurangzeb's Fundamentalism

However, a reverse trend was to set in. The Bhakti-Sufi synthesis, based on the rejection of dogma and ritual, had been disapproved from the beginning by the orthodox on both sides. Akbar's great-grandson Aurangzeb was orthodox, and regarded himself more as a Muslim than an Indian. He ascended the throne in 1658 after imprisoning his father Shah Jahan, and had his eldest brother Dara Shikoh, who was friendly to Sufism, condemned as a heretic and executed. Aurangzeb reimposed the Jeziya or poll-tax on the Hindus who were the great majority of his subjects. The Jeziya wasa great burden on the poor, who were already suffering from disabilities under the caste system. Large numbers of them changed their religion to Islam just to escape the tax. Aurang-

zeb's religious fundamentalism turned the Mughal empire into an Islamic instead of a national State. The sense of separateness between Hindus and Muslims, created by narrow-minded rulers or other fanatics, was to be exploited later by the British to divide and weaken the freedom movement. I led eventually to the partition of the sub-continent.

Aurangzeb offended the Rajputs who had been the props of the Mughal empire. He and his successors were involved in a series of wars with the Rajputs, the Sikhs, and with the Marathas led by Shivaji. These conflicts weakened the Mughal empire and made the country vulnerable to economic and military penetration by European powers.

THE EUROPEAN ADVENT

Decline of India's Sea Power

Indians had long been a seafaring people. There are references to the Mauryan empire's navy and to shipbuilding in the *Artha Sastra*, a treatise on statecraft dating back to the 4th century B.C. That there was trade in the early part of the Christian era with the Axumite kingdom of Ethiopia, in Africa, is shown by the discovery there of Indian gold coins of the 3rd century. The south Indian kingdoms were sea powers. During the reign of the Pallavas of Kanchipuram, from the 3rd to the 9th century, there were colonising expeditions to the countries of south-east Asia. Hindu and Buddhist kingdoms flourished there and sometimes quarrelled with each other. The subsequent Chola power, based in Tanjore, had commercial relations with the west and there are remains of a Roman trading station at Arikamedu on the Tamil coast, near present Pondicherry. Marco Polo who visited the Pandyan kingdom, based in Madurai, towards the close of the 13th century, wrote that the port at Kayal was full of ships from Arabia and China. The Pandyan power collapsed early in the 14th century following the Muslim invasion of the south.

It is an irony of history that a seafaring people like the Indians should subsequently have regressed so badly as to regard the crossing of the seas as an offence against

religion. Hindu society appears to have withdrawn into a shell as a defensive reaction to invasions by Muslim conquerors. It tried to retain its identity through a series of taboos, in the name of religion, on mixing with outsiders. The association of pollution with sea' travel seems to have been part of this reaction. It was one of the many superstitions which social reformers of a later period had to fight against.

With a vast sub-continent to conquer unify, the Mughals paid no attention to sea power. They did not realise the implications of the growing presence of the Portuguese and other Europeans, who were discovering and using sea routes the world over. Vasco-de-Gama of Portugal rounded the the southern tip of Africa and landed at Calicut on India's eastern coast in 1498. He went back after six months, his ships laden with spices, textiles and other precious articles he had bought in India. In the wake of the Portuguese came the Dutch, the Danes, the French and the English for trade with India and farther east. They wanted to displace the Arab middlemen in the trade between Europe and south and east Asia.

The Europeans established trading posts in these territories, and began to fortify them and to raise their own garrisons. It was an opening out, the world over, by Europe which was in transition from feudalism to a new era of science and technology, industrialisation, nationalism and the rudiments of a representative form of government. At one time the flow of knowledge and of skills had been from India and other countries of Asia to Europe : for example, the use of numerals in what was called the Hindu-Arab arithmetic ; the preparation of dyes' and the tempering of steel in India, not to speak of such Indian specialities in handicrafts as the weaving of fine muslin cloth and the carving of ivory ; or the making of paper and use of wood-blocks for printing, which travelled from China to Europe *via* west Asia. The roles of Asia and of Europe now stood reversed.

A Creeping Conquest

By Akbar's time the Portuguese became masters of the

Indian Ocean and were in control of Goa. In 1600 Queen Elizabeth granted a charter to "certain adventurers for the trade of the East Indies." This was the origin of the East India Company which was given the monopoly of the India trade. In 1615 the Company obtained permission from emperor Jehangir to establish warehouses.

The Dutch East India Company was formed in 1602 but it concentrated on trade with the islands of the East Indies. The chief rivals of the English in India were the French, who formed their trading company in 1668 and a few years later bought the town of Pondicherry on the eastern coast.

The Mughal empire began to disintegrate following the death of Aurangzeb in 1707. Provincial governors began to function in practice as independent rulers, and to fight each other for enlarging their dominion. In the absence of a common feeling of Indianness in the political sense, many of the contenders for regional power sought the aid of foreigners. The foreigners responded only too readily. The British and the French, in order to promote their own interests, sided with one Indian chieftain against another. They enacted on Indian soil the power struggle that was going on in Europe between Britain and France. Robert Clive and Francois Dupleix were the leading figures on the two sides. The British eventually got the better both of the French and of the mutually warring Indian rulers among whom India of the 18th century was divided.

The ordinary people meanwhile carried on with their occupations in the self-sufficient economy of India's villages, which was affected little by the changing fortunes of the regional rulers, Hindu or Muslim. In the costal settlements Indian merchants interacted with the foreigners. They found it profitable to act as intermediaries between the French or the British and the peasants and artisans of the hinterland. A diary left by Ananda Ranga Pillai, an 18th century merchant of Pondicherry who acted as the chief agent of the French, expresses great admiration for the rulership qualities of Dupleix. It shows vivid awareness of caste identity, but no trace of consciousness of an Indian national identity.

The conquest of India by the British was not through open invasion by the armed forces of their sovereign. It was a creeping conquest, in the guise of trade and through the practice of intrigue and taking of sides in quarrels between Indian rulers. In the south, for example, Chanda Sahib and Muhammad Ali were contenders for the nawabship of Arcot. The first asked for help from the French, and the other turned to the British. Robert Clive's forces, consisting of both Englishmen and Indian soldiers, prevailed over the French forces which also consisted predominantly of Indians. Muhammad Ali was placed on the throne of Arcot, as a puppet.

It was also Robert Clive who was responsible for installing a puppet as the Nawab of Bengal, based in Murshidabad, in place of Siraj-ud-Daula. When the English officials of the Company refused to take down the guns on the fort built by them at Calcutta, the Nawab's forces attacked and occupied the town. Clive came with his soldiers and gave battle to the Nawab at Plassey in 1757. The famous victory was won after Britain's empire-builder had forged a document and bribed the Nawab's minister, Mir Jafar, to play the traitor.

This was followed, in 1764, by another military victory for the British at Buxar. Its consequence was the reduction of the already notional Mughal 'emperor' in Delhi to the *de facto* status of a pensioner. But the pension was euphemistically described as an annual 'tribute' from the East India Company. Soon the Company secured from the emperor the *dewani* of Bengal, with the right to maintain law and order and collect land revenue in the vast province which at that time included Bihar, Orissa and Chota Nagpur.

The East India Company having become a territorial power, the British Parliament began to control its affairs. In 1774 a Governor-General, answerable to Parliament, was appointed in Calcutta and the Governors of Bombay and Madras were placed under his direction. Warren Hastings was the first Governor-General. But the Company continued to appoint its own officials.

After the victory at Buxar there was no looking back for the British. During the governor-generalship of Wellesley many

Indian rulers were persuaded or compelled to become subsidiaries of the East India Company. This was under treaties which permitted the Company to station its troops for protecting the ruler against his rivals. The ruler had to meet the cost of maintaining the garrisons or, in lieu, cede part of his kingdom to the British. Another Governor-General, Dalhousie, subsequently annexed several princely states including Oudh, Satara, Nagpur and Jhansi on the ground of misrule or if the ruler died without leaving a son as heir. With the final defeat of the Marathas in 1819 and of the Sikh power in 1849, the British became direct masters of two-thirds of the sub-continent. The remaining one-third was princely India, consisting of some large states like Travancore, Mysore, Hyderabad and Baroda and hundreds of small ones. The rulers enjoyed limited autonomy in local matters but were under the effective control of British Residents or Political Agents appointed by the Governor-General.

Meanwhile the East India Company drained India's wealth through the unfair terms of trade which it could dictate to Indian artisans and traders at the point of the gun. In addition, the servants of the Company, from the highest to the low, amassed private wealth through unscrupulous means. Robert Clive was the earliest to make a huge fortune. Englishmen who came out to India as petty officials of the Company returned home as prosperous 'nabobs'.

Unlike the earlier conquerors who either went back with the booty and the prisoners they captured in India, or made the new land their home and merged with its people, the British remained aliens. They had their national homeland and their cultural roots far away, across the seas. This made them the sub-continent's first foreign rulers in the true sense of the term.

REFERENCES

1. Quoted in *Prehistoric India* by Stuart Piggott, Cassell, London.
2. *The Great Integrations* (p. 49) by Dr. V. Raghavan, Publication Division, 1969.
3. *The Discovery of India* (pp. 235-241) Jawaharlal Nehru Memorial Fund, 1983 first published in 1946.
4. *The Discovery of India* (p. 259).
5. *Sources of Indian Tradition* (p. 362) ed. by Wm.Theodore de Bary *et. al.*, Motilal Banarasidass, 1963.

CHAPTER TWO

NATIONAL AWAKENING : THE REVOLT OF 1857

THE economic policy and practices of the East India Company caused widespread misery. The people resented the usurpation of the territories and powers of Indian rulers, the racial arrogance of the Company's functionaries, and the activities of the officially backed foreign missionaries. All these factors resulted in the great uprising of 1857. The introduction of modern education through English enabled many Indians to widen their mental horizons and learn about the nationalist and democratic revolutions in America and France. From the English-educated middle class emerged leaders who initiated social reforms and national awakening. This process culminated in the formation of the Indian National Congress in 1885.

CONSEQUENCES OF COLONIAL RULE

Unemployed Artisans, Exploited Peasants

We saw in the last chapter that the Company's officials were doing very well for themselves in India. So were its shareholders in England. The dividends declared by the Company were of the order of 100 to 200 per cent. All this was at the cost of the Indian artisan and the Indian peasant.

Robert Clive had in 1757 found the city of Murshidabad, a centre of the trade in Bengal's famed muslin and other cotton fabrics, "as extensive, popular and rich as the city of London, with this difference that there are individuals in the first possessing infinitely greater property than in the last". But the picture changed beyond recognition by 1834, when the Governor-General, Lord Bentinck remarked: "The bones of the cotton-weavers are bleaching the plains of India".

This was the result of colonial exploitation. In the ordinary course many of the Indian traders in urban centres like Murshidabad, who supplied raw material to the craftsmen in villages and towns and bought the finished goods from them, would have blossomed into industrial entrepreneurs. But India's industries were throttled so that England's might prosper. Spinning and weaving as household industries had for centuries provided employment on a large-scale. Textiles formed an important part of India's exports, to Britain among other countries. The British now levied heavy duties on Indian fabrics entering England. On the other hand, cloth manufactured in Lancashire mills was allowed into India with a nominal duty. Imported cloth penetrated from the port towns into the interior, thanks to the roads and, from 1853 onwards, the railways which the British constructed. These improved means of transport were designed to serve two purposes : the quick movement of British troops to places where they were needed, to defend or to expand control over territory ; and to carry raw material from, and British manufactures into, India. Indigenous industry and trade were hampered by duties on the movement of Indian-made goods and excise levies thereon. Indian textiles, once the country's pride, could no longer stand the competition from machine-made British cloth as it became progressively cheaper with improvement in the methods of mass production.

What happened to Indian textiles was repeated in respect of other industries such as the making of metal products, glass and paper. There was a drain of gold and silver from India, representing the profits extracted by the foreign masters. Adam Smith wrote in *The Wealth of Nations* in 1776 : "The

governments of an exclusive company of merchants is perhaps the worst of all governments for any country whatever. It is the interest of the East India Company considered as sovereigns that the European goods which are carried to their Indian dominions should be sold there as cheaply as possible; and that the Indian goods which are brought from there should be sold as dear as possible. But the reverse of this is their interest as merchants".

The weavers and other artisans who were thrown out of employment had to fall back on the land, either as cultivators of pitifully small holdings or as agricultural labourers. This pressure on the land coincided with increased burdens on those already engaged in agriculture. After securing the *diwani* of Bengal, the British introduced a new system of revenue settlement under which a parasitic class of Zamindars, or landlords, became intermediaries between the government and the cultivator. They collected as much rent from the cultivator as they could extract, pain to the government a fixed amount as land revenue, and pocketed the balance. Elsewhere, as in the south, there was no zamindari and the Company settled directly with the peasants ; but the land revenue was fixed at high levels and extorted through cruel methods. The peasant's land, which used to be virtually inalienable, began to be put on sale for realising arrears of land revenue ; it would pass into the hands of the *bania,* or moneylender, to whom the peasant became heavily indebted. The peasants thus came to be doubly exploited, by the foreign rulers as also by their own countrymen as zamindars or moneylenders. At certain places Englishmen themselves became landlords and introduced commercial agriculture. They compelled their tenants to grow indigo, for making dye, or other plantation crops for the international market. With the commercial market invading a hitherto self-sufficient village economy, villagers had less grain or none as a reserve to fall back on. Hundreds of thousands died whenever there was drought and famine.

The report of the Indian Famine Commission (1880), appointed by the British authorities to go into the terrible Bengal famine of 1769-70, said : "The loss to the country in

material wealth cannot be calculated ; the loss of life is believed to have been greater than has occurred in any subsequent or historical famine. In the north of Purnea the European supervisors believed that half the ryots were dead ; the Resident of Bihar calculated the famine mortality at 2,00,000 in May; the Resident of Murshidabad in June estimated that by that time three-eighth of the population of the province had died; in July 500 died daily in that town. The estimate made by the Council in November 1772 was that one-third of the population had died, and this implies the death of about 10 millions, as the whole population of Bengal in those days can hardly be estimated at less than 30 millions."[1]

British Missionaries

The Christian Church was a close ally of European colonialism. A Papal bull (order) of 1454, granting Portugal control over the East, read :

"Our joy is immense to know that our dear son, Henry, Prince of Portugal, following the foot of his father of illustrious memory, King John, inspired with a zeal for souls like an intrepid soldier of Christ, has carried into the most distant and unknown countries the name of God and has brought into the Catholic fold the perfidious enemies of God and of Christ, such as the Saracens and the Infidels.

"After having established Christian families in some of the unoccupied islands of the Ocean and having consecrated churches there, the Prince believed that he could give God the best evidence of his submission if by his effort the Ocean can be made navigable as far as India, which, it is said, is already subject to Christ. If he enters into relations with these people, he will induce them to come to the help of the Christians of the west against the enemies of the faith".[2]

Later, after the British had established themselves as the principal colonial power in India, missionaries of the Anglican and other Protestant churches came to India in addition to missionaries of the Catholic orders. The Christian missions did undertake educational and humanitarian work, but primarily as aids for converting Indians to their religion. If social service and

not proselytisation had been their motivation, there was plenty of work for them to do right at home, in England, where illiteracy and ill-health were rampant. As in other European countries which were at that time passing through the phase of the primitive accumulation of capital for industrial development, workers in Britin, women as well as men, worked long hours in crowded and ill-ventilated factories. More than the amelioration of the living conditions of their own countrymen, the prospect of saving the souls of heathens attracted the missionaries who came out to India. In 1813 the British Parliament included a clause in the Charter of the East India Company which said that "facilities shall be afforded by law to persons desirous of going to, or remaining in, India for the purpose of accomplishing those benevolent designs—the introduction of useful knowledge, and religious and moral improvement".

Because of the institution of army chaplains who were known as *padre lat*, and the aid and encouragement that the missionaries received from the authorities, it was widely believed that the missionaries were appointed and maintained by the government. They were to be seen everywhere and gave most offence at the market place where they poured ridicule on the beliefs and practices of Indians, both Hindus and Muslims. The Bible was introduced not only in missionary schools but also those run by the government. Indians who rose to the position of deputy inspectors of schools were popularly described as native clergymen. Prisoners were, proselytised within jails. So were orphans in large numbers, during the famine of 1847, after being given food and shelter. A law was passed in 1850 to enable converts to inherit ancestral property. Since Hinduism was a non-proselytising religion, and Islam forbade the inheriting of property from an infidel, the legislation was seen as a device to encourage the conversion of Hindus to Christianity.

Though state power loomed behind the missionary, large-scale conversions to Christianity took place because of its being armed with the purse rather than (as had been the case with Islam) the sword. On the inducements offered for conversion, an observer wrote : "If any native of low origin

becomes Christian from the desire of gain or from any other motives, these gentlemen (the missionaries) employ and maintain them as an encouragement to others to follow their example". As in the case of Islam, there were converts in large numbers from the exploited lower castes, for example the Sudra *thevars* and the untouchable *pariahs* of the Tamil region. In Bengal, on the other hand, the propagation of Christianity through modern educational institutions resulted in the conversion of a large number of persons belonging to the most notable families of Calcutta, including Brahmins.

Evangelical efforts were also successful among several groups of the tribal population. The missionaries brought education and health facilities to these people who had been neglected over the centuries by their fellow-countrymen, both Hindus and Muslims.

POSITIVE RESPONSE TO WESTERN IMPACT

The best part of the Christian missionaries' work was the contribution they made to the spread of modern scientific knowledge, as well as of political and economic thought, through education in the English language.

The East India Company in the early stages had shown little interest in promoting modern education. Such schools as it opened were for Sanskrit and Arabic studies. Classes in English were added, in the early 1820's, as an experimental measure in some institutions in Calcutta and Delhi. It was after the encouragement of missionary activity through amendment of the Company's Charter that modern education spread in a big way.

This was welcomed by the forward-looking section of the Indian intelligentsia since it opened the doors to scientific knowledge of the kind that had enabled Europe to make large strides in material civilisation. It was again through English that educated Indians became acquainted with the ideas of Thomas Jefferson and the American declaration of Independence of 1776, of Voltaire and Rousseau and the French Revolution of 1789, and with the works of the English poets who celebrated freedom.

Rammohun Roy : Initiator of a Renascence

Foremost among these Indian advocates of modern education through English was Rammohun Roy (1772-1833). He opened several English-medium schools at his own expense, and was distressed when the government decided in 1823 to open a new Sanskrit college in Calcutta. He wrote to Lord Amherst, the then Governor-General, that it would only "impart such knowledge as is already current in India", Rammohun Roy urged instead that the government should "promote a more liberal and enlightened system of instruction embracing Mathematics, Natural Philosophy, Chemistry, Anatomy, with other useful sciences, which may be accomplished with the sums proposed by employing a few gentlemen of talent and learning educated in Europe, and providing a college furnished with necessary books, instruments and other apparatus".

The origin of nationalism, imbued with an egalitarian spirit and therefore concerned with social reform besides self-government, can be traced to his life-work.

Born in a well-to-do family, Rammohun Roy acquired proficieny in Persian and Sanskrit as well as English. He joined the East India Company's service and assisted British officials in the revenue and judicial administration at district level. Though a rich Zamindar himself, he urged that a limit should be fixed on the rent payable by cultivators. He initiated an intellectual and social renascence by promoting the spread of modern knowledge through English education, and by fighting evil customs such as *Sati* (the practice of burning the widow on the husband's funeral pyre, which was prevalent among some of the upper classes). Endowed with a broad outlook, he studied the tecahings of Christianity and Islam and wanted to bring about a synthesis of the best values of all religions. He was the first Indian to bring out newspapers, and opposed restrictions on freedom of the Press.

Rammohun Roy was the first to advocate many of the reforms which were to be demanded in subsequent decades by leaders of the nationalist movement, such as equality before the law and separation of the office of judge from that of revenue collector, on the one hand, and magistrate on the other. However, he did not demand representative government. It

was too early for that, with an entrenched imperial power, and a people steeped in illiteracy and ignorance and with no sense of group identity beyond caste. But his consciousness of India's unfortunate status as a subject country is evident from his courageous criticism of the foreign missionaries' habit of ridiculing Hindu and Muslim religious beliefs : "It is true that the apostles of Jesus Christ used to preach the superiority of the Christian religion to the natives of different countries. But we must recollect that they were not the rulers of those countries where they preached. Were the missionaries likewise to preach the Gospel and distribute books in countries not conquered by the English, such as Turkey, Persia. etc., which are much nearer England, they would be esteemed a body of men truly zeal ous in propagating religion and in following the example of the founders of Christianity. In Bengal, where the English are the sole rulers, and where the mere name of Englishman is sufficient to frighten people, an encroachment upon the rights of her poor, timid and humble inhabitants and upon their religion cannot be viewed in the eyes of God or the public as a justifiable act".

Rammohun Roy visualised self-government as the eventual goal :

> "Supposing that a hundred years hence, the native character becomes elevated from constant intercourse with Europeans and the acquirement of general and political knowledge as well as of modern arts and sciences, is it possible that they will not have the spirit as well as the inclination to resist effectively any unjust and oppressive measures serving to degrade them in the scale of society ?"

In his own time, the practical steps forward, besides the spread of modern education, were the reformation of society by ending evil practices, encouraging the education and emancipation of women, and promoting inter-religious understanding. For these purposes Rammohun Roy founded in 1828 the Brahmo Samaj. It had a profound impact on the people of Bengal over several generations. The work of the Samaj was

continued by Dwarakanath Tagore and his son Debendranath, and by Keshub Chandra Sen.

When Alexander Duff, an English churchman, came to India and wanted to open in Calcutta an institution which would provide scientific knowledge alongside the teaching of the Christian religion, he found ready support from Rammohun Roy though the latter's interest was in promoting modern learning and not Christian evangelism. This institution came up in 1830. Some of the oldest and best colleges in India were established by various Christian missions in the years that followed : Wilson College, Bombay (1832); Christian College, Madras (1837) ; Noble College, Musulipatam (1841) ; Hislop College, Nagpur (1844) ; and St. John's College, Agra (1853).

Rammohun Roy died in 1833 while in England on a visit which was in defiance of the superstitious taboo on crossing the sea. He took the opportunity to present to a committee of the British Parliament recommendations on ways to improve the government of India.

Two years after Rammohun Roy's death, his cherished desire was fulfilled when the government's Committee on Public Instruction, headed by Thomas Macaulay, initially divided between the 'Anglicists' and the 'Orientalists', finally decided on English education. In his Minute on Education of 1835, Macaulay wrote : "The languages of Western Europe civilised Russia. I cannot doubt that they will do for the Hindu what they have done for the Tartar......It is impossible for us, with our limited means, to attempt to educate the body of the people. We must at present do our best to form a class who may be interpreters between us and the millions whom we govern ; a class of persons Indian in blood and colour but English in taste, in opinions, in morals, and in intellect. To that class we may leave it to refine the vernacular dialects of the country, to enrich those dialects with terms of Science borrowed from the Western nomenclature, and to render them by degrees fit vehicles for conveying knowledge to the great mass of the population." Even if the intention of the British was to turn out Brown Englishmen and an army of clerks to conduct the routine work of the Company, the effect was to

make possible the flowering of such great minds as those of Mahatma Gandhi, Rabindranath Tagore and Jawaharlal Nehru.

Emergence and Role of the Indian Press

Another notable contribution of the missionaries was to bring modern printing to India, thereby enabling the emergence of the Indian Press. The missionaries also contributed to the growth of Indian languages by compiling and publishing dictionaries and grammars.

The first newspaper to be brought out on Indian soil, in 1780, was the Bengal Gazette or Caclutta General Advertiser', a weekly published by James Augustus Hickey. It was a publication by a foreigner, addressed to other foreigners resident in India. It can be regarded at an Indian newspaper only in a technical sense, and hardly qualifies 1780 to be regarded as the year of birth of the Indian Press. We come closer to an Indian newspaper properly so called with the publication by the Baptist missionaries of Serampore, in 1818, of *Samachar Darpan*, a weekly in Bengali in which they attacked the religious beliefs and practices of Hindus and Muslims. In order to counter these attacks and to advocate social reform and English education, Rammohun Roy brought out about a year later three periodicals : the *Brahmanical Magazine*' in English ; *Sambad Kaumudi* in Bengali and *Mirat-ul-Akhbar* in Persian. These journals mark the emergence of a truly Indian Press, published and edited by Indians, for Indian readers. It is interesting that they should have been utilised for advancing the cause of progress which, in a country like India with a multi-religious society called for religious tolerance. Publishers and editors of Indian newspapers were strongly represented (next in numbers only to the large contingent of lawyers) in the Indian National Congress from its inception. They played a notable part in the freedom movement through their reports and writings about it, and several of them participated in the successive rounds of the struggle to the extent to courting fines and imprisonment. Some of the tallest leaders of the freedom movement were part-time journalists whose writing produced an even greater impact than that

of full time ones : Bal Gangadhar Tilak with his *Kesari* Maulana Azad (*Al Hilal*), Mahatma Gandhi (*Harijan*) ; and Jawaharlal Nehru (*National Herald*).

Rammohun Roy, a student of Vedanta as well as of the Quran and the Bible, propagated through his journals the fundamental unity of all religions. He turned the attention of Hindus from the beliefs and rituals of the Puranas, with their polytheism and idol worship, back to the higher monism of the Upanishads.

Rammohun Roy attacked the immorality practised in the name of Tantrism (a perversion of Hinduism as well as Buddhism), the superstitious fear and propitiation of planets, ghosts and evil spirits, discrimination against the lower castes and women, and the cruel customs of *Sati*, female infanticide and polygamy. He was forthright in his attack on caste prejudice : "The distinction of castes, introducing innumerable divisions and sub-divisions among the Hindus, has entirely deprived them of patriotic feeling."

Reaction of the Orthodox

Indian orthodoxy reacted quickly. Bhowani Charan Banerjee brought out *Samachar Chandrika*, which opposed English education as well as the social reforms propagated by Rammohun Roy. The mentality of the orthodox can be judged by their condemnation of the abolition of *Sati* by the British in 1929, during the Governor-Generalship of Lord Bentinck.

The conservatives among Brahmins (small as a proportion of the population but educated and vocal) similarly disapproved of the Hindu Widows' Remarriage Act of 1856. While it was permissible for a non-Brahmin widow to remarry if she wished, it was prohibited in the case of Brahmin women. Iswar Chandra Vidyasagar has been compaigning for ending this inequity. (A man could remarry as often as he became widower, if he did not exercise the privilege of having more than one wife at the same time).

Equally remarkable was the sense of outrage felt by the gentry, belonging to the upper castes, at being treated, under the laws made by the English, on a par with members of the

lower orders. One of the participants in the 1857 uprising, Birjis Qadr of Oudh, complained that the British "have brought the honour of the high classes on a level with that of the lower people—sweepers and leather workers. In fact the English show preference to the lower castes over the higher classes. On the complaint of a sweeper or a leather-worker, they seize the person of even a Nawab and a Raja and disgrace him". The complaint sounds ironic in the light of the abolition of untouchability becoming a major plank of the freedom movement.

There were, thus, two kinds of reaction to the impact of Western civilisation and values; one resilient and forward-looking, that sought a synthesis of the best in India's heritage and in what the English brought (alongside rejection of the anti-humanist elements in both); and the other, regidly orthodox and backward-looking which led to withdrawal into the protective shell of tradition for avoiding change.

1857 UPRISING : CAUSES AND COURSE

A great uprising shook British power in large parts of the country in 1857. It was the outcome of discontent caused by impoverishment under the East India Company's rule; the hurt to religious sentiment from the activities of the missionaries and the fear of losing cultural identity; the anger of the dispossessed princes and nobles; and the racial discrimination practised in all walks of life including the armies raised by the Company in different parts of the country.

The Sepoy's Psyche

The simple folk who enrolled themselves in the East India Company's armies to make a living, were closer in their beliefs and customs to the orthodox than to the innovating reformers like Rommohun Roy. The self-identity of the sepoy (from the Hindi *sipahi*) consisted in the caste and region he belonged to. Loyalty was to the local chieftain or king. There was no larger circle of identification—not yet a territorial nationalism comprehending all of India. In the case of both the Hindu and the

Muslim, religion served for patriotism as against the white Christian foreigner.

English officers of the Army, who had no understanding of the sepoy's psyche, introduced changes which the men resented. In 1806 in Madras, British officers of the local army of the East India Company decided to smarten up the appearance of the sepoys. They were ordered to discard their caste marks, trim their moustaches and to wear a leather cockade with the turban.

Leather was a sensitive article. In the context of the widespread fear that the foreigners were out to make Indians lose caste and convert to Christianity, Hindu sepoys feared that the cockade might be of cow's hide. Muslim sepoys suspected that it might be of pig's skin. The Hindu veneration of the cow and prohibition of its killing had its origin as a safeguard for preserving this valuable species of animal, provider of milk as well as of draught animals, from being eaten up and becoming extinct in times of famine. The Muslim abhorrence of the pig was out of aversion to the filth which the animal swallowed in and consumed. There was a near-mutiny at Vellore on the issue of the leather cockade, and the regulations requiring its use were withdrawn—but only after severe punishment of the protesters.

Hindu sepoys shared the superstition that going out of the country, or crossing the sea, was sinful. In the war of 1824 with Burma, Hindu sepoys of the Bengal army feared that they might be asked to embark from Chittagong port. During the Afghan wars they dreaded having to go beyond the boundary of the Indus river. These psychological anxieties worsened the frustration felt by the sepoys at their low emoluments and perquisites. In contrast their British counterparts were paid handsomely.

Lt. Col. J. Holmes wrote about the discrimination against the sepoy : "Though he might give the signs of the military genius of a Haider, he knew that he could never attain the pay of an English subaltern." And a retired officer noted : "The entire army of India amounts to 3,15,520 men costing pounds 98,02,235. Out of this sum no less than pounds 56,68,110 are expended on 51,316 European officers and soldiers." The

sepoys felt cheated when they were not paid *batta* (additional allowance) for serving at places far from their home. In 1849 some regiments at Rawalpindi refused to accept their pay without it.

When the East India Company dissolved the kingdom of Oudh and took the territory over in 1856, the soldiers from upper India, in the Bengal Army in particular, felt outraged It marked the beginning of a rebellious mood in the Company's forces. It was against this background that the greased cartridges caused an emotional explosion. The Brown Bess fire-arm of the sepoy was being replaced by the Enfield rifle manufactured at Dum Dum near Calcutta. Word got round that objectionable animal fat had been used for greasing the cartridges. Both Hindu and Muslim sepoys were enraged. According to one account, wax and oil were to have been used for greasing. That the sepoys' suspicion was not groundless is clear from what the correspondent of the London *Times* wrote from India at the time: "The government ordered mutton fat for the purpose. Some contractors, to save a few shillings, gave pigs' and bullocks' fat instead."

The first shots against the British were fired on 10 May 1857 at Meerut, where the horsemen who refused to bite the cartridge had been punished. The revolt spread like a forest-fire across upper India. But the rest of the country was largely uninvolved. Dispossessed princes, both Hindu and Muslim, joined the revolt and proclaimed their intention of restoring the Mughal emperor to effective power. But many Indian rulers stood aloof, or supported the British. The revolt collapsed in a little over a year because of the lack of unified leadership with an overall strategy, and dissension among the commanders. Moreover, the British were superior in respect of firearms. Indian generals had not yet acquired mastery of their use. Nor could they easily replace losses in guns and ammunition because of lack of knowledge of Science; they had to depend on foreign mercenaries who were unreliable. Above all, there was a crucial difference in morale. The defeat of a British general was only a temporary set-back ; he would be replaced by another and behind them was the nation. On the Indian side the polity was incorporated in

the person who led the army. The defeat of a prince in battle meant the collapse of the state in the absence of a larger Indian national entity. The rebel forces from Meerut took Delhi but could not hold it for more than four months. The emperor, Bahadur Shah Zafar, was imprisoned and exiled, and his sons killed in cold blood. Many patriots of later days derived inspiration from the revolt of 1857, and described it as India's first war of independence. In reality, however, it marked the end of an era rather than the beginning of a new one. The 1857 uprising was "the last flicker of feudal India", to qoute Jawaharlal Nehru, who added: "Not by fighting for a lost cause, the feudal order, would freedom come."

Heroes of the Uprising

Though the anti-British uprising of 1857 failed, the heroism of its leaders like Rani Lakshmibai of Jhansi and Tantya Tope became part of the country's proudly remembered heritage. The anger of the British against the Rani was mixed with admiration, as can be seen from an English writer's account in 1860: "The British soldiers were thirsting for vengeance. No maudlin clemency was to mark the fall of this city (Jhansi). The Jezebel of India was there—the young, energetic, proud, unbending, uncompromising Rani, and upon her head rested the blood of the slain, and a punishment as awful awaited her." But she could not be captured. Dressed in male garb, Lakshmibai escaped at night from the city and eventually died a soldier's death on the battlefied.

Tantya Tope was an able military leader who harried the British by his surprise attacks. The British were able to capture him because he was betrayed while he was asleep, by a professed friend. Sentenced to be hanged, he firmly climbed the scaffold and with his own hands wore the noose.

Other brave fighters included the Begum of Oudh, Hazrat Mahal; Liaqat Ali, highly respected by the people of Allahabad though he was only a schoolmaster of humble origin ; Ahmadullah Shah, the Maulvi of Faizabad; and Kunwar Singh, the ruler of a small state in Bihar who fought the British though he was eighty years old.

A major consequence of the 1857 uprising was the ending of Company rule and the assumption of responsibility for governing India by the British monarch, on whose behalf the Governor-General, now designated additionally as Viceroy, exercised authority.

SOCIAL REFORM AND NATIONAL AWAKENING

1857 marked a discontinuity. The revolt did not spring from the impulse generated by Rammohun Roy. Nor did it modify the later course of the work of social reform initiated by the Brahmo Samaj and similar movements which arose in various parts of the country. Then, in the latter half of the 19th century, came the formation of associations that were more explicitly political, expressing the aspirations of the growing English-educated middle-class for measures which would lead to self-government.

Country-wide Social Resurgence

An example from south India of the country-wide social resurgence witnessed in the second half of the 19th century is the reform movement initiated by Narayana Guru. He was born in Kerala in a humble family of Ezhavas, a community that was denied access to educational institutions and to temples. Overcoming the limitations imposed by the circumstances of his birth, young Narayana became proficient in Malayalam and Sanskrit. He made a special study of the philosophy of Advaita or non-duality.

Thus equipped, Narayana Guru gave fight to the forces of orthodoxy. He consecrated temples in various parts of Kerala which bore the inscription: "The ideal house, where all live in full fraternity without distinction of caste or prejudice of creed." In a shrine founded by him there is, in place of a deity, a light illuminating the words, 'Truth, Duty, Kindness, Love'. In the sanctum of another temple is installed a mirror, symbolically suggesting that divinity is to be realised within oneself.

Narayana Guru's teaching is summed up in the words:

'One Caste, one Religion, one God for all mankind'. It reminds us of the Tamil poet of the Sangam Age (2nd and 3rd centuries A.D.) who affirmed: "Every city is my city; all people are my people." One of the earliest social reformers in Maharashtra was Jotirao Govindrao Phule, popularly known as Mahatma Phule (1827-90). Born in a family of humble caste whose occupation was gardening, he took up, after his own schooling, the cause of education of women and the poor. Since women teachers were hardly available those days, he taught his wife Savitribai and made her a teacher in a school he opened in 1848 for women of the lower castes. He went on to start a night school for adults, a widows' home and an orphanage. Phule received encouragement both from the British authorities who in 1857 made a grant of six acres of land for constructing a school building, and from the enlightened Maharaja of Baroda, Sayajirao Gaikwad.

In Punjab and neighbouring areas, many nationalists were drawn to the Arya Samaj founded by Dayanand Saraswati (1824-83). A Gujarati by birth who lived in Punjab, Dayanand took his stand on the very Vedas which were invoked orthodox Hindus, to question idol-worship and to rescue Hinduism from the evils of untouchability, child marriage and the subjection of women. He advocated girls' education, free choice of husband by the woman, and the right of every person, not only the Brahmins, to study the Vedas. It is in his memory that the numerous D.A.V. (Dayanand Anglo-Vedic) schools and colleges in north India are named.

The 19th century combination of social reform and national self-respect is best exemplified by Swami Vivekananda (1863-1902) who established the Ramakrishna Mission. Vivekananda was a disciple of Sri Ramakrishna (1836-86), the saintly mystic who saw God in a variety of manifestations—as the Divine Mother, as Rama and Krishna, as Muhammad, as Jesus Christ—and worshipped in the manner of the various religionists, in each case suiting his dress, food and meditation to the particular tradition. Vivekananda's religious humanism made a great impact all over India as well as abroad. He addressed himself particularly to the youth. Vivekananda

condemned the notions of ritual purity, and the feasting and fasting of the upper-classes: "Our religion is in the kitchen. Our God is in the cooking pot—'don't touch me, I am holy'." He preached practical service and set an example by following up lessons on metaphysics, in a school founded by his followers in Calcutta, with helping to till the garden, dig a well and knead bread. Vivekananda told students: "I want sappers and miners in the army of religion. So, boys, set yourselves to the task of training your muscles. For ascetics, mortification is all right. For workers, well-developed bodies, muscles of iron and nerves of steel ! So long as the millions live in hunger and ignorance, I hold every man a traitor who, having been educated at their expense, pays not the least heed to them."

Political Associations: Surendranath Banerjea

Regional associations of the English-educated middle-class were formed in the 1850's in the three Presidency capitals of Calcutta, Bombay and Madras. They urged steps towards representative government and sent petitions to the British Parliament asking for a less expensive and more responsive administration in India. Outside the coastal cities, too, there came up organisations such as the Society for the Promotion of National Feeling started by Rajnarain Bose at Midnapore in Bengal; numerous district branches of the Mahajana Sabha of Madras, with its office room in the premises of *The Hindu*, which emerged as a newspaper forum for the expression of Indian political aspirations; and the Sarvajanik Sabha of Poona which was formed in 1870.

The first nationalist to achieve all-India influence was Surendranath Banerjea (1848-1925). Famed for his eloquence, he undertook a speaking tour of India during 1877-78 to protest against the reduction of the age limit for competing in the Indian Civil Service examination. An English officer of that time wrote: "The Bengalee Babus rule public opinion from Peshawar to Chittagong...and at the present moment the name of Surendranath Banerjea excites as much enthusiasm among the rising generation of Multan as in Dacca." When he was sentenced on the ground of contempt for criticising

in the columns of his *Bengalee* the Calcutta Chief Justice for ordering a Hindu to produce in the court the image of his household deity, there was a *hartal* all over Bengal, and protest meetings were held at places as far off as Agra, Lahore and Poona. Surendranath Banerjea convened in December 1883 in Calcutta a national conference of the Indian Association founded by him in 1876. The conference, attended by more than a hundred delegates from several parts of the country, was something like a national parliament and thus a precursor of the Congress sessions of subsequent years.

The credit for organising an all-India forum for expressing the political aspirations of educated Indians, which eventually emerged as the Indian National Congress, should therefore go at least as much to Surendranath Banerjea as to Allan Octavian Hume. A retired official of the civil service, Hume was concerned at the absence of a channel of communication between the rulers and the educated Indians, as distinct from members of the princely order with whom the British had plentiful contacts. He put it to the Viceroy, Lord Dufferin, that it would be very advantageous to the government to have a responsible body through which 'the best Indian opinion' could be gathered. Dufferin did not demur, though he was shortly to form an adverse impression both of Hume and of the Congress.

Birth of the Congress

In a celebrated letter addressed to graduates of Calcutta university, Hume said that if they, "the picked men, the most highly educated of the nation cannot, scorning personal ease and selfish objects, make a resolute struggle to secure greater freedom for yourselves and your country, a more impartial administration, a large share in the management of your own affairs, then...India truly neither desires nor deserves any better government than she enjoys." The upshot was the formation towards the close of 1884 of an Indian National Union which, in consultation with the Bombay Presidency Association, the Sarvajanik Sabha and others arranged to hold an all-India conference in December 1885. The aim was to "effect co-operation between the leaders of thought in

various parts of the country and decide upon a plan of political campaign."

The all-India conference was to have met at Poona, with the Sarvajanik Sabha forming the reception committee. But an outbreak of cholera led to the shifting of the venue to Bombay, where the trustees of the Goculdas Tejpal Boarding School at Gowalia Tank placed the spacious building at the disposal of the organisers. On the morning of December 1885, '72 good men and true', representing a cross-section of the most advanced political opinion, assembled at the Congress—as the gathering was appropriately named. They included such personalities of note as Pherozeshah Mehta, Subramania Iyer, K.T. Telang and Dinshah Wacha. Surendranath Banerjea was not present; he had been busy organising a similar gathering at Calcutta a few days earlier; and he soon merged his organisation with the Indian National Congress, their aims being identical.

Literary Impetus to Nationalism

Creative writers contributed significantly to the national awakening. One of the earliest among the patriotic writers was Bankim Chandra Chatterji (1838-94). While he valued English as a unifying link among educated Indians (Bankim Chandra was in the first batch of Calcutta university graduates), he cautioned against alienation of the English-educated intelligentsia from the masses. He stressed the importance of Indian languages for communicating with the masses. Bankim Chandra's song 'Vande Mataram', which he incorporated in the novel 'Ananda Math', became the battle-song of the mass movement against the partition of the province in 1905. The British banned its singing, and at the Bengal provincial conference held at Barisal in 1906, the delegates were severely beaten for singing the song in defiance of the ban. (Later, in 1918, the Rowlatt Committee was to hold the novel 'Ananda Math' responsible for the spread of the revolutionary—what it termed 'seditious'—spirit). 'Vande Mataram' has continued to be sung at patriotic gatherings throughout the country, and its two opening words have served as a slogan raised lustily by processionists.

Bankim Chandra advocated a change of outlook towards women, and the abandonment of practices such as polygamy and early marriage. At the same time he ridiculed those who blindly imitated Western fashions and manners. He stood for the preservation of cultural roots and the blending of the scientific outlook and humanist values. Another song that gained wide currency during the freedom movement and was sung along with 'Vande Mataram' was 'Jana Gana Mana', by Rabindranath Tagore (1861-1941). Composed on the occasion of an anniversary of the Brahmo Samaj, it celebrates India's unity in the midst of diversity and was adopted as the national anthem after independence. Tagore composed, and himself sang, the inaugural song at the second session of the Indian National Congress, at Calcutta in 1886. He came to be known internationally following the award of the Nobel Prize to him in 1913 for his English rendering of the *Gitanjali* verses. Knighed by the British sovereign in 1915, Tagore relinquished the title in protest against the massacre of unarmed men, women and children at Jallianwala Bagh by British troops in 1918. In Hindi literature the era of nationalism and social reform was inaugurated by Bharatendu Harishchandra (1850-85). The wide range of his writings extended from poems in celebration of Radha and Krishna to the play 'Bharat Durdasha', on India's decline into misfortune.

Then, inaugurating the modern period, came Mahavir Prasad Dwivedi, writer and editor of excellence who gave a new shape and style to *Khari Boli*, or Hindi as spoken and written today ; and Maithili Saran Gupta, the poet who dominated the scene for long. Nationalism was expressed in even stronger accents by subsequent writers : Siyaram Saran Gupta, Makhanlal Chaturvedi who sang in praise of the martyrs of the freedom struggle ; Bal Krishna Sharma 'Navin' ; Subhadra Kumari ; Ramdhari Singh Dinkar ; and Prem Chand whose novel 'Rang Manch' became a bible for Gandhian Satyagrahis. Notable among the poets of freedom of south India is Subramania Bharati (1882-1921), who wrote in Tamil. He sang not only of national freedom but also of women's emancipation, economic equality and liberation of the lower castes which independence should herald. He says in 'Vidudalai' (Freedom) a

widely popular song : "There shall be none of low degree, and none shall be oppressed ; born in India, all are of noble birth."

Bharati, like Bankim and many other patriotic writers, used the imagery of gods and goddesses of the Hindu pantheon. Bankim visualised the motherland as the ten-armed goddess Durga. This became the subject of some controversy. According to an article in the British-owned *Statesman* of 14 August 1937, "The Muslims objected to the singing of 'Bande Mataram' because in 'Ananda Math' this song was sung by the main character of the play whose 'sole aim was to turn out the Muslims from Bengal, and the song was also idolatrous in spirit".

It is only to be expected that the literature and the arts of a people should bear the impress of the mythology and symbolism of their religion. The impress of Hinduism on Indian culture is like that of Christianity in the western world or of Islam in the Muslim-majority countries. Seventy years after the Bande Mataram controversy, it seemed entirely natural to M. F. Hussain, the great Indian artist, to pay tribute to the strength and determination of the then Prime Minister, Indira Gandhi, by depicting her as Devi Durga.

As regards wars between Hindu and Muslim rulers, there were quarrels over power, not religion. For example, Shivaji was a Hindu and it is a fact of history that he defied and fought the Mughal empire which was headed by a Muslim. But it is also a fact that one of the constant bodyguards of Shivaji was Siddi Ibrahim. Similarly, the Foreign Minister of the Sikh ruler Ranjit Singh was Fakir Azizuddin. Haider Ali of Mysore used to let his Hindu soldiers perform their worship in a temple before embarking on an expedition. The true difference among rulers lines not in their religion but between the broad-minded and the narrow-minded. We noticed in the first chapter the contrast between Akbar's respect for other religions and the fundamentalism of Aurangzeb.

The best among poets, as among statesmen, are also broad-minded. Subramania Bharati composed a poem in praise of Jesus in which he says of the symbolism of the death on the Cross : "God will enter our body and save us from destruction

if only we destroy our ego." He wrote another poem in praise of Allah "Who has decreed out of His grace that, in illimitable space, a million worlds should roll unceasingly in all directions; all who come and worship Him, He saves, destroying the fear of death."

REFERENCES

1. *India's Struggle for Independence* : *Visuals & Documents* (p. 16) National Council of Educational Research and Training, New Delhi 1985.
2. *Ibid.* (p. 2).

CHAPTER THREE

RESISTANCE TO BENGAL'S PARTITION

THE uprising of 1857 had taken the British unawares, breaking out as it did within eight years of the destruction of the Sikh State in Punjab which completed the British conquest of India. They were quick to draw their lessons from the trauma.

DIVIDE AND RULE

A Calculated Policy

The British noticed the loyalty commanded by the princes and nobles who raised the standard of revolt. It was therefore decided to keep the princes in good humour with the baubles of rulership, honours and decorations. Princely India, consisting of several hundred distinct states, was to be kept separate from British India.

Hindus and Muslims had stood together in all the affected areas, at every level : among the sepoys, the civilian population and the princes and chieftains. It was desirable, from the viewpoint of the British rulers, to create a Hindu-Muslim cleavage, specially since many educated Hindus had begun to voice political aspirations. It was decided therefore to patronise the Muslims and keep them away from nationalist mischief. The

Sikhs had kept aloof from the uprising. They were now to be favoured, and a sense of separate Sikh identity encouraged among them. Later, as we shall see, the British were to support the non-Brahmin Justice party in Madras as against the 'Brahmin' Congress, and to promote separatist feeling among the Depressed Classes (the so-called Untouchables). For the purpose of representation in the legislatures in British India, distinct identity was to be ascribed, through separate electorates, to a half-dozen communities : Muslims, Sikhs, Depressed Classes, Europeans, Anglo-Indians and Indian Christians.

Five years after the revolt, the Secretary of State for India, Sir Charles Wood, gave detailed advice on the art of divide-and-rule to Lord Elgin, then Governor-General. In a series of communications starting from 3 March 1862, the Secretary of State said : "We have maintained our power by playing off one part against the other, and we must continue to do so. Do what you can, therefore, to prevent all having a common feeling...... I have been always very anxious to avoid any fraternising and combining amongst the troops. It obviously is a cardinal point in India to keep races and classes so far away from each other as to obviate as far as possible the danger of combined action. Do the ordinary work of the North-West Provinces with North-Western troops, Punjab ditto, and then have your Punjab troops ready to beat the Eastern with, and your Eastern troops to beat the Sikhs with, if occasion should arise......The natural antagonism of the races is no inconsiderable element of our strength. If all India was to unite against us, how long could we maintain ourselves ?"

Lord Dufferin was assured by an English official, Sir W. H. Gregory, in a letter of 24 February 1886, that the policy of encouraging Muslims in education and in employment was sound, and would pay off : "I am confident that it will bear good fruits ; indeed it seems to have done so already, by the complete abstention of the Mohammedans from Brahmin and Baboo agitation. It will be a great matter to sweeten our relations with this portion of the Indian population, the bravest and at one time the most dangerous. They all with one voice declare they got their whipping in 1857, and they take it like men. They now look to us alone, not to be subjected to Hindu domination."

Muslim Ambivalence towards the Congress

The above letter was written within two months of the first session of the Indian National Congress at Bombay. The outstanding Muslim personality in public life of that time, Badaruddin Tyabji (1844-1906), had been invited and was to attend, but was detained outside Bombay on urgent business and could not come. He had to miss the second session too. His absence led some loyalist Muslims to claim that he was, like themselves, keeping away from the newly formed Congress. Apparently Lord Dufferin's informant thought so too.

Badruddin Tyabji not only attended the third session of the Congress, at Madras in 1877, but presided over it. And in his address he said that he failed to understand why Muslims should not work shoulder to shoulder with their fellow-countrymen for the common benefit of all.

Tyabji, who was the first Indian to become Chief Justice of the Bombay High Court, pulled up a British barrister who had made disparaging remarks about the Indian National Congress: "I have always regarded it (Congress presidentship) as the highest honour, higher than being on this Bench. Let me tell the counsel, that in my Court no contemptuous references to that body will be permitted."

When Syed Ameer Ali invited Tyabji to attend a Muslim political conference that was proposed to be held at Calcutta, he replied : "You are no doubt aware that I have always been of opinion that in regard to political questions at large, the Mohammedans should make a common cause with their fellow countrymen of other creeds and persuasions, and I cannot help deprecating any disunion on such questions between ourselves and the Hindus and Parsees. If, therefore, the proposed Mohammedan Conference is started simply as a rival to the National Congress, I should entirely oppose it, as it seems to me that the proper course is to join the Congress, and take part in its deliberations."

A section of the Muslim intelligentsia shared Tyabji's robust nationalism. Others shared the fear voiced by an older Muslim leader, Syed Ahmad Khan, that democracy based on representative government in India would result in Hindu domination and would be harmful to Muslim interests. Ahmad Khan

argued : "The first requisite of a representative government is that the voters should possess the highest degree of homogeneity. In a form of government which depends for its functioning upon majorities, it is necessary that the people should have no difference in the matters of nationality, religion, ways of living, customs, mores, culture and historical traditions. Only when such homogeneity is present can representative government work or prove beneficial. It should not even be thought of when these conditions do not exist. I consider the experiment which the Indian National Congress wants to make, fraught with dangers and suffering for all the nationalities of India, specially for the Muslims." Syed Ahmad Khan wanted the Muslim community to offer its loyal co-operation to the British Government. This attitude was welcome to the British authorities, who did everything to encourage it.

Modernisation : the Hindu-Muslim Gap

At the root of this separatist trend was the delayed start of Indian Muslims on the path of modernisation through English education as compared to the Hindus, not to speak of Indian Christians and Parsees who had taken to western education with alacrity. The gap which was to have profound consequences for the development of the sub-continent's polity, is marked by the respective life-spans of Rammohun Roy, namely 1772-1833, and of his counterpart as the initiator of social reform and modern education among the Indian Muslims, Syed Ahmad Khan, which was 1817-1898.

The Hindu-Muslim gap in modern education was cited by 'The Mohammedan Observer' in January 1887 to justify the policy of abstention from the Congress pursued by the Central National Mohammedan Association : "English education has not made such progress among Muslims as among Hindus. To insist upon open competition as the only mode of selection for state employment means the absolute exclusion of the Mohammedans from the public services. To ask for representative institutions, without sufficient guarantees for the repesentatives of the minority, means swamping of the minority by the majority. There is more hope of a fair equilibrium being maintained from the political wisdom of a neutral

government than from the generous instincts of a majority looking primarily but naturally to the interests of its own bulk. The minority have a right to see their interests safeguarded. And we say advisedly that until our people have come abreast of the Hindus in education and political intelligence, political concessions to the majority, without sufficient guarantees for the protection of the minority, would be destructive to the latter."

The Muslim elite withdrew into sullen isolation after the 1857 revolt had been crushed. Immediately after the uprising, the British ragarded the Muslims as unreliable and treated them with special harshness. According to one account, whereas the first batch of Hindus who had fled from Delhi during the months of fighting were allowed in October 1857 to return to their homes after paying a tax of ten per cent of their estimated wealth, the return of Muslims was allowed only after April 1858, and they were required to pay a tax of twenty-five per cent. Muslim parents who could afford at all to educate their children sent them to traditional schools of religious instruction rather than the schools opened by missionaries or by the government, where English was taught. It was only after two or three decades that the Muslims started coming out of the protective shell of orthodoxy into the sunlight of the contemporary world and modern knowledge. Virtually a whole generation thus missed the process of modernisation.

Ahmad Khan cited the Prophet to urge his co-religionists to come out of the isolation which was keeping them backward, and to acquire scientific knowledge : "The adoption of the new system of education does not mean the renunciation of Islam. The Prophet said that knowledge is the heritage of the believer, and that he should acquire it wherever he can find it. He also said that the Muslims should seek knowledge even if they have to go to China to find it. It is obvious that the Prophet was not referring to theological knowledge in these sayings. China at that time was one of the most civilised countries of the world, but it was a non-Muslim country and could not teach the Muslims anything about their own religion. Islam, Islamic culture and the Muslims themselves prospered as long as the Prophet was followed in respect of these teachnigs ; when

we ceased to take interest in the knowledge of others, we began to decline in every respect. Did the early Muslims not take to Greek learning avidly ? Did this in any respect undermine their loyalty to Islam?" It was Ahmad Khan who founded in 1875 the Muhammedan Anglo-Oriental College, which was raised in 1921 to the status of a university as the Muslim University of Aligarh. In the sphere of social reform, Ahmad khan attacked the Purdah system which symbolised the seclusion of women. He also deprecated the tendency to attribute supernatural powers and miracles to the Prophet and saints. Ahmad khan stood for social harmony between the Hindus and Muslims : "Do you not inhabit the same land ? Remember that the words Hindu and Mohammedan are only meant for religious distinctions : otherwise all persons, whether Hindu or Mohammedan, even the Christians who reside in this country, are all in this particular respect belonging to one and the same nation."

The affirmation here of a single Indian nationhood in a political sense runs contrary to the passage quoted earlier, in which Ahmad Khan said that India lacked the pre-requisite of homogeneity required for reprsentative government. This is an example of ambivalence which, as we shall see, marked also two tall Muslim figures of a later period in India's public life: the poet Mohammed Iqbal, who composed a patriotic song celebrating Hindustan's unity in diversity which is widely used in post-partition India to this day, but who also envisioned the creation of a north-west Indian Muslim state; and Mohammad All Jinnah, who began as nationalist but became a separatist and brought about the partition of the sub-continent. Thus the ambivalence, or feeling a pull in two directions was profound.

A BLOW AIMED AT NATIONALISM

Though the Congress was established in 1885 with official blessing, its resolutions and the speeches thereon soon dismayed the British rulers. By 1900 the Viceroy had decided to destroy the Congress. In the hope of accomplishing this purpose, he effected the partition of Bengal, the birth-place of nationalism, in 1905. The mass resistance to the partition marked the

beginning of the Indian Revolution. As Gandhiji said later, the partition of Bengal led to the partition of the British empire.

Congress on lap-dog

The resolutions of the Congress were moderately worded, and in the early years included expressions of loyalty to the British Crown. But it was evident from the start that the Congress was not going to be a lap-dog of the administration. The very first Congress session, in 1885, adopted a resolution asking for reform of the provincial legislative councils by including elected members, in addition to the official and nominated members, submission of budgets to the councils, and the right of interpellation, i.e. of putting questions to and eliciting information from the official members. From the chair, W.C. Bonnerji said: "Our desire to be governed according to the ideas of government prevalent in Europe is in no way incompatible with our thorough loyalty to the British Government. All we desire is that the basis of the government should be widened and that the people should have their proper and legitimate share in it."

In this plea for a first step towards democratic self-government at least one member of the English ruling class saw a sinister move for installing an oligarchy—rule of the many by a few. In a letter of 2 June 1886 to Dufferin, Sir Henry Maine said, "Though the educated natives have learnt to use our democratic language, they are really trying to set up a narrow oligarchy. I cannot bring up the total number of educated, university-bred Indians to more than 5000. Any machinery which enables 5000 men to govern 180 millions of souls creates an aristocracy and, in this case, an aristocracy which is not powerful, nor representative, nor friendly to any social reform."

At the second session in Calcutta, Dadabhai Naoroji (1825-1917) as president defined the goal of the Congress as Swaraj or self-government for India within the British Empire, in the manner of the white Dominions. Dadabhai was on one of his many visits to India from London. He had taken up residence there both to attend to the business of a firm in which he

was a partner, and to educate British public opinion on the problems of India and what the drain of wealth from the country meant to its people. It was a measure of the respect he gained in Britain that he was elected to the British House of Commons in 1892 on the Liberal Party's ticket.

At the third session in Madras, one of the delegates—and an Englishman to boot, by name Eardley Norton—said: "If it be seditian to insist that people should have a fair share in the administration of their own country and affairs, to mutiny against injustice, to uphold the liberties of the individual to vindicate our common right to gradual but ever advancing reforms, if this be sedition I am rightly glad to be called a seditionist, and doubly, aye, trebly glad when I look around me to know, and feel, that I am ranked as one among such a magnificent array of seditionists."

All this was more than the British authorities could stomach. At the time of the fourth Congress session in 1888 at Allahabad, in the then North-West provinces, the Lt. Governor, Sir Auckland Colvin, placed obstacles in the way of the Reception Committee's work. He wrote to Dufferin assuring the Viceroy that the Muslims of his province would be bitterly hostile to the Congress, which they saw as a claim for Hindu supremacy. Colvin described the theory of a national movement in India as absurd, and one to which the Muslim would not subscribe.

When the Congress met again at Allahabad in 1892, Lala Murlidhar from Punjab denounced the destruction of Indian handicrafts and the flooding of the Indian market by British goods, and upbraided his fellow-delegates : "You, it seems, are content to join with those accursed monsters in battening on the heart's blood of your brethren (Cris of 'no', 'no'). I say, yes. Look round. What are these chandeliers and lamps, and European-made chairs and tables, and smart clothes, and hats, and English coats and frocks, and silver-mounted canes and all the luxurious fittings of your houses but trophies of India's misery, monuments of India's starvation ! Every rupee you have spent on Europe-made articles is a rupee of which you have robbed your poor brethren, honest handicraftsmen who can now no longer earn a living." The British had

"repealed the import duties and flung away three crores a year of revenue, which the rich paid, and to balance this wicked sacrifice, raised the salt tax which the poor pay...Free trade, free play, between these two nations ! How I hate the sham ! What fair play in trade can there be between impoverished India and the bloated, capitalist England ?"

There was an outbreak of plague at Poona in 1896, and an English official called Rand was killed following misbehaviour by British soldiers during their search of houses for plague cases. Bal Gangadhar Tilak, the fiery nationalist, was arrested and sentenced to 18 months' imprisonment. These events caused disquiet. Tilak's arrest dominated the 1897 session, presided over by Sankaran Nair who had resigned from the Viceroy's Executive Council in protest against the repressive policies of Lord Chelmsford.

The same year came a signal from London reiterating the policy of divide-and-rule. Lord Hamilton, Secretary of State for India, wrote to the Viceroy, Lord Elgin, on 7 May 1897 : "I am sorry to hear of the increasing friction between Hindus and Mohammedans in the North-West and the Punjab. One hardly knows what to wish for ; unity of ideas and action would be very dangerous politically ; divergence of ideas, and collision, are demonstrably troublesome. Of the two the latter is the least risky, though it throws anxiety and responsibility upon those on the spot where the friction exists."

Curzon's Hostility to the Congress

The next man on the spot, as Viceroy, was Lord Curzon. A more effective instrument could not have been chosen for implementing the policy of divide-and-rule. Curzon had a poor opinion of Indian character, and detested the Congress. He said in a letter of 18 November 1900 to Lord Hamilton : "My own belief is that the Congress is tottering to its fall, and one of my greatest ambitions while in India is to assist it to a peaceful demise." The partition of Bengal, mooted in 1903, was Curzon's brainchild. Of the 18 annual sessions of the Congress between 1885 and 1902, four had been hosted by Calcutta. Bengali nationalist leaders had presided over as many as six of the annual sessions held outside Calcutta. The

Bengali presence was thus conspicuous on the stage of Indian nationalism. And the Bengali nationalist intelligentsia was largely Hindu. Curzon deeided to strike where, as he thought, it would hurt the cause of Indian nationalism most. Ironically, the partition of Bengal was, instead, to mark the beginning of the Indian struggle for freedom.

Diabolical Purpose of Partition

It was ostensibly for improvement of the administration that the division of Bengal, a Presidency of unwieldy size, was undertaken. It included, besides Bengal proper, Bihar, Orissa and Chota Nagpur. If administrative considerations had been primary, there were rational ways of reorganisation : for example, a reduction of the Bengal Presidency's size by constituting a new Chief Commissioner's province comprising the non-Bengali areas of Bihar and Chota Nagpur.

The aim was different. Curzon initially proposed to detach the Chittagong division and the districts of Dacca and Mymensigh from Bengal and to incorporate them with Assam. This would have separated the bulk of Bengal Muslims from Bengali Hindus. The proposal met with strong and unanimous opposition. This only confirmed Curzon in his view about Bengali nationalism and the danger it held for British rule. He now improved upon his earlier plan: the whole of Northern and Eastern Bengal, with Assam, was to form a new Province of Eastern Bengal and Assam ; and Western Bengal with Bihar and Orissa was to constitute the Province of Bengal. Bengalis in Western Bengal would be separated from their kith and kin ; and Bengali Hindus would be a minority in both the provinces.

Commending the scheme to London, the Viceroy said in a despatch :

> "Calcutta is the centre from which the Congress party is manipulated throughout the whole of Bengal and indeed the whole of India. Its best wire-pullers and its most frothy orators all reside here. The perfection of their machinery is truly remarkable. They dominate public opinion in Calcutta, they affect the High Court. They

> frighten the local government and they are not sometimes without serious influence upon the Government of India. The Bengalis who like to think of themselves as a nation, and who dream of a future when the British will have been turned out and a Bengali Babu will be installed in Government House, Calcutta, of course bitterly resent any disruption that will be likely to interfere with the realisation of this dream. If we are weak enough to yield to their clamour now, we shall not be able to dismember or reduce Bengal again, and you will be cementing and solidifying in the eastern flank of India a force already formidable and certain to be a source of increasing trouble in the future."

To the Muslims of Eastern Bengal, Curzon's appeal was frankly communal. Addressing a gathering at Dacca, he said : "When a proposal is put forward which would make Dacca the centre and possibly the capital of a new and self-sufficing administration, which must give to the people of these districts by reason of their numerical strength and their superior culture, the preponderating voice in the province so created, which would invest the Mohammedans in Eastern Bengal with a unity which they have not enjoyed since the days of old Musalman viceroys and kings, which must develop local interests and trade to a degree that is impossible so long as you remain the appendage of another administration—can it be that the people of these districts are to be advised by their leaders to sacrifice all these great advantages from fear ? Do you mean to be so blind to your future as to repudiate the offer ?"

Salimullah, the Nawab of Dacca, was at the beginning opposed to the proposed partition. He was won over with a combination of inducements : a large loan at a nominal rate of interest ; the prospect of Dacca, his home town, being raised to the position of a capital ; and the likelihood of Muslims dominating the administration of the new province. The first Lt. Governor of the province of Eastern Bengal and Assam, Joseph Bamfylde Fuller, said with reference to the two main communities—Muslims and Hindus—that they would be like two queens of his, the first being the favoured one.

BEGINNING OF THE INDIAN REVOLUTION

Economic Boycott of Britain

The decision to partition of Bengal was announced by the Government on 20 July 1905. It set off a mass movement of protest in Bengal, with sympathetic reaction in other parts of the country, the like of which had not been witnessed before. The repressive measures adopted by the British authorities were also unprecedented. Economic boycott of Britain was forged during this movement as the weapon of a weak nation against a strong nation. Starting with cloth made in Manchester, the boycott movement soon widened to cover Liverpool salt and foreign sugar, and social boycott of those using British goods. (See I under select Documents).

Hundreds of public meetings were held throughout Bengal. About one of the demonstrations in Calcutta, which was to culminate in a meeting at 5 p.m. in the Town Hall, the *Englishman* reported : "From two o'clock there were in the streets of Calcutta processions of students marching, two by two, with blue pennons inscribed in Bengali with the words 'United Bengal'. The students were marshalled under their teachers in College Square. There they stood in groups, each holding aloft black flags bearing words such as 'Unity is Strength', 'Bande Mataram' and 'No Partition'. A huge procession of students, estimated at not less than 5,000 in number, marched from College Square to the Town Hall, as if in a funeral procession. The shops were closed since the morning." At the Town Hall itself, the crowd was so large that two over-flow meetings had to be held. As a report put it, "Rajas and pleaders and Babus jostled each other and the gathering shaded off into the poorest class." The main meeting, presided over by Maharaja Manindra Chandra Nandi of Cossimbazar, demanded the withdrawal of the partition decision and endorsed the decision taken at many meetings in the districts to abstain from the purchase of British manufactures. Such was the strengh of popular feeling in favour of Boycott that shopkeepers took down their signboards proclaiming, 'English goods are sold here'. Instead, they displayed placards saying that Swadeshi wares alone were to be purchased within.

The effect of the economic boycott can be judged from the telegram sent by Indian merchants of the Marwari Chamber of Commerce, Calcutta on 1 September 1905 : "We appeal to you to intervene and persuade the Secretary of State for India to prevent the partition of Bengal which has created a great tension of feeling here. The Bengalees have resolved in numerous public meetings to boycott British goods. The sale of Manchester goods has been practically stopped. We shall be ruined and shall not be able to make future contracts unless the Secretary of State withdraws the Partition, and the boycott ceases."

The momentum of the campaign was maintained over the years, even in Muslim-majority Eastern Bengal. Writing from there, Henry W. Nevinson said in the *Manchester Guardian* of 3 January 1908 : "Late the other night, as I sat on the river steamer after a long day of listening to leaders of Hindu opinion, leaders of Mahomedan opinion, and English officials, five or six dark forms gathered round me with gestures of secrecy. They were merchants who had large dealings in Manchester cotton and in consequence were generally shunned. Barbers would not shave them, milkmen would not sell them milk, friends would not go to their daughters' marriage. It was distressing and inconvenient. Would I please set everything as it was before ? I have no doubt all they said was entirely true, except perhaps their assertion that the Mahomedans insisted on having Manchester goods. The Mahomedans in this province have most to gain by the Swadeshi movement, for they form the great majority of the handloom weavers, and owing to Swadeshi, that industry, for which Dacca was long famous over the world, has in the last two years not only revived but redoubled."

The Swadeshi movement spread to other parts of India. Confidential reports received by the Government from the intelligence bureau showed that, by the end of 1905, the Boycott Swadeshi movement had affected 23 districts in the United Provinces, 15 towns in the Central Provinces, 24 towns in the Bombay Presidency, 20 districts in the Punjab and 13 districts in the Madras Presidency. In rural Delhi, the people of Larsoli village took an oath to discard the use of imported

sugar. When a trader was caught selling it, he was fined ten rupees. The Panchayat announced that any person who informed it of such a breach would be given a reward of ten rupees and the culprit would suffer eviction from the village. Even priests, not ordinarily involved in public affairs, participated in the movement. From Puri, Lahore and Hardwar, instances were reported of *pandas* (Brahmin priests) refusing to accept offerings, at shrines and in domestic rituals, of sweetmeats made with imported sugar. This was perhaps on account of rumours that had been set afloat, and statements reported in Bengali-language newspapers, to the effect that Liverpool salt and foreign sugar were refined by the use of the blood and bones of swine and cows. Vows to boycott foreign goods began to be taken before the images of deities in temples. Since the imported articles, owing to the fiscal and economic policies of the British government, were in most cases cheaper than the indigenous substitutes, some people succumbed to the temptation of ignoring the boycott. Picketing was therefore organised of the shops which sold foregin goods.

Swadeshi : Fillip to Indian Industry

Swadeshi, the counterpart of Boycott, came as a boon to Indian industrialists, specially those who owned and ran spinning and weaving mills manufacturing cotton yarn and cloth. Since the supply of Indian-made cloth was much short of the demand generated by the Boycott movement, the textile mills of Bombay and Ahmedabad increased their production. Their owners thus helped to sustain the Swadeshi movement at the same time as they increased their sales and profits.

The supply of mill cloth was supplemented by handloom production of coarser cloth. Bengalis accepted this in the spirit of Swadeshi. A widely popular song urged the people : "Give the place of honour to the coarse cloth which is the gift of the Mother, too poor to offer a better one." There were problems of distribution, which were sought to be met by opening Swadeshi stores. Some shop-keepers began to charge exorbitant prices for Swadeshi goods. National volunteers

sold indigenous articles at a fair price from door to door in towns.

The Swadeshi movement launched in 1905 marked the beginning of a mutually supportive relationship that was to develop in the coming decades between the national movement and the growing class of industrial entrepreneurs. A section of the capitalists remained aloof, not wishing to risk giving offence to the British. Similarly, some Leftists in the national movement did not want to have anything to do with capitalists, foreign or indigenous. But the national movement in general looked with sympathy, and admiration at the pioneering efforts of Indian industrialists such as Jamshedji Tata who wanted to start steel manufacture in India. He had to struggle against great odds. The government refused to give Tata the information available with the Geological Survey of India about iron ore and coal deposits that had been discovered in Bengal and Bihar. He had to hire geologists to prospect all over again, for several years, to secure data already in the possession of the government.

The Congress, over the years, urged the adoption of tariff and foreign exchange policies that would benefit Indian rather than British industry and trade. In turn industrialists made substantial donations to support Congress activities, and helped to maintain the families of Congress workers who gave up their careers and courted imprisonment.

Repression and National Education

The repression with which the authorities responded to the anti-partition movement is illustrated by an example reported by W. H. Nevinson : "By a succession of orders and circulars Mr. Fuller has taken away the right of public meeting. The police are authorised to treat as criminals any student or other person who may so far forget himself as to shout 'Bande Mataram' (Hail, Motherland !) in the street. Under the threat of guarding against a breach of the peace, which was never threatened, the recalcitrant gentry of Rangpore, who refused to join in an address to Mr. Fuller, have been ordered to act as special constables, to 'drill with belt & baton' by the side of ordinary policemen, and to bring daily information

regarding 'disloyal movements' in the town. To the credit of Rangpore it must be added that these gentlemen declined to obey these preposterous and humiliating orders—preposterous because they are not according to the law, and humiliating because they were obviously designed to punish them for their inconvenient shows of independence —and they have been threatened with prosecution which they have cheerfully undertaken to face."

The repressive measures bore heavily on students. On 10 October 1905 a government circular was issued over the signature of R.W. Carlyle, saying that students were being used for political purposes and "it is impossible to tolerate this in connection with institutions which Government either assists or countenances." The circular warned that unless heads of educational institutions prevented students' participation in the Swadeshi movement, their grant-in-aid would be withdrawn and the University would be asked to disaffiliate the institutions. If the head of an institution was himself loyal to the government but unable to prevent student participation, he should prove his loyalty by furnishing to the educational authorities a list of the offending students.

This produced a strong reaction in the two Bengals. The outcome of the 'anti-Circular' movement was the establishment of the Jatiya Siksha Parishad, or Council of National Education. The Council wanted to impart education—literary as well as scientific and technical—on national lines and exclusively under national control, not in opposition but standing apart from the existing systems of primary, secondary and university education." It stood for education ordinarily through the medium of the vernaculars, but with English as a compulsory subject.

The Bengal National College was inaugurated on 14 August 1906, with Aurobindo Ghose as principal. The example inspired the formation of similar institutions under the auspices of national education councils in various parts of the country.

Inspiration for the Resistance

The Indian National Congress had little to do with all

these stirring events. It was dominated at that time by moderates. Those who joined the anti-partition movement derived their inspiration from such eminent sons of Bengal as Surendranath Banerjea and Bepin Chandra Pal, Rabindranath Tagore and Aurobindo Ghose.

Surendranath Banerjea attended the annual Bengal provincial conference which was held at Barisal in 1906, at the height of the anti-partition agitation. When some delegates moving in a procession were lathi-charged for singing 'Vande Mataram,' he said to the English Superintendent of Police. "Why are you thrashing our men? If they have done anything, I am the person to be punished. I am responsible." The police officer promptly replied, "You are my prisoner, Sir", Surendranath's arrest only spurred further resistance.

Bepin Chandra Pal (1858-1932) started a Bengali daily newspaper under the title 'Bande Mataram' in 1906 to strengthen the movement. Closely associated with the paper was Aurobindo Ghose (1872-1950). He had turned his back on a career in the Indian Civil Service and served for 13 years in Baroda where he taught and served as principal at the state college. He now returned to Bengal to head the National College. Aurobindo became the virtual editor of 'Bande Matram'.

The rousing articles in the newspaper attracted the adverse attention of the government. A formal warning was issued to the editor on 8 June 1907 "for using language which is a direct incitement to violence and lawlessness". The newspaper's office was searched in July, and the next month Aurobindo was charged with sedition, along with the printer of the newspaper. Only the printer could be convicted and sentenced since Aurobindo had no formal connection with the paper. When, during the trial, the government called Bepin Chandra Pal as a witness, he refused to testify since he wanted neither to say an untruth nor any harm to come to Aurobindo. B.C. Pal gave as his reason for refusing to testify, that the prosecution was injurious to the interests of the country. He was sentenced to six months' imprisonment.

Rabindranath Tagore's poems contributed greatly to the stirring of the Swadeshi spirit. "The more they tighten our

fetters", he said, "the more will our fetters snap ; the more their eyes redden the more will our eyes open." Tagore was among the participants in the conference at Calcutta on 16 November 1905 where the Council of National Education adopted the resolution on the content and aims of national education. He was soon to establish his own Santiniketan school and Viswa Bharati University.

Among the many newspapers which were proceeded against under the Newspapers (Incitement to Offences) Act was *Sandhya*, a popular Bengali daily edited by Brahmabandhab Upadhyaya. A Catholic who retained the Brahamin observances and way of life, he was intensely patriotic. He refused to take part in the proceedings of his trial, saying : "I do not believe that, in carrying out my humble share of the God-appointed mission of Swaraj, I am in any way accountable to the alien people who rule over us."

Though the Congress was at that time dominated by moderates who had no stomach for courting imprisonment and facing lathi-charges, there were several Congress leaders outside Bengal who admired and fully supported the anti-partition agitation. Notable among them were Bal Gangadhar Tilak and Lala Lajpatrai. The similarity of one element in the names of the three led to the description of the 'extremists' as the Bal-Lal-Pal group.

Muslim League and Separate Electorates

A natural sequel to the creation of a Muslim-majority province by dividing Bengal was the encouragement by the British of the formation of an all-India Muslim political organisation. Lord Minto, Curzon's successor, received on 1 October 1906 a Muslim delegation headed by the Aga Khan. That the delegation was sponsored by the British authorities is clear from an entry of the same date in the diary of Lady Minto : "This evening I have received the following letter from an official : 'I must send Your Excellency a line to say that a very, very big thing has happened today. A work of statesmanship that will affect India and Indian history for many a long year. It is nothing less than the pulling back of sixty-two

millions of people from joining the ranks of the seditious opposition.'

What was this momentous event ? It was the Viceroy's acceptance of the principle, urged by the delegation led by the Aga Khan, of a separate Muslim electorate. This was the beginning of the process which was to break up the sub-continent four decades hence.

The delegation told Lord Minto that representative institutions of the European type should be "adapted to the social, religious and political conditions obtaining in India, and in the absence of such care and caution their adoption is likely, among other evils, to place our national interest at the mercy of an unsympathetic majority." Pointing out that the Muslims formed between one-fifth and one-fourth of the total population of India, the delegation wanted that they should be given a more than proportionate share both in the legislatures and in public employment : "The position accorded to the Mahomedan community in any kind of representation, direct or indirect, and in all other ways affecting their status and influence, should be commensurate not merely with their numerical strength but also with their political importance and the position which they occupied in India a little more than a hundred years ago, and of which the traditions have naturally not faded from their minds."

Lord Minto responded most sympathetically. He agreed that "any electoral representation in India would be doomed to mischievous failure which aimed at granting a personal enfranchisement regardless of the beliefs and traditions of the communities composing the population of this continent."

Shortly after this, Nawab Salimullah proposed the formation of a central Muslim organisation to the leaders of the community who had gathered at Dacca for the Mahomedan Educational Conference. Accordingly, on 30 December 1906, a political association called the All India Muslim League was formed. Its objects were to promote feelings of loyalty towards the British government and to protect and advance the political and other rights of the Muslims of India.

In this atmosphere of separatism, a series of Hindu-Muslim riots broke out in Eastern Bengal, particularly in the districts

of Mymensigh and Comilla. These were followed by a chain of communal disturbances in the ensuing years in Peshawar, U.P. and Bihar. Separate electorates for Muslims—or the election of Muslim members of legislatures by Muslims only—were provided for in the Indian Councils Act of 1909. This Act incorporated the 'reforms' formulated by the Viceroy, Lord Minto, and the Secretary of State, Lord Morley. The main features of the Act were : appointment for the first time of an Indian member on the Viceroy's Executive Council; appointment of Indian members in the provincial executive councils and the creation of such councils where they did not exist ; and enlargement of the legislative council, at the centre and in the provinces, by an increase of both nominated and elected members. But the central legislative council was to have a majority of official members. Non-official majority could mean a majority of nominated, and not necessarily elected members. The Government reserved the right to disqualify any candidate regarded as undesirable. The franchise, based on property and education qualifications, was very narrow, with lower qualifications in the case of Muslims. There was weightage for Muslims, through reservation of seats in excess of their share in the population. Over the years, the British rulers carried their flattery of Indian Muslims so far that they treated the basic Indian identity as Muslim and described the rest of the Indian population as 'non-Muhammadan'. Thus we find, in the officially published proceedings of the Central Legislative Assembly of February, March 1927, that not only is Lala Lajpatrai of Muslim-majority undivided Punjab described as member from 'Jullundur Division: Non-Muhammadan' but members from the south too, where the Muslims are a small minority, are similarly described. Thus A. Rangaswami Iyengar is member from 'Tanjore-cum-Trichinopoly : Non-Muhammadan Rural', and C. Duraiswamy Aiyangar is member from 'Madras ceded districts and Chittoor: Non-Muhammadan Rural' !

Annulment of Partition

Lord Hardinge, who replaced Minto as Viceroy towards the close of 1910, realised that there could be no peace till the

partition of Bengal was ended. The annulment was announced on the occasion of the visit of the British king and queen, George V and Mary, for the Delhi Durbar in December 1911. Bihar, Chota Nagpur and Orissa were formed into a Lt. Governor's province ; Assam reverted to Chief Commissionership ; and the rest of the area constituted the province of Bengal. Simultaneously, it was announced that the capital would be shifted from Calcutta to Delhi.

The annulment of partition was widely welcomed, but it was too late to check the militant nationalism which had been generated. And if made no difference to the divide-and-rule policy, which was continued. The mischief of communal electorates introduced in the Act of 1909 made inevitable a second partition of Bengal during the political break-up of the sub-continent in 1947.

WAITING FOR THE MAHATMA

The agitation against the partition of Bengal resulted in a split in the Congress. The majority were moderates who believed in persuading the authorities rather than defying them. The minority, known as extremists, had no faith in petitioning the government; they wanted to mobilise the masses by rousing patriotic feeling. A third group emerged from the anti-partition movement. They were the revolutionaries, who believed in armed struggle and tried to demoralise the enemy by killing British officials and their Indian accomplices. There was also the Home Rule movement started by Mrs. Annie Besant, a notable figure among the British friends of India and of Indian freedom.

While these streams of the nationalist movement were running their course, far away, in South Africa, a man who was to change the whole character of the freedom movement was experimenting with an alternative to all of them: a war without violence and without hatred. Mohandas Gandhi called it Satyagraha (holding fast to truth, or firmness in a righteous cause).

The Moderates' Argument

The moderates denied that they were practising political

mendicancy. Dadabhai Naoroji observed : "Petitioning is not begging for any favours, any more than the conventional 'Your obedient servant' in letters makes a man an obedient servant. It is the conventional way of approaching higher authorities. The petitions are claims for rights or for justice or for reforms, to influence and put pressure on Parliament. The fact that we have more or less failed hitherto is not because we have petitioned too much, but that we have petitioned too little."

Gopal Krishna Gokhale (1866-1915), the educationist, social reformer and tireless advocate in Imperial Legislative Council of greater Indian representation in the executive, was an exponent of gradualism. He cautioned against making the better the enemy of the good : "Some have gone so far as to talk of independence as an object of practical pursuit. We owe it to the best interests of the country to resist the propaganda with all our resources. It means the sure destruction, or at any rate the indefinite postponement, of all the opportunities for slow but peaceful progress which are at present within our reach. The attainment of a democratic form of government is bound to be a slow and weary affair. It must depend upon the average strength in the character and capacity of our people taken as a whole and our average today is far below the English average. The most important work before us therefore now is to endeavour to raise that average."

On the other hand, Gokhale urged the British authorities to effect reforms quickly. Minto, the Viceroy, wrote to the Secretary of State, Morley, about his meeting with a deputation led by Gokhale : "He pressed of course for increased representation, and amendments to the Budget. He asked for two Native Members on the Viceroy's Council and three on the Secretary of State's. He says that the whole younger generation of India is going over to the extremists' side ; that they are quite unreasonable, and attracted by the idea of getting rid of British rule which is the doctrine preached to them ; that the glamour of the British Raj, which in the old days fascinated the people, had departed, and that the only way to recover our moral control is to do something that will appeal to the Native imagination."

The rift between the moderates and the extremists was

evident even before the partition of Bengal. At the 1897 session of the Congress at Amraoti, the moderates successfully resisted the adoption of a special resolution on Bal Gangadhar Tilak, who had been convicted on a charge of sedition and sentenced, on 14 September, to eighteen months' imprisonment.

Any difference of opinion in the nationalist ranks being welcome, the British did everything to promote it. On 9 August 1899, the Secretary of State, Lord Hamilton, wrote to Curzon the Viceroy : "I think the real danger to our rule in India, not now but fifty years hence, is the gradual adoption and extension of Western ideas of agitation and organisation. If we can break the educated Hindu party into two sections holding widely different views, we should ; for, such a division will strengthen our position against the subtle and continuous attack which the spread of education must make upon our present system of government."

In connection with the anti-partition agitation, the moderates said that boycott was futile because, in the Indian conditions, if one Indian resigned a paid or honorary office under the government, a hundred would apply for the post with in 24 hours. As regards the boycott of Indian universities and educational institutions affiliated to them, it was 'suicidal folly' to deprive people even of the meagre facilities that were available. And, finally, the moderates said that after a year and a half of Boycott, more cotton goods and sugar were being imported into India than before ; and in Bengal the movement had not succeeded in keeping out a harmful article of luxury, the foreign cigarette, 'in spite of patriotic vows innumerable, and self-denying ordinances many.'

When the Congress split in 1907, the London *Times* advised the moderates to sever all connections with extremists : "They (Indians) must show that self-government does not mean for them, as it would today, the substitution of the Brahmin for the Englishman and the subjection of all India to the control of Bengali lawyers and clerks." Two late-converts to the moderate ranks were, ironically, Surendranath Banerjee and Bepin Chandra Pal. The popularity of both declined when they turned moderate.

Surendranath, who had fired the imagination not only of

Bengal but of all India, ceased to be an extremist after 1906. He advocated the acceptance of the Montagu-Chelmsford report (so named after the Secretary of State and the Viceroy of the time). And when the Government of India Act of 1919, based on the reforms recommended in this report, came into force, Surendranath accepted office as a Minister. He also received knighthood, which made him 'Sir Surendranath'. It is a pointer to the temper of the times that Surendranath was defeated in the elections to the Bengal Legislative Council in 1923.

The popularity of Bipin Chandra Pal similarly declined when he kept aloof from the non-cooperation movement of 1919 and declared his opposition to the pan-Islamism of the Khilafat agitation.

Tilak : 'Swaraj is My Birthright'

The difference between the moderates who addressed their pleas to the rulers and the militants who mobilised the masses is illustrated by the life-work of Bal Gangadhar Tilak (1856-1920). On completing his education, Tilak spurned government service and engaged himself in teaching and journalism. He ran two journals, *Kesari* (in Marathi) and *Mahratta* (in English) to spread the message of militant nationalism.

During the Bombay famine of 1896, he asked people not to pay government dues by selling their lands and cattle : he told them not to join food riots either : "Why loot the bazars ? Go to the Collector and tell him to give you work and food. That is his duty." He brought out pamphlets and leaflets to familiarise the people with the provisions of the Famine Relief Code.

Tilak transformed the observance of the annual Shivaji festival at Raigarh, birth-place of the Maratha hero, by utilising it as an occasion for rousing patriotic consciousness. This practice, begun by Tilak in March 1895, spread to other parts of India, notably Bengal where it contributed to rousing nationalist sentiment during the anti-partition agitation. A section of Muslims saw an anti-Muslim slant in the Shivaji festival. When this objection was raised at a public meeting in Calcutta in 1906, Aswini Kumar Datta who was in the chair

explained that it was a political and not a religious festival. Tilak, who was present, said : "Shivaji did not fight against the Mohammedans but against the tyrannical power that existed at the time. That is the true spirit in which you must read the life of Shivaji." Tilak utilised the Ganapati festival, popular in Maharashtra, in similar manner. He regarded festivals as 'opportunities for the tutored class to come into close contact with the untutored'. Such use of festivals was, however, criticised by liberal Hindus of Ranade's school who were trying to reform orthodox beliefs, and by those Congressmen who regarded it as an aggressive challenge thrown at Muslims.

Tilak's ringing declaration, 'Swaraj is my birthright, and I will have it' was widely echoed. Along with Aurobindo Ghose, he was the first to enunciate a programme of total non-cooperation with the British rulers : "We shall not give the government assistance to collect revenue and keep peace. We shall not assist them in fighting beyond our frontiers. We shall not assist them in carrying on administration of justice, and when the time comes we shall not pay taxes. If you can do that by your united efforts, you are free tomorrow."

Tilak became a national hero when he was sentenced in July 1908, for his part in the anti-partition agitation, to transportation. He spent six years in jail at Mandalay in Burma. Hailed as the father of the Indian unrest, Tilak initiated the mass awakening which Gandhiji was to develop into a mass movement.

Revolutionary Violence

The dividing line between the extremists and the revolutionaries, who organised secret societies like the Anusilan Samiti of Bengal and Abhinav Bharat of Maharashtra, was thin. Tilak was in touch with the revolutionaries of his time, and was not unappreciative of their strategy of opening another front in the struggle for freedom. Surendranath Banerjea is said to have offered to raise funds to assist anyone prepared to kill Bamflyde Fuller, Governor of the newly created province of Eastern Bengal.

An early journal of the revolutionaries was *Yugantar*, founded in March 1906 by Barindra Kumar Ghose, younger

brother of Aurobindo Ghose. About the writings in this journal, a sessions judge remarked: "They exhibit a burning hatred of the British race; they breathe revolution in every line; they point out how revolution is to be effected." The articles referred to the history of revolutions in France and other countries and commended the winning over to the cause, of soldiers along with their arms, adding that the revolutionists in India had the additional advantage of the rulers being foreigners.

Barindra Kumar Ghose and his associates Abinash Bhattacharya and Bhupendra Nath Datta propagated through pamphlets the need for secret societies and the collection of arms to fight for independence. They also sent out members of their group to other parts of the country, even as far south as Madras, to preach the gospel of revolution. Aurobindo Ghose was among those arrested and charged for conspiracy in connection with a bomb attack aimed at Kingsford, chief presidency magistrate at Calcutta who had ordered the sever flogging of several young men. The bomb actually killed some others. It was in this conspiracy case conducted at Alipur in Calcutta that Khudiram Bose, one of the early martyrs, was tried and hanged.

The bomb incident took place on 20 April 1908, at Muzaffarpur in Bihar where Kingsford was posted at the time. It was betrayal by a colleague named Narendra Gosain who turned approver, which led to the arrest of this group of revolutionaries in a public garden in Calcutta. Prafulla Chaki, companion of Khudiram Bose in the bomb attack, shot himself dead, as the armed police approached them in the garden. The revolutionaries killed the public prosecutor who conducted the case at Alipur, and a police officer who was present at the hearing of the appeal in the Alipur conspiracy case in the High Court at Calcutta. Narendra Gosain was murdered inside jail by two revolutionary prisoners, Kanailal Datta and Satyen Bose, with the consequence that his confession could not be treated as evidence. When Kanailal was hanged for his crime, the funeral procession in Calcutta was like that of a conquering hero, with the body being covered by heaps of flowers thrown by weeping women from the

balconies of houses on the two side of Kalighat Road. The government never again allowed the dead bodies of revolutionaries to be carried in public procession.

The example of Khudiram inspired a number of other revolutionaries. Among them was Madanlal Dhingra, who on 1 July 1909 shot dead Sir Curzon Wylie, an adviser to the Secretary of State for India, at a meeting at the Imperial Institute in London. During his trial at the Old Bailey, Madanlal acknowledged his action, and on the sentence of death being pronounced, thanked the judge and said: "I am proud to have the honour of laying down my humble life for my country."

A legendary figure among the revolutionaries was Vinayak Damodar Savarkar (1883-1966). As a youngster he was moved by accounts of how the Chapekar brothers, who killed the plague officer Rand in Poona, went to the gallows singing verses from the *Gita.* During the anti-partition agitation he organised a big bonfire of foreign cloth at Poona and addressed the gathering along with Tilak. For this he was fined and expelled from his college residency. Proceeding to England on a scholarship, he procured a book on bomb-making and sent cyclostyled copies to India. He prepared a Marathi translation of Mazzini's writings with a long Introduction, and celebrated the 50th anniversary of the 1857 Uprising with a treatise in English on 'The First War of Independence', which was prescribed. In London he met Hardayal who later went to the U.S.A. and founded the Ghadar (Revolt) Party.

Savarkar was assaulted at a meeting of Indians in London convened for condemning the action of Madanlal Dhingra, as he opposed the move. He was not called to the Bar since he would not give an anti-sedition undertaking to his Inn of Court. Extradited to India, he escaped from the ship through a porthole and landed near Marseilles, but was captured and brought to India. Sentenced to two consecutive transportations, he spent many years in jail in the Andamans and on the mainland.

Bhagat Singh, who was to achieve great fame and popularity, his martyrdom came into prominence when he and Batukeshwar Dutt created a country-wide sensation by hurling

two bombs along with a bunch of pamphlets in the Central Legislative Assembly in New Delhi on 8 April 1929. Though no one was hurt, both were sentenced to transportation for life. It was in connection with an earlier event, the shooting dead in December 1928, at Lahore, of Saunders, a police official, that Bhagat Singh was sentenced to death along with Sukhdev and Rajguru. Mahatma Gandhi tried hard but in vain to persuade the Viceroy, Lord Irwin, to commute the sentence. The hanging was carried out on 23 March 1931.

Less than a month earlier, at Allahabad, Chandraskhar Azad, after shooting at and hitting a couple of members of an armed police party that had come to capture him, used the last bullet of his pistol to shoot at his own temple. This young revolutionary thus fulfilled his resolve that he would never be arrested and dragged to the courts to be hanged. Brave even as a lad, when Chandrasekhar, then about fourteen years old, was arrested in the non-cooperation movement of 1920, the handcuffs proved too big for his wrists. He defiantly gave the magistrate his name as Azad; his fathers' name as Swatantra and his residence as prison—and was awarded 15 lashes of flogging. After joining the Hindustan Socialist Republican Army, he was involved in an attempt in 1926 to blow up the Viceroy's train, and other revolutionary acts of violence, before being betrayed and encountering the police at Allahabad.

A revolutionary from the Telugu-speaking region of south India was Alluri Sitarama Raju (1897-1924). Coming under the influence of Mahatma Gandhi, he persuaded the tribal people of Visakhapatnam district to give up drink. When the government did not respond to peaceful pressure for respecting the rights of the tribal people to forest resources, he led a revolt for two years from 1932, caputring arms and ammunition from the Chintapalli police station and defeating the police in two encounters. He was eventually captured, and shot and killed while trying to escape from custody.

Kalpana Dutt, the woman revolutionary, joined the movement in her college days in 1930 and participated in the raid on the Chittagong Armoury in 1933. Sentenced to life

imprisonment, she was released in 1942 and joined the communist party. The following year she married the Communist leader, P.C. Joshi.

A negative feature of the revolutionary movement was that dacoities were committed to raise the resources for buying arms and sustaining the participants through their fugitive life. It also had its quota, like similar movements in other parts of the world, of betrayers, real or suspected, and of rivalry between leaders of factions. The revolutionary movement declined in the thirties, following the emergence of a mass movement for freedom. But the martyrs did not die in vain because they inspired, by their death-defying dedication to the country's freedom, the participants in the non-violent struggle led by Gandhiji.

British Friends of India

We come now to Annie Beasant-British born but a friend of India, who contributed significantly to the raising of nationalist consciousness. She was in a line of Britons who were exceptions to the rule of the typical Britisher in India, who was either racially arrogant or remained aloof from and uninvolved in the life and problems of the Indian people. These friends of India functioned in various spheres—literature, administration, politics and religion.

The earliest was Sir William Jones (1746-94), a pioneer of Asian studies who helped to found the Asiatic Society in Calcutta. He commended to Europeans the study of the Sanskrit language for its "wonderful structure; more perfect than the Greek, more coplous than the Latin, and more exquisitely refined than either." William Jones's translation of Kalidasa's *Shakuntala* (1789) created a sensation among European intellectuals. This, and Edwin Arnold's *Light of Asia* (on the life of the Buddha) and *The Song Celestial* (*Bhagavad Gita*) fostered among English-educated Indians a pride in their own past. This played an important part in the 19th century Indian renascence.

The next notable friend of India was none less than a Viceroy, Lord Ripon (1827-1909). Before coming out to India he had entered the House of Commons in 1852 as an

advanced liberal and served as Under Secretary for India and Secretary for War in the British government. On assuming office as Viceroy in 1880, he laid the foundations of local self-government in India's cities. This served as a training self-government in India's cities. This served as a training ground for Indian leaders in framing and implementing administrative policy. In addition to extending the rights of Indians in this manner, Ripon wanted to curtail some of the privileges of the Europeans in India. The Law Member of Ripon's Executive Council, Sir Courtney Ilbert, introduced in the Imperial Legislative Council a Bill to remove the restriction placed by the Criminal Procedure Code on the jurisdiction of Indian magistrates over Europeans charged with offences. Anglo-Indians (as Englishmen living in India used to be called those days) were furious. They swore by the racist creed of Lord Roberts who had said that "no rank which we could bestow on him (the Indian) would cause him to be considered as an equal by the British officers."

Ripon was broad-minded and large-hearted enough to argue in favour of the Ilbert Bill in the Legislative Council in January 1884: "I have read in a book that righteousness exalteth a nation, and my study of History has led me to the conclusion that it is not by the force of her arms or by the might of her soldiery that a great empire is permanently maintained, but that it is by the righteousness of her laws and by her respect for the principles of justice." But so clamorous were the Whites in their campaign against the Ilbert Bill that its provisions had to be watered down.

Unlike Allan Octavian Hume who had thought of an all-India association of educated Indians to function primarily as a safety valve for expressing their grievances and aspirations, so as to make British rule stable and secure, Annie Beasant (1847-1933) worked for full self-government through elected institutions. She came to India in 1893 after a remarkable record of work in England in women's education, trade unionism, and free thinking as against Christian dogma. A theosophist from 1889, she was elected as president of the Theosophical Society to succeed Col. Henry Steel Olcott on his death in 1907. Theosophy induced her to study Indian

religion and culture, on which she lectured extensively in India and abroad. She made Adyar, in Madras, her headquarters.

Annic Beasant was a delegate to the Indian National Congress in 1914. The same year she founded two journals, 'Commonweal' and 'New India', to propagate Home Rule. After a spirited speech by her on the subject at Cuddalore in 1916, the year in which she formed the Home Rule League, the Governor of Madras, Lord Pentland, asked her to leave India but she refused. Her consequent internment at Ootacamund led to countrywide protests. Mrs. Beasant regarded the Montagu-Chelmsford reforms embodied in the Government of India Act of 1919 as inadequate, but was in favour of giving a trial to self-government in the provinces. She had a deep distrust of massive law breaking, and stood aloof from the Satyagraha movement launched by Gandhiji.

Her contributions ranged beyond the field of politics to national education (she helped to found the Banaras Hindu University and the National College at Madanapalle besides a national university at Adyar) and to the organisation and emancipation of Indian women. Several more friends of India came in her wake from Britain. Among them were Sister Nivedita (Margaret Noble), disciple of Vivekananda and sympathetic to the revolutionaries of Bengal ; Gandhiji's friend and follower C.F. Andrews (whose initials were amplified by his admirers as Christ's Faithful Apostle) ; and Mira Behn (Madeleine Slade), disciple of Gandhiji, who joined the Satyagraha movement and was arrested on many occasions.

From average Youth to Mahatma

There is no parallel in the world's history for the leader of a country's freedom struggle attracting a large number of supporters and admirers, as Gandhiji did, from the very nation whose rule he was fighting. C.F. Andrews and Madeleine Slade, mentioned above, are only illustrative instances. They were attracted, as were the Inaian people—the educated and the uneducated, women as well as men—by his extraordinary moral force. He imbued with something of this force the large number of persons who volunteered for Satyagraha—the

active and large-scale but non-violent resistance to evil, without hatred for the wrong-doer.

Mohandas, born to Karamchand Gandhi and Putlibai on 2 October 1869 at Porbandar on the Gujarat coast in western India, bore no sign of genius or divine grace in his adolescence. He was married very early according to the custom of that time, at the age of 13, to Kasturbai. On completing his high school education, Gandhi went to England to study law. He disregarded the threat of ex-communication by the people of his caste of Modh Bania if he should commit the sin of crossing the sea.

It was during the three years spent in London that something out of the ordinary began to develop in Gandhi's ideas and personality. After a brief effort to conform to the customs and manners of the natives of England, he began to live abstemiously in order to lessen the financial strain on his elder brother who was supporting him, their father having died when Mohands was still at school. He had stuck to the vow he had made to his mother not to touch meat, but the obligation turned into a cheerful mission when he came to know a circle of vegetarians in London and was introduced to literature on vegetarianism. It was on this subject that Gandhi, who was to become a prolific journalist, wrote his first articles. The London *Vegetarian* published these as well as an interview with him.

More important, Gandhi was introduced to the teachings of Buddha and the *Gita* (through Sir Edwin Arnold's *Light of Asia* and the *Song Celestial*), the New Testament, and Carlyle's essay on the 'Prophet of Islam'. He often attended church to hear good preachers of the day. This was the beginning of a comparative study of religion, not as a cold and academic exercise but as a guide to right living. This led him to delcare in 1928: "After long study and experience, I have come to these conclusions: (i) that all religions are true ; (ii) all religions have some error in them; and (iii) all religions are almost as dear to me as my own Hinduism. My veneration for other faiths is the same as for my own faith. Consequently the thought of conversion is impossible."

It is interesting that both Gandhi and Nehru, who were

the greatest mass communicators in the Indian freedom movement and were among the great communicators of all time anywhere, began by being terrified of speaking in public. On return to India, Gandhi got his first brief in Bombay after a long wait but returned the fee of thirty rupees because he was unable to cross-examine a witness. He had to turn to petition-writing to make a living, and jumped at the opportunity when there was an offer of a year's contract to work in South Africa for Dada Abdullah, an Indian Muslim merchant. Gandhi landed at Durban, in Natal, in May 1893 to discover soon that South Africa was a land to racial arrogance and oppression at its worst. Indians, most of whom had come to South Africa as indentured labour, were despised as 'coolies'.

The newly arrived lawyer had to leave after a few days for Pretoria, capital of the Transvaal, in connection with a court case. Though he held a first class ticket, when the train reached Maritzburg a white passenger who boarded the train objected to a coloured man sharing the compartment. A railway official ordered Gandhiji to remove himself to a lower class compartment. On his refusal, he was thrown out on the platform. He spent the cold night in the waiting room wondering whether he should arrange to go back to India. He decided that he should complete the work for which he had come.

Worse humiliation was to follow. On another part of the journey, by a stage-coach, he was made to sit with the coachman on the box outside. When the white conductor, who was sitting inside with the white passengers, wanted to have a smoke, he asked Gandhiji to sit on the footboard so that he himself could sit beside the coachman and smoke. Gandhi refused. The conductor thereupon began to rain blows on Gandhi and tried to throw him down. Gandhi did not hit back, but did not yield either. He clung to the rails of the coach box till some of the white passengers intervened and restrained the conductor. Gandhi kept his seat. It was an early exercise in Satyagraha.

Indians in Transvaal were worse off than in Natal. They had to pay an annual poll tax of three pounds. They had

no right to vote, and could not own land except in a certain area allotted to Indians. They could not use the pavement, or move out of doors at height without a pass.

Moved by what he experienced and saw, Gandhiji asked Indians to form associations, overcome the distinctions of religion and caste, reform their habits and work for the welfare of the community. But he did not at that stage think of leading a campaign in South Africa himself. It was in fact at a farewell dinner, when he was about to return to India on completion of his assignment, that he decided to stay on. He noticed a newspaper report that the Natal Government intended to introduce a bill to disfranchise Indians. When he advised his hosts to resist this legislation they begged him to postpone his departure by at least a month to help them do so. His involvement in the struggle of Indians in South Africa was to stretch out to two decades, during which he developed the philosophy and technique of Satyagraha.

After three years, Gandhi visited India in 1896 to bring his family over. He utilised the occasion to inform public men and newspaper editors about the condition of Indians in South Africa, and published a pamphlet on the subject. Among the national leaders he met were Badruddin Tyabji, Pherozeshah Mehta, Surendranath Banerjea, Tilak and Gokhale.

On return to South Africa he resumed his work of protest and petition which were directed to the local authorities as well as the British Government. In his personal life he gradually reduced his wants and expenses, and took a vow of *brahmacharya* or absolute continence. This was on the reasoning that one could not live both after the flesh and the spirit." He read widely. Among the books which deeply influenced him were Ruskin's 'Unto This Last' with its message of voluntary poverty and bread labour ; Tolstoy's 'The Kingdom of God is Within You', with its Christian pacifism ; and Thoreau's essay on civil disobedience.

Against Racism in South Africa

Gandhi's work as a publicist was successful, to the extent that the London *Times* wrote several editorials on Indian settlers in South Africa. But it made little difference to the

attitude of the local authorities. The passage of the Asiatic Registration Act in Transvaal in 1907 convinced Gandhi that the time had come for organised and active resistance. Known as the 'Black Act', it required all Indians—men, women and children—to have their fingerprints taken. Gandhiji advised resistance to this law by refusing to submit to the indignity. He cautioned them that they might be punished, to the extent of imprisonment. He himself was arrested in January 1908, and sentenced to two months. Other Satyagrahis defied the law and followed him to jail.

When General Smuts sent Gandhiji word that the Black Act would be repealed if the Indians registered themselves voluntarily, he agreed to it in line with the friendly approach of Satyagraha. For this moderation he was physically attacked by some *Pathans* who thought he had betrayed the Indian community. General Smuts, for his part, went back on his word. The Indians made a bonfire of their registration certificates, and the struggle continued for long years till, in January 1914, the government conceded the principal Indian demands.

Before leaving South Africa after two decades of momentous work, Gandhiji sent to General Smuts as a gift a pair of sandals he had made during one of his spells of imprisonment. Recalling this present General Smuts wrote a quarter-century later : "I have worn these sandals for many a summer since then, even though I may feel that I am not worthy to stand in the shoes of so great a man."

CHAPTER FOUR

GANDHIJI : CONGRESS AS A MASS MOVEMENT

THE return of Gandhiji to India led to a transformation of the freedom movement. He changed the Congress, which used to bring together nationalists from among English-educated Indians of the middle and upper classes once a year, into a round-the-year movement with mass participation. Peasants and workers, shopkeepers, students and housewives, joined the movement along with teachers and lawyers, writers and doctors. It became a movement not only for political independence but simultaneously for internal social justice and for economic betterment of the poorest.

After the advent of Gandhiji, the story of the Congress and of the freedom movement which it led was the story of his life and work—with Jawaharlal Nehru emerging by the Mahatma's side, from the late 'twenties, as disciple and critic rolled into one, and in 1942 designated as the 'successor'.

MILITANCY WITHOUT VIOLENCE

Satyagraha : a Radically New Method

The method of Satyagraha brought by Gandiji combined the virtues of, and was yet radically different from, the methods of the moderates, the extremists and the revolutionaries. Trust

in the basic goodness of human nature and therefore of the opponent, and readiness to reach a settlement through compromise instead of rigid insistence on all of one's initial demands-these were merits which belonged to the moderates at their best. Raising the level of consciousness of the masses and rousing their patriotic feelings, and defying, unjust laws at the risk of imprisonment, were right out of the extremists' book. Readiness to face death in struggling for the cause was the example set by the revolutionaries. Gandhian Satyagraha combined all these virtues, and made two crucial additions : the eschewing of violence towards the opponent, in thought and in deed ; and (ii) identification with and service of the poorest and the oppressed.

Charisma of a Saintly Revolutionary

Gandhiji was able to get hundreds of thousands of Indians, from foreign-educated intellectuals to the non-literate, women as well as men, to accept the method of Satyagraha even if they could not all live up to it all the time. The secret of his success was that he was a saintly revolutionary, the adjective being paramount. He was and looked every bit, a man of god, and not just another nationalist. Present in him were all the attributes of the *Rishi* and the *Sanyasi* whom the people of India have revered over the centuries : renunciation of worldly ambitions, minimisation of personal wants, control of the sexual appetite, and dedicated service of fellow human beings. He not only wore home-spun Khadi but was himself a home-spun revolutionary, in the tradition of the egalitarian Bhakti saints.

This endowed him with a charisma comparable to that of Lenin and MaoTse-tung but greater than theirs because no part of his power came out of the barrel of a gun. He combined good religion-humanistic and respectful towards other faiths with the good politics of striving for national independence and a just society. Hence, in his hands, the combination of religion and politics did not become an explosive mixture, except perhaps in the sole case of Khilafat in which he handled a religion other than his own. Instead, the combination acted as a leaven which invested politics with a moral quality.

Gandhiji did not plunge into public life immediately on his return to India. He travelled round for a year, as advised by Gopal Krishna Gokhale, with 'his ears open but his mouth shut'. [illegible]e end of this tour of observation and learning, he settl[illegible]n in May 1915 at Ahmedabad with his close associates at a spot on the bank of the river Sabarmati. It became an Ashram (which he defined as "group life lived in a religious spirit"). As in the Phoenix colony and Tolstoy farm established by him in South Africa, the inmates had to do all the work themselves, from cooking and washing and seavenging. There was a strict code of conduct. Everyone had to do manual work : spinning, weaving, or minding the cowshed or farm. There was, of course, to be no untouchability or caste hierarchy.

In the same year Gandhiji visited Rabindranath Tagore. This was the occasion when the sage of Santiniketan first applied to him the title of '*Mahatma*' (Great Soul). There were to be occasions when Tagore would differ with Gandhiji, as on the latter's call for the burning of foreign cloth. Though the Mahatma defended this flaming demonstration of Boycott as a necessary deflection of the people's anger from men (the British) to things, the Poet could not endorse the action. But Tagore's admiration and regard for the moral awakener of the Indian people was profound : "The Mahatma has won the heart of India with his love. He has given us a vision of the Sakti (power) of truth. For that our gratitude to him is unbounded. We read about truth in books ; we talk about it ; but it is indeed a red-letter day when we see it face to face."

In the words of Jawaharlal Nehru. "Tagore was primarily the man of thought, Gandhi of concentrated and ceaseless activity. Both, in their different ways, had a world outlook, and both were at the same time wholly Indian. They seemed to represent different but harmonious aspects of India and to complement one another." In the concentric circles of human belonging, Gandhiji was more engrossed in the circles of the nation while Tagore dwelt more in the larger circle of the family of man. But while the Mahatma was intensely bound to his motherland to his mother religion, his catholicism was quite

extensive. "Indian culture", he wrote, "is neither Hindu, Islamic nor any other, wholly. It is a fusion of all." Again, "I want the cultures of all lands to be blown about my house as freely as possible. But I refuse to be blown off my feet by any."

Organising Peasants' Struggles

It is significant that it was on behalf of the exploited peasants of India that Gandhiji organised his first Satyagraha in India. It took place in the Champaran district of Bihar. The poor tenant farmers there had for long been compelled by British indigo planters to apply at least 15 per cent of their land to the cultivation of indigo. The planters took all of the indigo crop as rent for the land. A group of peasants met Gandhiji in 1917 and requested him to come and see their plight. When the Mahatma reached there, thousands of peasants travelled from their villages to look at and make obeisance to him in the manner in which the people have traditionally sought *darshan* of temple deities and holy men. But this was a holy man with a difference. He told them of how they could secure justice by fighting for it fearlessly-but non-violently. Gandhiji was ordered by the police to leave the district. When he refused and was asked to appear in court the next day, an army of peasants marched be hind him. At the court he refused to furnish bail, not having violated any law, and was released without condition.

Gandhiji, typically, made efforts to promote hygiene and elementary education in the villages of Champaran at the same time as he was organising them to fight for their rights. After some months the Government set up a committee of inquiry, with Gandhiji as one of the members, and the committee's report brought relief to the indigo cultivators. Thus the first experiment in Satyagraha on Indian soil proved successful.

Another peasants' struggle was led by Gandhiji shortly afterwards in the Kheda district of Gujarat. Though the crops had failed on accunt of drought, the peasants were being compelled to pay the land tax as usual. Gandhiji advised Satyagraha through non-payment of land revenue both by the rich and the poor till remission was granted to the poor

peasants who could not pay. After four months of the no-tax campaign the authorities agreed to exempt the small peasants from the revenue assessment.

It was during the Kheda Satyagraha of 1918 that the lifelong association of Vallabhbhai Patel (1875-1950) with Gandhiji began. Born in Gujarat, Patel had come up the hard way, becoming a lawyer after studying borrowed books. He gave up his practice and joined the movement launched by Gandhiji. In the course of a later struggle against a steep increase in the revenue rates imposed on the peasants of Bardoli, he came to be known as the Sardar (leader of men)—a title by which his name came to be pre-fixed thereafter.

Another prominent participant in peasants' struggles was Lala Lajpat Rai. He was arrested while leading an agrarian movement in Punjab, and was deported to Burma.

In addition to bringing relief to the peasants, the work among them initiated by Gandhiji brought the urban intelligentsia of the Congress in touch with the realities of Indian rural life. Jawaharlal Nehru wrote : "He sent us to the villages, and the countryside hummed with the activity of innumerable messengers of the new gospel of action. The peasant was shaken up and he began to emerge from his quiescent shell. The effect on us was different but equally far-reaching, for we saw, for the first time as it were, the villager in the intimacy of his mud-hut, and with the stark shadow of hunger always pursuing him. We learnt our Indian economics more from these visits than from books and learned discourses. The emotional experience we had already undergone was emphasized and confirmed, and henceforward there could be no going back for us to our old life or our old standards."

Working Class and the Freedom Movement

There were friendly links from the beginning between the nationalist leaders and the trade union movement which emerged in the early years of the 20th century. There was a strike by workers of the East Indian Railway in 1906 against low wages, poor living conditions and racial discrimination. Bepin Chandra Pal and C.R. Das were among those who attended the workers' meetings and expressed their support.

Two years later, when Tilak was arrested, industrial workers in Bombay went on a week-long strike in protest. The first major political strike by industrial workers (as distinct from *hartal* or a general cessation of business activity), it was described by Lenin as a sign of the political consciousness of the Indian working class.

The Madras Labour Union was formed in 1918 by B.P. Wadia, an associate of Annie Besant. Shortly afterwards Gandhiji founded the Majdoor Mahajan Sabha (Ahmedabad Textile Workers' Union).

One of the earliest successes achieved by the textile workers of Ahmedabad was when they requested Gandhiji, at the conclusion of his campaign in Champaran, to intervene in their dispute with the mill owners. Gandhiji found that the workers' demands were reasonable and certainly deserved to be referred to arbitration if the employers could not accept all the demands. When the mill owners would not agree, Gandhiji advised the workers to strike work but to remain non-violent. When the situation was becoming tense, he went on a fast and said he would not break it till a settlement was reached. The parties agreed to arbitration at the end of three days.

The All India Trade Union Congress, nursed and led for long by N.M. Joshi, was formed in October 1920. The Congress session the same year adopted a resolution expressing its "full sympathy with the workers in India in their struggle for securing their legitimate rights." The first session of the A.I.T.U.C. in Bombay was presided over by Lala Lajpat Rai.

C.R. Das was president of A.I.T.U.C. in 1923 and 1924, and Jawaharlal Nehru elected to the office at Jharia towards the close of 1928. The radical group wanted to put up a railway worker for election, but Nehru was proposed and elected in absentia. He wrote about this : "If I had been present at Jharia on the day of the election I am sure that I would have withdrawn in favour of the worker candidate. It seemed to me positively indecent that a newcomer and non-worker should be suddenly thrust into the presidentship. This was in itself a measure of the infancy and weakness of the trade union movement in India."

Subhas Chandra Bose presided over the Calcutta session

of the A.I.T.U.C. in 1931. Other notable Congress figures associated with the trade union movement included orthodox Congressmen like V.V. Giri and Gulzarilal Nanda, and Congress socialists like Acharya Narendra Deva, Jayaprakash Narayan and Ram Manohar Lohia.

The Communists with their solid base in the Girni Kamgar Union of Bombay's textile workers, led by Sripat Amit Dange, gradually acquired controlling influence in the A.I.T.U.C. As we shall see in Chapter V, the attitude of the Communists during World War II and their opposition to the Quit India struggle of 1942 caused a vertical split in the working class movement.

NON-COOPERATION AND KHILAFAT

Gandhiji was in South Africa when the Boer War broke out in 1899, his sympathies were with the Boers who were fighting for their independence, he called for support by the Indian community to the British on the ground that the demand for the rights of Indians in South Africa, as British subjects, carried with it the obligation to support the British at a time of crisis. He raised an ambulance unit and offered its services to the government. During the Zulu rebellion he again raised an ambulance corps which helped to nurse the victims of the fighting, including the Zulus whom white doctors and nurses did not like to serve.

World War I broke out when he was on his way back to India in 1914. Gandhiji decided that "If we would improve our status through the help and cooperation of the British" (a possibility which he still believed in). "it was our duty to win their help by standing by them in their hour of need." Hence his abstention from political agitation during the war and his campaign to promote Army recruitment.

Massacre at Jallianwala Bagh

Gandhiji was sadly disillusioned when, instead of offering a substantial measure of self-government at the end of the war, the British authorities in India set out early in 1919 to arm themselves with extraordinary powers. The Rowlatt Bill was

ostensibly aimed against seditition but drastically curtailed all civil liberties. He gave a call for country-wide *hartal*, the response to which was overwhelming. When Gandhiji was arrested, there was great public excitement in which there was violence in some cities including Amritsar where five Europeans were killed. Gandhiji undertook a three-day fast in penance for his 'Himalayan miscalculation'. On 13 April 1919, the very day on which Gandhiji announced his fast in Ahmedabad, occurred the gruesome massacre at Jallianwala Bagh, in Amritsar. General Dyer ordered his troops to fire on unarmed people who gathered for a public meeting. Nearly 400 persons were killed in the ten minutes of sustained firing. The outrage shocked and angered the nation.

Meanwhile, many leaders of the Indian Muslims felt uneasy about the terms that seemed likely to be imposed by the victorious Allied Powers on Turkey, whose Sultan was the Khalifa. The propriety of regarding the Sultan as having any jurisdiction over Muslims outside Turkey had been questioned by Syed Ahmed Khan, writing newly four decades earlier ; "Khilafat literally means succession, and the person who succeeds is called the Khalifa,....Their Khilafat or government is confined to the Muslim inhabitants of that country alone over which they rule. . . . He (the Sultan of Turkey) can in no sense be the Khalifa for those over whom he has no such authority, the conditions for his Khilafat being altogether absent."

In any case, Gandhiji offered to support the Muslim community on the Khilaft issue if they would accept his method of Satyagraha and his leadership. The offer was made at a Muslim conference held in Delhi in November 1919. The movement was launched on a full scale in August 1920 with a six-point programme : boycott of the law courts by lawyers, who would see up popular tribunals for administering justice; boycott of schools and colleges owned or aided by the government, and the establishment of national educational institutions; boycott of elections; surrender of honours and titles and boycott of official functions; boycott of British goods and the encouragement of Swadeshi, especially Khaddar (handspun, hand-

woven cloth); and the prohibition of liquor through the boycott of liquor shops.

Massive Popular Response

A wider, eleven-point programme (see *II* under *Select Documents*) was drawn up by Gandhiji after the Nagpur Congress of December 1920 approved the policy of non-violent non-cooperation. The movement generated an unprecedented wave of enthusiasm throughout the country. Leading lawyers commanding a large income gave up their practice : for example Motilal Nehru in Allahabad and Chitta Ranjan Das in Calcutta, Rajendra Prasad in Bihar and C. Rajagopalachari in the south. Thousands of students left government schools and colleges, and teachers volunteered to work on a pattance at newly started institutions of national education. A number of students of the Aligarh University left their studies at the bidding of Muhammad Ali, Gandhiji's comrade-in-arms in the Khilafat movement. Many teachers, including Dr. Zakir Hussain, also left. Thus was founded the Jamia Millia Islamia which later shifted to Delhi from Aligarh. Subhas Chandra Bose resigned from the Indian Civil Service and worked as a Principal of the National College, Calcutta. The scale of popular participation in the Satyagraha movement can be guaged from the fact that about 30,000 non-cooperators were arrested.

It was during a tour of South India in September 1921 that, on hearing of Muhammad Ali's arrest in the Khilafat movement, Gandhiji decided on the reduction of his dress to the barest minimum—a loin cloth covering the body from the waist to the knee. It was a mark of sorrow at his comrade's arrest, and served also to reduce personal expenditure on clothing and as a symbol of identification with the half-naked poor. Willingdon, Governor of Madras, expressed the hope in a letter to the Vicerory that Gandhiji would not die of pneumonia as a result—"though his demise might save us all a lot of trouble!"

At places, the Khilafat meetings where the wrongs done to Islam were recounted, served to rouse sectarian religious feeling. When the movement reached Kerala in 1921, the Muslims of

Malabar, known as Moplahs, rose in a violent revolt in disregated of the leaders, insistence on non-violence. They committed atrocities not only on officials of the administration but also on their Hindu neighbours. Hindu-Muslim relations suffered a set-back instead of being strengthened.

Chauri Chaura : An anti-Climax

On 4 February 1922, processionists in a village named Chauri Chaura, near Gorakhpur in Eastern Uttar Pradesh, clashed with the police. The outnumbered policemen ran inside the police station for shelter. The police station was set on fire by the mob, and 22 policemen were killed.

Gandhiji called the movement off, to the dismay of virtually all his colleagues. The non-cooperation movement, which was then at its height, thus ended in an anti-climax. The British took advantage of the demoralisation in the Congress to arrest Gandhiji. He told the trial judge who was an Englishman : "I have no personal ill-will against any single administrator, but I hold it a virtue to be disaffected towards a government which in its totality has done more harm to India than any previous system. . . .The only course open to you, the Judge, is either to resign your post and thus dissociate yourself from evil, if you feel that the law you are called upon to administer is an evil and that in reality I am innocent; or to inflict on me the severest penalty if you believe that the system and the law you are assisting to administer are good for the people of this country." who was judging whom?

The judge awarded six years' imprisonment. This was one of the many 'arrest cures', as Tagore called them, which Gandhiji was to receive in the course of his strenuous public life, enabling him to rest, read and reflect. In the case of Jawaharlal Nehru the jail terms yielded such masterpieces of writing as his *Autobiography* the *Glimpses of World History*, and the *Discovery of India*. C. Rajagopalachari applied his prison terms to study Sanskrit, and write short stories and literary criticism. Here is a found comment on the Indian epics : "I believe with Bapu that most of our mythological stories are allegories, including the Ramayana and Mahabharata. Only, I don't believe in the attempts sometimes made to weave a systematic

allegory running throughout a book. I think it is a wild collection of isolated and valuable allegories.

Gandhiji's prison term ended in January 1924, when he fell ill with acute appendicitis and was released after surgery. By that time the Khilafat movement had become redundant. The Turkish people themselves decided, under the leadership of Kamal Ataturk, to do away with the Sultanate and proclaim a republic.

CONSTRUCTIVE PROGRAMME

Political Advance First or Social Reform ?

We saw in Chapter II that social reform and political awakening reinforced each other during the 19th century. While this continued to be the case by and large, views differed on the priority to be given to social reform *vis-a-vis* advance on the political front.

Dadabhai Naoroji wanted reformation of the practices of each religious community to be left to reformers from within that community. He said in his presidential address at the Second Congress Session in Calcutta, in 1886 : "The National Congress must confine itself to questions in which the entire nation has a direct participation and it must leave the adjustment of social reforms and other class questions to class congresses." There was to be a notable instance of the impulse for reform coming from within the ranks of a religious community when, in the early 1920's, the Akalis launched a movement for reform of the management of Sikh shrines. The Gurudwaras had become, in the words of a Sikh leader, "dens of drunken vice and debauchery". The movement met with resistance from the vested interests, who received police support. The British, as a further step in the strategy of divide-and-rule, had conferred separate electorates on the Sikhs in 1919. But this did not prevent co-operation between the Akalis and the Congress, which fully backed the reform movement.

Badruddin Tyabji was of the same view as Dadabhai Naoroji, namely that different communities should attend to problems of social reform pertaining to them. At the third Congress Session at Madras in 1887, Tyabji said : "Whereas

any question of social reform must of necessity affect some particular part or some particular community of India . . . the only wise and, indeed, the only possible course we can adopt is to confine our discussions to such questions as affect the whole of India at large."

Mahadev Govind Ranade (1842-1901), social reformer and a moderate in politics, held that social reform and political progress were inextricably connected : "You cannot be liberal by halves. You cannot be liberal in politics and conservative in religion. The heart and the head must go together. It is an idle dream to expect men to remain enchained and enshackled in their own superstitions and social evils while they are struggling hard to win rights and privileges from their rulers." Ranade founded the Social Conference, an all-India organisation which ran as an adjunct to the Indian National Congress for several years.

In contrast, W.C. Bonnerji was impatient with those who linked political rights with social change. He was himself an ardent advocate of the education of women and a rightful place for them in society, and was opposed to child marriage. But he asked : "Are we unfit for political rights because our widows remain unmarried and girls are given in marriage earlier than in other countries? Because our wives and daughters do not drive about with us, visiting friends? Because we do not send our daughters to Oxford and Cambridge?"

In a quite different category was Bal Gangadhar Tilak. He was radical in politics but very conservative in social matters. On one occasion he did penance for having taken tea in a Christian missionary school. He attended and spoke at an All India Depressed Classes Conference held in March 1918 under the presidentship of Sayajirao Gaikwad. But he refused to join others in signing a personal pledge adjuring untouchability. Tilak was emphatically for concentrating attention on the struggle for political freedom. When the Congress met in 1895 at Poona, those opposed to Congress involvement in social reform had their way by threatening to burn the *pandal* if the Social Conference was also allowed to use it as in the past.

Surendranath Banerjea explained in a letter to Justice

Ranade : "The reason for excluding social questions from our deliberations is that were we to take up such questions, it might lead to serious differences culminating in a schism, and it is a matter of the first importance that we should prevent a split. The request of the other side is very unreasonable; but we have sometimes to submit to unreasonable demands to avert greater evils."

In November 1917 there was a meeting of the Depressed Classes in Bombay, organised in the context of anticipated political reforms that were promised by the British Government. The meeting asked for Depressed Classes being given the right to elect their own representatives to legislative councils in proportion to their population. It also requested the Indian National Congress "to pass at its forthcoming session a distinct and independent resolution declaring to the people of India at large the necessity, justice and righteousness of removing all the disabilities imposed by religion and custom upon the Depressed Classes. These disabilities, social in origin, amount in law and practice to political disabilities and as such fall legitimately within the political mission and propaganda of the Indian National Congress."

The request could not obviously be ignored. The Calcutta Congress of 1917 passed the following resolution : "This Congress urges upon the people of India the necessity, justice and righteousness of removing all disabilities imposed by custom upon the Depressed Classes, the disabilities being of a most vexatious and oppressive character, subjecting those classes to considerable hardship and inconvenience." But little appears to have been done by Congressmen in follow up of the resolution. Action to end untouchability had to await the Mahatma taking the helm of Congress affairs.

The Eight Points of the Programme

Improvement of the condition of the Depressed Classes formed the fourth item in the eight-point work plan which came to be known as the Constructive Programme. The programme was incorporated in a resolution adopted by the Congress Working Committee during its session at Bardoli on the 11th and 12th February 1922. It was at this session that

the civil disobedience movement was called off because of the violence at Chauri Chaura, near Gorakhpur, on the 4th of February. The two decisions were inter-linked, the constructive programme having been drawn up for strengthening the moral fibre of the Congress and of its members. The resolution said : "Whereas the Gorakhpur tragedy is a powerful proof of the fact that the mass mind has not yet fully realised the necessity of non-violence as an integral, active and chief part of mass civil disobedience, and whereas the reported indiscriminate acceptance of persons as volunteers, in contravention of the Congress instructions, betrays want of appreciation of the vital part of Satyagraha, and whereas in the opinion of the Working Committee the delay in the attainment of the national aim is solely due to the weak and incomplete execution in practice of the constitution of the Congress, and with a view to perfecting the internal organisation, the Working Committee advises all Congress organisations to be engaged in the following activities :

1. To enlist at least one crore members of the Congress.
2. To popularise the spinning wheel and to organise the manufacture of hand spun and hand-woven Khaddar.
3. To organise national schools.
4. To organise the Depressed Classes for a better life; to improve their social, mental and moral conditions; to induce them to send their children to national schools; and to provide for them the ordinary facilities which the other citizens enjoy.
5. To organise the temperance campaign amongst the people addicted to the drink habit by house-to-house visits, and to rely more upon appeal to the drinker in his home than upon picketing.
6. To organise village and town Panchayats for the private settlement of all disputes, reliance being placed solely upon force of public opinion and the truthfulness of Panchayat decisions to ensure obedience to them.
7. In order to promote and emphasise unity among all classes and races and mutual goodwill—the establishment of which is the aim of the movement of

non-cooperation—to organise a social service department that will render help to all, irrespective of differences, in times of illness or accident.

8. To continue the Tilak Memorial Swaraj Fund collections and call upon every Congressman or Congress sympathiser to pay at least one-hundredth part of his annual income for 1921. Every province to send every month twenty-five per cent of its income from the Tilak Memorial Swaraj Fund to the All India Congress Committee.

War on Untouchability

The mild wording of the fourth item is curious. It gives no hint of the crusading zeal with which Gandhiji was to wage an unremitting war on untouchability in the ensuing years. His attitude is expressed in the following extracts from his writings in *Harijan* (the choice of title for the weekly Journal edited by him is itself significant) :

> "If you consider the Harijans untouchable because they perform sanitary service, what mother has not performed such service for her children ?"
> "If untouchability lives, Hinduism dies."
> "No scripture which labels a human being as inferior or untouchable, because of his or her birth, can command our allegiance."

Gandhiji might be in or out of jail, a non-cooperation movement might be launched or withdrawn, but the removal of untouchability was to him an unceasing engrossment. Jawaharlal Nehru was all for social reform, but could not understand the Mahatma's preoccupation with it. In the early 'thirties, when a Bill for removing obstacles to Harijans' entry into temples was introduced in the Central Legislative Assembly, Gandhiji sent an appeal to the members, through C. Rajagopalachari, asking for their votes for the Temple Entry Bill. Nehru was amazed by this because the Assembly has been boycotted by the Congress, and a majority of those inside it were opposed to the Congress and supported the

Government. Moreover, a civil disobedience movement was on, though suspended temporarily. "To me," wrote Nehru "for Gandhiji or any Congress leader to countenance such activities appeared immoral and almost a breach of faith with the large numbers of people in goal or carrying on the struggle. But I knew that his way of looking at it was different." Soon thereafter, Gandhiji went on a fast in Yeravada prison, where he had been sent back on rearrest, in protest against denial of the facilities given to him earlier for carrying on Harijan work from within jail. To Nehru, "It seemed an extraordinarily trivial matter for such a tremendous step." To him freedom came first, not social reform. He recalls in his *Autobiography* that the British government took no steps to popularise the Child Marriage Restraint Act of 1929, popularly known as the Sarda Act after the name of its sponsor, Har Bilas Sarda. He goes on to raise the question why, in that case, the Congress did not propagate the message of the Act, and says in reply : "We suffer from the disease of nationalism, and that absorbs our attention and it will continue to do so till we get political freedom." After independence, Nehru was to be in the forefront of the battle for social reform through legislation for punishing the practice of untouchability, enforcing monogamy and permitting divorce, and giving the daughter a share in succession to property.

Ambedkar's Criticism

If Nehru thought that Gandhiji was unduly preoccupied with the Harijan question, Bhimrao Ramji Ambedkar (1891-1956), leader of the Depressed Classes Federation, was unimpressed by Gandhiji's exertions on behalf of the untouchables. Chief among his complaints was that the Mahatma did not disown the concept of Chatur Varna or the Four Castes which was at the root of the feelings of superiority and inferiority based on caste.

Ambedkar took the stand that equal voting rights and fundamental freedom in a Constitution arc of no help to socially persecuted minorities such as the American Negroes, Jews in Hitler's Germany and the untouchables of India. He therefore wanted, prior to and as a condition for self-

government in India, constitutional safeguards by way of a guaranteed quota of representation in the legislatures, separate electorates so that the Depressed Classes could elect persons of their own choice, and quotas in the provincial Cabinets and in public services.

It is true that Gandhiji did not question the Varna Ashrama Dharma which traditionalists regard as being at the heart of Hinduism. The Ashrama part of the Dharma (Ethical Code) is essentially descriptive and contains nothing repugnant to humanist values or the modern social conscience. It enumerates the four stages in the round of a man's life as it was to be lived, ideally, in Indo-Aryan society of the Vedic period : Brahmacharya or studentship during which the adolescent, vowed to celibacy, is instructed in knowledge and skills; then the stage of the Grihastha or householder; the third stage of Vanaprastha or retirement to a forest to lead a life of calm reflection; and finally Sanyasa, the renunciation of worldy interests by donning the yellow robes and becoming a wandering ascetic and teacher.

Chatur Varna, however, is based on heredity since caste is determined by birth; on a hierarchy of supposedly superior and inferior castes; and on skin colour, which in turn is based on race. Obviously in order not to alienate and frighten away a large section of Hindu society by a frontal attack on their beliefs, Gandhiji said that he accepted Chatur Varna; but he gave it an interpretation which stood the whole thing on its head. He wrote in *Harijan* of 12 October 1934, for example : "If we must talk in terms of Varna, there is only one Varna today for all, whether men or women : we are all Sudras." This was in the ideal sense of Sudra as one who selflessly serves others. Gandhiji's primary interest was in reforming social practice, rather than theory. On another occasion he said that if he had to be born again, he would like to be born as an untouchable "so that I may share their sorrows, sufferings and the affronts levelled at them, in order that I may endeavour to free myself and then from that miserable condition." The thrust is again on changing the content, namely human conduct, without attacking the traditional form whose hoary antiquity made it seem sacred to the orthodox.

Gandhiji's approach was to reform an inherited institution rather than to repudiate and abandon it. He defined his philosophy of Swadeshi in these words in February 1916 : "Swadeshi is that spirit in us which restricts us to the use and service of our immediate surroundings to the exclusion of the more remote. Thus, as for religion, in order to satisfy the requirements of the definition I must restrict myself to my ancestral religion, that is, the use of my immediate religious surroundings. If I find it defective, I should serve it by purging it of all its defects. In the domain of politics I should make use of the indigenous institutions and serve them by curing them of their proved defects. In that of economics I should use only things that are produced by my immediate neighbours, and serve those industries by making them efficient and complete where they might be found wanting."

The very special interpretation of Varna by Gandhiji was set out by him in an introduction, written in 1934, to 'Varna-Vyavastha', a collection of his writings on the subject : "I would define the law of Varna briefly thus : The law of Varna means that everyone shall follow as a matter of Dharma—duty—the hereditary calling of his forefathers insofar as it is not inconsistent with fundamental ethics. He will earn his livelihood by following that calling. He may not hoard riches, but devote the balance (beyond his needs) for the good of the people. Fulfilment of the law would make life livable, spread peace and content, end all clashes and conflicts." Also, according to Gandhiji, there is nothing in the Varna system to prohibit a Sudra from learning or a Kshatriya from serving his fellow-men; only, these should not become the means of earning a living.

Ambedkar, on the other hand, went by Varna as ordinarily understood, which simply means sticking to one's ancestral family calling, be it money lending or scavenging, with no conditions regarding fundamental ethics' or philanthropic utilisation of surplus income. And he bluntly denounced it. Himself a member of the depressed class of *Mahars* of Maharashtra, Ambedkar attained a high level of education. He was stung to the quick by the derogatory remarks made by some Congress leaders about the untouchable castes.

Bal Gangadhar Tilak is stated to have said at a public meeting in Sholapur in 1918, when there was an agitation for the separate representation of non-Brahmins and the Backward Classes in the legislature, that he could not understand why oil-pressers, tobacco shopkeepers, washermen and the like should want to go into the legislatures.

Gandhiji's Fast and the Poona Pact

The attitude of Depressed Classes leaders like Ambedkar, who stood aloof from the Congress and opposed the grant of representative government without prior constitutional safeguards, fully suited the British rulers. At the Round Table Conference sessions of the early thirties in London, Ambedkar was among the invitees. Since no agreement could be reached by the Indian participants who, at the 1931 session, included Gandhiji as sole Congress spokesman, on the question of representation of the depressed classes in the legislatures, it was left to the British Prime Minister to decide.

Gandhiji was arrested in January 1932, within a few days of his return to India from the Round Table Conference. The idea of separate electorates for the Depressed Classes was already in the air in connection with the new Government of India Act (eventually enacted in 1935). This would have extended the area of the himself done already by the provision of separate electorates for Muslims in the Government of India Act of 1919. Gandhiji dreaded the prospect of the further fragmentation of the Indian society and polity. He wrote from jail in Poona on 11 March 1932 to the Secretary of State, Sir Samuel Hoare, saying that he would feel constrained to embark on a fast till death if separate electorates were created for the Harijans. He said in the course of the letter : "I am not against their representation in the legislatures. I should favour every one of their adults, male and female, being registered as voters irrespective of education or property qualification, even though the franchise test may be stricter for others.... I feel that no penance that the Hindus may do can in any way compensate for the calculated degradation to which they have consigned the Depressed Classes for centuries. But I know that separate electorate is neither a penance nor any remedy."

What came to be known as the 'communal award' was announced on 17 August 1932. It segregated the Harijans for the purpose of elections. They were to have two votes, in special constituencies where their population strength was considerable : One to be cast for candidates of their community in the manner of a separate electorate ; and the other to be cast in the normal course, along with other electors, for candidates who might be caste Hindus or might be from a Depressed Class. Gandhiji sensed in this formula "the injection of a poison that is calculated to destroy Hinduism and do no good whatever to the Depressed Classes". He embarked on a Fast on 20 September 1932.

The fast had an electrifying effect on public opinion. All over the country, temples, wells and public places were thrown open to Harijans. Caste Hindu leaders declared themselves willing to give Harijans more seats in the legislatures than the communal award gave them, if only Harijan leaders would accept joint electorates Sir Tej Bahadur Sapru, the Liberal statesman, suggested a way out : Harijans could elect for each reserved constituency, a panel of their representatives only those whose names figured on such panels could contest the reserved seats ; and voting would be jointly be caste Hindus and Harijans. Both Gandhi and Ambedkar agreed to this. The British Government could not but accept the agreement, and the fast was broken. The event was celebrated with more tokens of fraternisation between caste Hindus and Harijans. An untouchability abolition week was observed throughout the country. Poet Tagore had spoken at Santiniketan on September 20, when the fast began, about the urgency of fighting the age-old evil of untouchability. He greeted the Poona Pact and the ending of the Mahatma's Fast with the words, "Before our very eyes the wonder has happened." The *Economist* of London expressed the opinion that the fact was "the most important event that has occurred in the history of Hinduism for centuries."

Ambedkar later wrote about the Poona Pact: "As to myself, it is no exaggeration to say that no man was placed in a greater and graver dilemma than I was then. It was a baffling situation. I had to make a choice between two alternatives.

There was before me the duty, which I owed as a part of common humanity, to save Mr. Gandhi from sure death. There was before me the problem of saving for the Untouchables the political rights which the (British) Prime Minister had given them. I responded to the call of humanity and saved the life of Mr. Gandhi by agreeing to alter the Communal Award in a manner satisfactory to Mr. Gandhi."

The spirit of mutual accommodation was to culminate in the generous offer to Ambedkar by Jawaharlal Nehru, as Prime Minister of the first government of independent India, to join the Cabinet as Law Minister. Ambedkar accepted the offer, and played a notable part in the drafting of the Constitution of free India. It included reservation of seats in the national and State legislatures for the Harijans and the Scheduled Tribes, as well as constitutional sanction for discrimination-in-reverse, in favour of these two categories, in the matter of employment in public services and to promote their education and general advancement.

Rajaji : the Mahatma's Southern Apostle

Congress workers in their hundreds and thousands took up the constructive programme all over the country. Each concentrated on one or more of the items in accordance with his or her inclination and the local conditions : anti-untouchability ; Khadi : prohibition : or basic education, and the spread of Hindi as the national language, which also came to be part of the Gandhian programme.

Foremost among constructive workers in the South was C. Rajagopalachari (1878-1972). A leading lawyer of Salem, in the Tamil-speaking region of Madras Presidency, C.R.—or Rajaji as he came to be popularly known—had given up his practice to join the freedom movement. He began to work closely with Gandhiji over the years. His acceptance of the Gandhian approach to life, public and private, was so complete that the Mahatma asked him in 1922 to take over the editing of the journal *Young India* in the event of his arrest. Following Gandhiji's arrest in May, the weekly continued to be printed in Ahmedabad and the editor functioned from Salem.

A by-product of the freedom movement, with the occasions it provided for men and women from different parts of the country to meet and to work together, was a crop of inter-regional marriages, some of them between persons belonging by birth to different religions or castes. Among such was the marriage of Devadas, son of Mahatma Gandhi, and Lakshmi, daughter of Rajaji. After the two fathers put the young people to the test of a long wait and made sure that they were in earnest about marrying, in June 1933 Rajaji wrote to Kasturba saying that he would reach Poona with his daughter around the 12th, and expressed the hope that "with your concurrence I hope God will enable Lakshmi to become formally and finally your own child on some auspicious day thereafter." Among other notable instances of such marriage were of Indira Nehru and Feroze Gandhi ; Aruna Ganguly and M. Asaf Ali ; and Sucheta and J.B. Kripalani.

Khadi : the Livery of Freedom

Rajaji commended the constructive programme formulated by the Congress Working Committee in February 1922: saying: "We should concentrate all our energy on the tastelelss but health-giving economic and social reform." He himself set up an Ashram at the hamlet of Pudupalayam near Tiruchengode. As in innumerable villages of India, the women here used to ply spinning-wheels but had put them away in the attics after the advent of manufactured yarn took away from them, this means of supplementing the family income. The Ashram now supplied cotton and paid them for spinning. This was welcome, but not the Ashram's acceptance of five untouchable boys who ate and lived with the other members. The 'Caste Hindus' boycotted the Ashram. It took quite so time to get them to accept social change.

A lost industry was thus revived around the Ashram, and as a result a number of half-starved families were getting a little more food. It was only the beginning. Gandhiji had once remarked about Rajaji that he had "the patience to wait for a century and the desire to succeed tomorrow". By 1927-28 Tamil Nadu led all the provinces in Khadi production, accounting for more than a third of the country's output.

Khadi had both a symbolic and an economic function. It came to be valued by every patriot, as Jawaharlal Nehru put it, as the livery of freedom ; Nehru himself used to spin regularly, especially during the frequent spells of imprisonment. It was also a provider of part-time employment to very many, at a small investment. Speaking at Poona in May 1928, Rajaji pointed out that the textile industry was providing employment, after more than two decades of development, to four lakhs of people. Khadi, in four years and with a tiny fraction of the investment, had given supplementary work to one lakh in their own homes.

In 1931, during the Round Table Conference in London, Gandhiji said : "You, even the Indian members of the sub-committee, will perhaps be astonished to know that today the Congress through its organisation, the All India Spinners Association, is finding work for nearly 50,000 women in nearly 2,000 villages, and these women are possibly 50per cent Muslim. We have in this constructive manner penetrated these villages and the effort is being made to cover every one of the seven lakh villages."

Fighting the Demon Drink

Prohibition was of paramount interest to Rajaji. He regarded it as essential for saving the poor from ruin and misery. Not all of his colleagues among Tamil Nadu Congress leaders shared this zeal. One of them, S. Satyamurti, to whom Swaraj was the only issue, exclaimed : "I would rather be a member of a free nation of drunkards than belong to a slave nation of teetotallers."

Rajaji worked indefatigably for the cause, addressing—as his diary entries show--as many as 62 prohibition meetings in the course of 1929. The last of them was at the Temperance Conference held that year at Lahore along with the Congress session over which Jawaharlal Nehru presided. "The undisputed leader of the prohibition movement in India". Nehru called Rajaji.

The war against Demon Drink entailed the picketing not only of liquor shops but also of the auction of liquor-vending by the government. The picketing in the various districts was

so effective that during 1938 about 3,000 out of the 9,000 liquor licences in Madras Presidency were still unsold till September. And the licences fetched the government a revenue of only Rs. 50 lakh in 1931 against an anticipated collection of Rs. 150 lakh.

Some of Rajaji's most eloquent writing and public speaking were against the evil of drink. He edited two magazines, *Prohibition* which was a quarterly journal of the Prohibition League, a non-political forum ; and *Vimochanam* ('Liberation') in Tamil, devoted to the same cause. He would present, vividly and with pathos, the misery caused by the drink habit to the poor man, his wife and children.

In this multi-pronged work of social and economic regeneration under the constructive programme, countless numbers of unsung heroes joined as volunteers in villages and towns, responding to the example set by leaders like the Mahatma and Rajaji. Among the institutions formed by Gandhiji to carry on the work on an organised basis were the All India Village Industries Association, the Spinners' Association, the *Goseva Sangh* to improve the condition and breed of cows which were venerated but ill treated, and the Hindustani Talimi Sangh to promote education related to practical living, which was known as basic education.

Ahimsa as Creed or Policy

Gandhiji knew, while suspending the non-cooperation movement when it was at its peak, in February 1922, that it was not good tactics. He admitted that "the drastic reversal of practically the whole of the aggressive programme may be politically unsound and unwise." But to him the moral principle of Ahimsa or non-violence was paramount. "There is no doubt", he said, "that it (the decision) is religiously sound." In fact the Mahatma's objection to violence was on practical and political grounds besides the moral. He warned on a later occasion, referring to the cult of violence of the revolutionaries : "You will not stop at using the violent weapon against your rulers ; you will use it against your brothers and sisters too, and others of your way of thinking will use it against you."

Gandhiji's decision made no sense to persons like Jawaharlal Nehru whose impulse in joining the freedom struggle was not religious. He wrote about his reaction, and that of several of his colleagues : "If this was the inevitable consequence of a sporadic act of violence, then surely there was something lacking in the philosophy and technique of a non-violent struggle. For it seemed to us be impossible to guarantee against the occurrence of some such untoward incident. Even if we succeeded, what of the numerous *agents provocateurs*, stool pigeons and the like who crept into our movement and indulged in violence themselves, or induced others to do so ?" To Nehru, and several other Congress leaders, non-violent resistance was a sensible policy for an unarmed people to adopt in face of a mighty imperial power, but not a creed or an article of faith.

Even Rajaji, who was more closely attached to Gandhiji's moral philosophy, felt constrained to say : "In spite of my tenderest and most complete attachment to my master and the ideal he stands for, I fail to see why there should be a call for stopping our struggle for birthrights because of every distant and unconnected outburst." Yet so complete was the hold of the Mahatma on the loyalty of his colleagues and so indispensable was he was the only one who could mobilise the masses behind the Congress, that the Congress Working Committee at its meeting in Bardoli in February 1922 adopted a resolution which reaffirmed non-violence as the Congress creed.

While calling for the enlistment of "at least one crore of members" of the Congress, the resolution added this explanatory note : "Since peace (non-violence and legitimateness) and truth are the essence of the Congress creed, no person should be enlisted who does not believe in non-violence and truth as indispensable for the attainment of Swaraj. The creed of the Congress must, therefore, be carefully explained to each person who is appealed to join the Congress." So soon after Chauri Chaura, and after the sad events that had occurred in Malabar, how could Gandhiji have expected to find ten million and more persons who would accept non-violence as an article of faith ? It was a case of hope triumphing over experience.

Congress Ideology : A Multi-Stream Ganga

The difference of opinion over Ahimsa as creed or as policy is only one example of the presence of different schools of ideology in the Congress during the freedom struggle. The Congress movement was like the Ganga, a mighty river which gathers to its bosom diverse sreams which all add to the volume of the river as it flows towards its destination.

We have seen, in the discussion of the trade union movement, that there were Socialists within the Congress. They formed themselves into a Congress Socialist Party in 1937. It acted more as a ginger group within the Congress than as a distinct party. Many Congress leaders sympathised with the aims of the C.S.P. though they did not join it. Foremost among them was Jawaharlal Nehru, who did more than anyone else to popularise the socialist idea among the Indian intelligentsia. Nehru did not join the C.S.P. because he did not want to break with Gandhiji whose leadership, he was convinced, was indispensable for preserving the broad-based mass appeal of the Congress. A number of other Leftists, who might be described as Nehru Socialists, were sympathetic to but sayed out of the C.S.P. They were non-dogmatic about Marxism, receptive to Gandhiji's moral idealism, and above all overwhelmed by his practical example of identification with and service of the poor and the oppressed.

Different in temperament from Jawaharlal Nehru, but also friendly to the C.S.P.'s aims, was Subhas Chandra Bose. He said in February 1938 : "There has been a good deal of controversy over the formation of the Congress Socialist Party. I am not a member of the C.S.P. But I must say that I have been in agreement with the its general principles and policy from the very beginning. To my mind it is quite immaterial whether you call it a bloc, a group or party. Socialism is not an immediate problem for us ; nevertheless, socialist propaganda can be conducted only by a party, like the C.S.P., which stands for and believes in socialism." Subhas Bose was soon to form a separate Leftist party, the Forward Bloc, when after re-election to preside over the Tripuri Congress in March 1939, he found himself unable to function because of differences with Gandhiji.

The Communists were another organised group within the Congress. During the many years when, because of a legal ban imposed by the British, the Communists could not function openly as a party, they did so under the cover of the C.S.P. This led to tensions. While some Congress Socialists were admirers of the achievements of the Soviet Union and differed from the Communists only on the question of civil liberties and democracy being feasible in a socialist India, there were others who (like many democratic socialists of Western Europe) thoroughly disapproved of the totalitarian Soviet State with its thought control and harsh suppression of dissent.

Then there were the large numbers of active and prominent Congressmen drawn from the middle and upper classes who had no ideology other than the *status quo* which they were content with ; it was the political dimension of the Congress which drew them into the freedom movement, rather than the social and economic concerns of Gandhiji and Nehru.

There were the shrewd ones, saw that the Congress would sooner or later over state power from the British, and who wanted to be on the winning side. But even these contributed to the movement by providing funds and facilities to freedom fighters.

And, of course, there were the Gandhians. Many of them exhibited the externals of Gandhism, and tended to be complacent and self-righteous. A few, like Vinoba Bhave, were truly dedicated beings.

In contrast to the criticism of each other, often acrimonious, which some of the above groups indulged in, the Mahatma himself treated them all with goodwill. He did not question the *bona fides* of those holding an ideology or a particular view different from his. Along with Ahimsa and *Aparigraha* (non-attachment), Anekanta (non-absolutism, or the many-sidedness of truth) is a principle of jainism, widespread in his native Gujarat, which deeply influenced Gandhiji. "I very much like the doctorine of the many-sidedness of reality. It is this doctrine that has taught me to judge a Muslim from his standpoint and a Christian from his." He likewise bore cheerfully with the Communists. As we shall see in the next chapter, he admired the courage and dedication of the underground

fighters of the 'Quit India' movement even while trying to persuade them to give up the path of the secrecy and violence.

JAWAHARLAL NEHRU : SOCIALIST ORIENTATION

The year 1929 marks the beginning of a socialist accent in the articulation of economic policy by the Congress. This was largely under the influence of Jawaharlal Nehru (1889-1964). Two years earlier when he was invited on the occasion of the tenth anniversary of the Bolshevik revolution, Nehru had visited Soviet Russia. On return he wrote extensively in the Indian Press giving his impressions and expressing his admiration for much that had been achieved in that country.

In response to urgings by the Congress Committee of U.P., Nehru's home province, the All India Congress Committee at its meeting in Bombay in May 1929 adopted a resolution calling for drastic changes in the economic and social structure : "In the opinion of this Committee, the great poverty and misery of the Indian people are due not only to foreign exploitation in India but also to the economic structure of society, which the alien rulers support so that their exploitation may continue. In order therefore to remove this poverty and misery and to ameliorate the condition of the Indian masses, it is essential to make revolutionary changes in the present economic and social structure and to remove the gross inequalities."

Later in the year, at Gandhiji's instance, Nehru who was then only 40 years of age—was elected to preside over the Lahore session of the Congress. How did the Mahatma sponsor Nehru despite their ideological differences?

Rama Rajya and Socialism

The rule of righteousness, depicted in the Ramayana epic, is known to the common people of India as Rama Rajya or the rule of Rama. This is the homely expression which, characteristically, the Mahatma employed to indicate the kind of India which the people should join in building. On one occasion he described the India of his dreams as "an India in which the poorest shall feel it is their country, in whose making they have an effective voice, an India in which there shall be

no high class and low class of people, an India in which all communities shall live in perfect harmony. There can be no room in such an India for the curse of untouchability. Women will enjoy the same rights as men."

Gandhiji's Rama Rajya was socialism with an Indian face. The means on which the Mahatma would rely was not expropriation of the 'haves' through nationalisation of the means of production. He would induce in them—through persuasion if possible and through Satyagraha if necessary—a change of attitude so that they would act as trustees of the poor. He believed that a change of heart would bring about more enduring improvement than changes in economic structure or in the legal framework of a society.

"The socialism and communism of the West," Gandhiji said, "is based on certain conceptions which are fundamentally different from ours. One such conception is their belief in the essential selfishness of human nature. Our socialism and communism should be based on non-violence and on the harmonious co-operation of labour and capital, landlord and tenant." This sounded to Jawaharlal Nehru and other Leftist intellectuals, at the time, as old-fashioned and naive. But events a half-century later in Poland and other countries of Communist Europe were to show that State capitalism has its own problems of harmonious relations with labour, since a part of the value created by labour must be withheld from consumption and invested if the aim is more and more economic growth.

We have already noticed the divergence between the two on the subject of non-violence. To Nehru it was not a creed but an effective policy for resisting British rule in the circumstances in which India was placed.

These differences notwithstanding, Nehru recognised the Mahatma as a true revolutionary. Referring to the criticism by some Leftist intellectuals that Gandhiji was backward-looking, he wrote : "These parlour socialists are hard on Gandhiji as the arch-reactionary, and advance arguments which in logic leave little to be desired. But the little fact remains that this 'reactionary' knows India, understands India, almost is peasant India, and has shaken up India as no so called revolutionary

has done." Could any affirmation of the need to eradicate poverty be more emphatic than Gandhiji's ? : "I may as well place before the dog over there the message of God as before these hungry millions who have no lustre in their eyes. To them God can only appear as bread and butter."

Just as the Mahatma was certain that British rule must collapse if Indians refused to cooperate, he had full faith that non-violent non-cooperation could be applied effectively against indigenous exploitation : "The rich cannot accumulate wealth without the cooperation of the poor in society. If this knowledge were to penetrate to and spread among the poor, they would become strong and would learn how to free themselves by means of non-violence from the crushing inequalities which have brought them to the verge of starvation." If Gandhiji's distaste for class war and preference for change of heart was tempered with the advocacy of Satyagraha for securing social justice, Nehru's emphasis on class conflict was tempered with his firm attachment to democracy and civil liberties.

Who but one of the world's greatest democrats of all time could have argued against his own re-election to political office as Nehru did in a pseudonymous article in the *Modern Review* of November 1937 ? : "For two consecutive years Jawaharlal has been President of the Congress and in some ways he has made himself so indispensable that there are many who suggest that he should be elected for a third term. But a greater disservice to India and even to Jawaharlal can hardly be done. By electing him a third time we shall exalt one man at the cost of the Congress and make the people think in terms of Caesarism. We shall encourage in Jawaharlal the wrong tendencies and increase his conceit and pride. We want no Caesars." "There is a heart union between us," the Mahatma said of Nehru, "which no intellectual differences can break." The next big step which Nehru induced the Congress to take in the direction of socialism was with Gandhiji's consent and even collaboration.

Fundamental Rights and Economic Pro. ramme

Two years after the Bombay resolution of May 1929, a

resolution on Fundamental Rights and Economic Programme was adopted by the Karachi session of the Congress. Nehru recalls in the 'Autobiography' : "During my early morning talks in Delhi with Gandhiji in February and March 1931. I had referred to this matter, and he had welcomed the idea of having a resolution on economic matters. He asked me to bring the matter up at Karachi, and to draft a resolution and show it to him there. I did so at Karachi, and he made various changes and suggestions....It was a new subject for the Subjects Committee and some members were surprised. However, it was easily passed by the Committee and the (plenary) Congress."

The resolution (see iii under *Select Documents*) was a landmark in the development of the Congress ideology and anticipated many of the Fundamental Rights and Directive Principles of State Policy which were later incorporated in the Constitution of free India.

The Lucknow Congress, in April 1936, reiterated the Karachi formulations and referred, in addition, to the worsening rural poverty and indebtedness as the result of the slump in prices of agricultural commodities.

In December 1936 the Faizpur Congress adopted a resolution on the agrarian programme which said that the "final solution involves the removal of British imperialistic exploitation and a radical change in the antiquated and repressive land tenure and revenue systems." The resolution also said that "effort should be made to introduce co-operative farming".

After these formulations of the policy approach, the next step was to draw up the broad outlines of a national economic plan. This become practicable after the assumption of office by the Congress in 1937 in several parts of the country in terms of the Government of India Act of 1935 which introduced provincial self-government.

Meeting in August 1937, the Working Committee asked Congress Ministries to form committees of experts to collect data for framing schemes of "national reconstruction and social planning." They were also asked to initiate consultations with neighbouring provinces and princely states on the feasibility of inter-state river valley projects.

Subhas Bose : National Planning Committee

It was appropriate that the National Planning Committee should have been formed during the term of Subhas Chandra Bose as president of the Congress. Like Nehru, Bose was a votary of a non-limitative and democratic socialism. Addressing the Bengal provincial conference at Rangpur in March 1929, Bose had said : "New ideas of socialism are nowadays travelling to India from the West and they are revolutionising the thoughts of many, but the idea of socialism is not a novelty in this country. We regard it as such only because we have lost the thread of our own history." Recalling the fiery words of Swami Vivekananda, 'Let a new India emerge through the workshop and from the huts and bazaars', Bose said : "This socialism did not derive its birth from the books of Karl Marx. It has its origin in the thought and culture of India."

At the Haripura Congress in February 1938, Bose in his presidential address affirmed his agreement with the general principles and policy of the Congress Socialist Party though he was not a member of that group.

In October 1938, a Conference of Industries Ministers of the Congress-ruled provinces, presided over by Subhas Bose, adopted a resolution on planning for promoting industrial development : "The problems of poverty and unemployment, of national defence and of economic regeneration in general cannot be solved without industrialisation including heavy key industries, medium scale industries and cottage industries. Steps should be taken to start manufacture of machinery and plant and tools of all kinds ; automobiles, motor boats etc. ; electrical plant and accessories ; heavy chemicals and fertilisers ; and metal production." For giving effect to this, the resolution called for the formation of a National Planning Committee whose personnel would be announced later by the Congress president.

Jawaharlal Nehru was the natural choice for chairmanship of the National Planning Committee. The membership was broad-based and included industrialists and scientists besides Congressmen. K.T. Shah, the economist, was the honorary general secretary. The Committee's questionnaires were finalised at the first session held in December 1938, and in June 1939 the Committee urged the provincial governments to introduce

industrial licensing for new industries and for the expansion or change of control of existing industries.

In a memorandum of 4 June 1939, Jawaharlal Nehru pointed out to members that though the resolution adopted by the industries ministers' conference did not mention agriculture specificially, "it is impossible to conceive of any scheme of national planning in any country, and least of all in India, which does not include agriculture. Agriculture is and will remain the largest single industry of this country, and it is associated with a host of subsidiary industries."

Numerous sub-committees were formed to study different sectors of development. Nehru asked them to avoid falling into "the bad habits of official committees and commissions which are notorious for spending on themselves large sums of public money." Provincial governments and co-operating (princely) States should send more contributions to meet the expenditure because "the work this Committee is doing is essentially their work". The travelling allowance for members of the National Planning Committee and its sub-committees was austere : "not exceeding second-class railway fares."

The work of the sub-committees got off to a brisk start but the outbreak of the Second World War and the resignation of the Congress Ministries diverted the attention of the leaders to pressing political problems. It was only after the end of the war that the reports of the sub-committees and the resolutions of the main Committee thereon could be consolidated and issued in the form of reports. They furnished valuable data and policy approaches for the Planning Commission that was to be formed after independence.

THE HINDU-MUSLIM PROBLEM

Swarajists and no-Changers

The years that followed Chauri Chaura were a bad patch for the country. Hindu-Muslim riots broke out in many cities. Congressmen were divided between those who wanted to fight elections and enter the provincial legislative councils, and others who were for no change from the policy of boycott. Motilal Nehru, C.R. Das and Hakim Ajmal Khan were prominent

among those favouring council entry ; and Rajendra Prasad and C. Rajagopalachari among the no-changers. Gandhiji, with his appreciation of the many perceptions of truth and the many paths to it, brought about a compromise on the basis that those who wished to contest the elections, and had formed the Swaraj Party for the purpose, could do so without having to leave the Congress.

Though the green signal was given only in September 1923 and the elections were held in November, the Swarajists captured a large number of seats both in the Central Legislative Assembly and in the provincial councils. Motilal Nehru led the Swarajist bloc in the Gentral Assembly, and C.R. Dass in the Bengal provincial assembly where his followers had been successful even in many constituencies reserved for Muslims under the scheme of separate electorates. This was because he had allayed Muslim fears by making the offer that when the Congress secured power in Bengal, it would reserve 60 per cent of all new appointments for the Muslims until such time as their representation in the services came up to the level justified by their population share.

Meanwhile, no-changers like Rajaji carried on with the constructive programme. By the time of the 1937 elections, most Congressmen including Rajaji had become pro-changers.

Economic Roots of Social Conflict

The Hindu-Muslim riots of the 'twenties nearly drove Gandhiji to despair. He said at a public meeting at Comilla in January 1927 : "I dare not touch the problem of Hindu-Muslim unity. It has passed out of human hands, and has been transferred to God's hands."

The despair was, of course, momentary. No one knew better than he the root causes and the immediate provocations of the conflict that erupted from time to time. One of the root causes was the competition for jobs and economic opportunity between the educated and privileged classes of the two the communities; and the other the fundamentalists. The common people of both the communities, sunk in poverty and illiteracy, had to be insulated from incitenent in the name of religion by both the groups of vested interests.

We saw in Chapter III that the Indian Muslim middle class made a delayed start on the path of modern education leading to positions in the civil services and the professions, public life and political office. Job opportunities in the provincial government departments increased with each instalment to political reforms in the direction of self-government. This intensified the scramble for crumbs from the table of the British rulers. Gandiji said with reference to Punjab : "The Mussalmans complain that the Hindus have raised a storm of protest on Mr. Fazlul Hussain trying very timidly to give a fair proportion of government employment to Mussalmans. The causes of tension are thus more than merely religious." And on another occasion : "Does not the Hindu-Muslim question centre round a division political power—the spoils of office?"

Hoodlums from both the communities were active in Hindu-Muslim riots and profited from the looting and arson, but they did not start the trouble : "The gondas come on the scene because the leaders want them." Similarly, cow killing or music before mosques was often a deliberately organised provocation.

Gandhiji had tried, and failed, to bring about Hindu-Muslim unity 'from the top' during Khilafat period. He had joined hands with religious leaders whose strength depended on keeping alive the sense of distinct identity and special interest of the Muslim community. It must have been deeply disappointing to Gandhiji when Maulana Muhammed Ali said that he prayed for the day when he would convert the Mahatma to Islam. Gandhiji issued a rejoinder when Maulana Shaukat Ali dubbed the civil disobedience movement of 1930 as a bid to achieve Hindu Raj and advised Muslims to keep aloof. Earlier, some Muslim leaders would not condemn the Moplah atrocities in Kerala, including forced conversions. Hindu leaders like Madan Mohan Malaviya and Swami Shraddhanand reacted by organising *shuddhi* (purification) and *sangathan* (unity) movements among Hindus.

"Fortunately," Gandhiji noted in *Young India* of 29 January 1925, Hindu-Muslim unity does not finally depend upon religious or political leaders. It depends upon the enlightened selfishness

of the masses belonging to both the communities." For this reason he commended Motilal Nehru's proposal to organise Hindu-Muslim friendship forums : "If he succeeds in forming genuine Hindu-Muslim Sanghtans, he will have done service of a first-class order to the country. His decision to work from the bottom, instead of through middlemen, must result in nothing but better relations between Hindu and Mussalman masses."

This is of course what the Mahatma himself was doing all the time. In the tradition of Bhakti-Sufi saints of India who in their time kept separating the chaff of dogma and superstition from the humanist grain of religion, he did more than any other person in the 20th country to promote fellowship among the various religious communities of India—not only Hindus and Muslims—as members of the Indian family and of the larger family of humankind.

An altogether different approach to the problem of Hindu-Muslim unity was available. India has had its own tradition of Charvakas or atheists from ancient times, and this was revived when, after the opening to the West, free thinking reached the country along with other currents of modern thought. There were, during the freedom movement, some who propagated rationalism and atheism along with social reform. But they did not meet with any significant measure of public response. Gandhiji would never have consented to throwing the baby out with the bathwater of religious fanaticism. And, knowing the Indian psyche as he did, he would if he were living doubtless tell those secularists of our time who advocate rationalism as the cure that it will take a long, long time for the bulk of Indians to turn agnostic or atheist.

NON-VIOLENT WAR : SECOND ROUND

The British government's announcement in November 1927 of a Royal Commission to Examine the Working of the 1919 Act and recommend the lines of further progress towards self-government in India shook the country and the Congress out of political torpor.

Headed by Sir John Simon, it was to be all-white, consisting entirely of British politicians and no Indian. The Congress

decided on boycott. The commission was greeted everywhere with cries of 'Simon, go back!'

Lahore Congress : Complete Independence

For its part the Congress was divided on the formulation of its objective : should it be Dominion status or complete independence? Entrusted with the task at an all-party conference, Motilal Nehru and some others had drawn up a blueprint of reforms based on Dominion status. This was not acceptable to Jawaharlal Nehru or to Subhas Bose and other radicals. The Calcutta Session of the Congress in December 1928 adopted a compromise resolution which was to have momentous consequences. It said that if the Nehru report was not accepted within a year, the Congress would opt for complete independence and would forge sanctions for securing it, through nonviolent non-cooperation.

A year passed. At the Congress Session of December 1929 at Lahore the president, elected at Gandhiji's instance, was Jawaharla Nehru. The Mahatma himself moved the Resolution on 31 December, defining the Congress objective as complete independence. It called upon Congressmen to abstain from participating directly or indirectly in future elections, and the present Congress members of the legislatures to resign their seats. The All India Congress was authorised to launch, at the appropriate time, a programme of civil disobedience including non-payment of taxes.

Gandhiji called for country-wide observance of 26 January as Independence Day, when people would take a pledge (see IV under Select Documents) to the effect that it was "a crime against man and God to submit to British rule". The response to the call was overwhelming.

Salt Satyagraha

Gandhiji then decided to launch a civil disobedience movement, choosing salt as the article on which no tax would be paid. Salt is a basic need, and a free gift of nature. But even the poorest had to pay the tax on it. As far back as in August 1844, a new duty on salt had met with resistance in Surat where a mob attacked the courthouse. Gandhiji, with

his finger on the common man's pulse, chose a symbolic article.

Gandhiji inaugurated the Salt Satyagraha by setting out, on 12 March 1930, on a 24-day foot march from Ahmedabad to Dandi, on the Gujarat coast, a distance of 241 miles. He broke the law there, by asserting the right to make his own salt. The example was followed by hundreds of thousands of persons all over India—city dwellers and village folk, men and women, students and elders.

The British authorities deployed the police to prevent the law-breaking. But there was little they could do, beyond savage assaults on the Satyagrahis at some places, in face of the massive participation by the people at thousands of venues in the country. Police violence was particularly severe at Dharsana, where volunteers had planned to raid and take possession of the salt depots. The famed poetess Sarojini Naidu flagged off the Satyagrahis after impressing on them that there should be no retaliation against the police.

An American newspaper correspondent sent out this eye-witness account of what followed : "In eighteen years of reporting in twenty-two countries, I have never witnessed such harrowing scences as at Dharsana. Sometimes the scenes were so painful that I had to turn away momentarily. One surprising feature was the discipline of the volunteers. It seemed they were thoroughly imbued with Gandhi's non-violent creed."

Women's Participation

A notable feature of the Salt Satyagraha was the large-scale participation by women. The women's movement in India began in the second decade of the 20th century, inspired by Annie Besant and Margaret Cousins. Gandhiji's leadership of the freedom movement from 1920 gave a new impetus to women's role in public life. Rajkumari Amrit Kaur, from a Christian and princely family of Punjab, and Sushila Nayyar, a medical practitioner, were for long years members of Gandhiji's Ashram encourage. Motilal Nehru's was one of the earliest families of note whose women joined the movement, braving *lathi* charges and imprisonment : his wife, daughters Vijayalakshmi and Krishna; daughter-in-law Kamala; and

grand-daughter Indira. From numberless homes of ordinary people came women volunteers who (and whose menfolk) felt no fear in joining a movement led by such a one as the Mahatma. Women were active in the constructive programme as well as the civil disobedience movements, and made a special contribution to the picketing of shops selling liquor or foreign cloth.

During the Salt Satyagraha women went out with earthen and metal vessals to collect sea water. In land-locked places like Delhi, marshy and saline areas were chosen. The men and women volunteers would distribute the illegal salt freely, or sell packets of it to raise funds for sustaining the civil disobedience movement. The collection was made up of the ordinary man's paisa as well as high bids at auctions of Gandhi's salt, or the salt of independence, as it would be called. A bid of as much as Rs. 30,000 for one packet was reported at an auction in the neighbourhood of Bombay's bullion market.

Rukmini Lakshmipati and Durgabai in the South, Kamala Devi Chattopadhyaya in Bombay, and Satyawati in Delhi were among prominent women workers of the Congress who took part in the civil disobedience campaign.

Because of this close involvement in the freedom movement, Indian women did not have to struggle for political franchise in the manner of their sisters in the West. Having fought for independence side by side with men, it was natural that they should have been fully enfranchised under the Constitution that came into force in 1950.

Looking an Empire in the Face

A Round Table Conference was called by the British Government in London, in 1930, to discuss constitutional reforms. Everyone was there—princes, zamindars, leaders of communal groups—except those who mattered, they being in jails on account of civil disobedience. The Labour Prime Minister of Britain, Ramsay MacDonald, expressed the hope that the Congress would be represented at the Second Round Table Conference. This led to the release of Gandhiji and other leaders without conditions, on 26 January 1931. There

were talks between the Viceroy, Lord Irwin, and the Mahatma, and a pact emerged which enabled the suspension of civil disobedience. An interesting comment on the Gandhi-Irwin talks was the statement by the arch British Conservative, Winston Churchill, expressing his unhappiness at "the nauseating and humiliating spectacle of this one-time Inner Temple lawyer, now seditious *faqir*, striding half-naked up the steps of the Viceroy's palace, there to negotiate and parley on equal terms with the representative of the King Emperor."

Nothing came out of the second R.T.C. which met in the closing months of 1931. By this time the Labour government had been succeeded by a coalition cabinet in which the Conservatives were heavily represented. Gandhiji was arrested on return to India in January 1932, and the civil disobedience was resumed. The wide extent of participation is indicated by the figures of arrests : about 60,000 during 1930, and a slightly larger number during 1932.

Neither the first round of the non-violent war against British rule during 1920-22 nor the second in 1930-32 yielded any immediate or substantial political concessions from the British. But they eroded the moral base of British rule in India. The true gain from them was that they enabled the people of India to stand erect, look a mighty Empire in the face, and assert their rights.

It is no surprise that when the Congress contested the elections to provincial assemblies early in 1937, the people voted over-whelmingly in its favour, sweeping away the loyalist and communal elements who had been basking under official favour.

STATES PEOPLES MOVEMENT

The opening of Banaras Hindu University in February 1916 was the first occasion when Gandhiji made a public speech after his return to India after two decades of work in South Africa. The Viceroy was there, and bejewelled Maharajas and princes. Many among the latter walked out when he said to them : "There is no salvation for India unless you strip yourselves of this jewellery and hold it in trust for your countrymen."

This was early in his 32-year innings in India's public life. After observing the good work done by some Indian rulers, as in Baroda and Mysore, in the fields of education and social reform, as also the divide-and-rule strategy of the British, Gandhiji adopted a friendly tone towards the princes. He continued to advocate the trusteeship principle contained in his words at Banaras, but witout belligerence. He commended the same change of heart to landlords and capitalists. But his rejection of class hatred and class war did not mean that victims of oppression and exploitation should wait patiently till the end of time for a change of heart to take place on the part of their masters. On the contrary, he placed at their service—the peasants of Champaran and textile workers of Ahmedabad, for example—the weapon of Satyagraha to secure redressal of wrongs.

Against Autocratic Rule

Many Indian states had rulers who wallowed in luxury and self-indulgence, were autocratic, and paid little attention to the welfare and progress of their people. The All India States Peoples' Conference, was formed with the objective of democratisting the administration in the princely states, and grew alongside the freedom movement. Many prominent Congressmen such as Pattabhi Sitaramayya and Balwantraj Mehta took part in its work.

Jawaharlal Nehru did not share what seemed to him to be a soft approach on the part of Gandhiji towards the princes. In a letter of July 1934 to the president of the States Peoples' Conference, the Mahatma advised non-interference in the internal administration of the princely states and said ; "I would like the states to grant autonomy to their subjects and would like the princess to regard themselves and be, in fact, trustees for the people over whom they rule." If so, asked Nehru, why should we object to the claim of the British government that they are governing India as trustees? Nehru set an example of militancy, as during his visits to Nabha in 1923 and Kashmir in 1946, which encouraged the people of the princely states in their efforts to secure a better and more democratic government.

Veer Savarkar, in 1939, organised under the auspices of the Hindu Mahasabha a Satyagraha to secure a measure of popular representation in the legislature of the Nizam's Hyderabad State. It had at that time no Hindu member though the population was overwhelmingly Hindu. Thousands of persons from outside the State joined this struggle. As a result, representation to the extent of 50 per cent was granted to the majority community.

CHAPTER FIVE

BRITAIN QUITS INDIA

THE clouds of the Second World War were already gathering in Europe when in 1937 the Congress decided, after initial hesitation, to accept office in the provinces where it had won a majority of seats in the assemblies. The Ministries resigned in protest against India being dragged into the war on its outbreak, without consultation with the people's representatives or the promise of India's freedom at the war's conclusion. The Congress served notice on Britain in August 1942 to quit India so that the people of a free country could defend themselves against the impending invasion. The notice was complied with after five years of heroic struggle by the people, and tortutous negotiations which ended in the sub-continent's partition. Having undergone a necessary amputation, free India emerged into freedom on 15 August 1947 to build a new life for its people.

PROVINCIAL SELF-GOVERNMENT

We saw in the previous chapter that Lord Ripon as Viceroy introduced local self-government—an expression which covers city corporations, town municipalities, and district boards. Congressmen contested the local elections and served on local bodies not only in the early period before the freedom

movement developed militancy, but even thereafter. This was a paradox because a section of Congressmen were opposed to entering the provincial legislative councils or the central assembly on the ground that their powers were severely limited. The powers of local bodies are even more severely limited; yet Jawaharlal Nehru, an opponent of legislature entry and office acceptance right till 1937, served as elected chairman of the Allahabad municipality.

Experience of Municipal Government

The experience of municipal government showed that there was a fair amount of elbow room for doing good to the people in terms of education and other social services even within the limited powers, of decision making and of finance, available to municipalities.

In Bombay, Sir Pherozeshah Mehta (1845-1915), one of the early presidents of the Congress, became Chairman of the City Corporation while still young. He is gratefully remembered by the citizens of Bombay for making it a self-governing city and giving of his best over a period of forty years for its improvement. Vitthalbhai Patel (1875-1933), who became the first elected President of the Indian Legislative Assembly in 1925, secured passage of the Primary Education Bill as a member of the Bombay Provincial Legislative Council. This Act empowered municipalities to introduce free and compulsory primary education in their respective areas. As a member of the Bandra municipality, Vitthalbhai introduced compulsory primary education in that suburb. Later, as president of the Bombay Municipal Corporation, he promoted the teaching of Hindi, introduced Swadeshi in all departments of the Corporation, and gave special encouragement to the education of children from the scheduled castes.

In the South, C. Rajagopalachari, who was to enjoy the reputation of a skilled administrator, acquired his first administrative experience as chairman of the Salem municipality. In this capacity he fought the evil of untouchability in relation to municipal water supply, besides improving the civic services.

In Calcutta, an extension of the programme of Council entry to the civic field resulted in a thumping victory for the

Swaraj Party (consisting of Congressmen) in the mayoral election of March 1924. C.R. Das became the city's mayor. Subhas Bose was appointed as the Corporation's chief executive officer at the early age of 27. He took only half of the salary attached to the post, and revolutionised the relations between the Corporation and the public of Calcutta. The British interests in the city suddenly found themselves deprived of their importance, while the people began to feel for the first time that municipal officers and employees were public servants and not merely bureaucrats. The arrest of Bose in October 1924, ostensibly to scotch a revolutionary conspiracy, was widely seen as a calculated blow at the Swarajist administration of the Corporation.

Among prominent Congressmen elected to the Delhi Municipal Committee was M. Asaf Ali (1888-1953). When the local administration, as part of 'improvement', began to demolish the Daryaganj section of the wall round the old city, built in Shahjahan's time, to make room for a road and buildings, he organised a Satyagaraha against the vandalism. Asaf Ali was imprisoned for a term, but saved the rest of the historic city wall.

Jawaharlal Nehru served for two years as Chairman of the Allahabad Municipality during 1923-25. He promoted the use of *Khaddar* by municipal employees, of Hindu and Urdu in official transactions, and the singing of Iqbal's "Sare Jahan se achha" in schools. He has discussed in the *Autobiography* the hurdles in the way of his effort to rectify the neglect of the city's congested old areas while spending large sums on spruce maintenance of the new areas where "all the Big Noises and Little Noises live". Jawaharlal Nehru contested again for chairmanship of the Allahabad municipality in 1928 but lost by one vote.

Congress Ministries : Half Way to Freedom

The Government of India Act of 1935 widened the franchise compared to the predecessor Act of 1919. But it was very far from universal adult suffrage, which was to come only after independence. A fair range of subjects were allotted to the popular Ministries to be formed in the provinces. But the

Governor was given overriding powers even in respect of these, over and above the subjects reserved for him. The Act as a whole, and in particular the federal part of the scheme (in which the Indian states would have been represented by nominees of the princes rather than elected representatives) was unacceptable to the Congress. However, it was decided to contest the elections, keeping open the issue of office acceptance.

Jawaharlal Nehru who was, as a biographer puts it, "by now as indispensable to the Congress as the party was to him". campaigned vigorously on the basis of an election manifesto which rejected the Act of 1935. The election results were overwhelmingly in favour of the Congress, which was in a position to form Ministries in eight provinces (Assam, Bihar, Bombay, Central Provinces, Madras, N.W.F.P., Orissa and United Provinces). Many Congressmen were in favour of doing so but Nehru and some other were opposed to it.

Prominent among those favouring the assumption of governmental responsibility by the Congress was C. Rajagopalachari. In his home province of Madras, the Governor did not wait for the Congress to make up its mind but invited the Justice party and depressed classes leaders to form the government. The Justice party claimed to represent non-Brahmins, who form the bulk of the population, as against the 'Brahmin-dominated' Congress. It had been in office in earlier years too, with powers that were extremely limited but enough to promulgate recruitment rules which would help non-Brahmins to secure a larger share of jobs in the provincial government services. The encouragement of the Justice party was in line with the British policy of trying to weaken the Congress and the nationalist movement by promoting divisions based on religion and caste.

The issue was clinched when Gandhiji supported the formation of Congress governments. He did so on the ground that, notwithstanding the deficiencies of the 1935 Act, Congressmen in power would be able to implement items of the constructive programme such as khadi, village industries and prohibition, and could also reduce the burden of the peasants.

But a technical hitch remained. The Congress wanted an assurance that the Cabinet's would be binding on the Governors in respect of the subjects transferred to the popular Ministries. This hitch was overcome when the Secretary of State made a tortuously worded statement in the House of Commons: "There is no foundation for any suggestion that the Governor is free, or is entitled, or would have the power to interfere with the day-to-day administration of a province outside the limited range of the responsibilities specially confided to him."

Gandhiji's hope was fulfilled in large measure, at least in the case of Madras province where the Ministry was headed by Rajaji as Prime Minister (that was the designation those days, when there was no Prime Minister in Delhi). A notable step was the legislation for rural debt relief. In terms of this law, if a farmer had paid back, in interest and in principal instalments, more than twice the principal, his debt stood cancelled. Properties interests—big landlords, traders and moneylenders—raised a hue and cry complaining that it would shake the roots of social life, with some even calling the reform 'un-Hindu'. The debt relief example set by Madras was seen followed by Bombay.

The Madras government also introduced prohibition in several districts, and gave encouragement to Khadi and handloom industries. The sales tax introduced by Rajaji to make up the loss of excise revenue consequent on prohibition came to be adopted all over India as a prolific source of revenue—prohibition or no prohibition.

At the beginning, specially when employees of local bodies in Madras were banned from joining the Congress or other political party, Jawaharlal Nehru who was then Congress president felt that it was 'perilously like the old government'. But later he acknowledged the good work done by the Madras Congress Ministry : "The Madras government did more during its brief career than any other provincial government." Even about the 1935 Act, Nehru took the view that it "proved to be an organic connecting link between the old and the new."

For the common people—including government employees—throughout India it was a strange and heart-warming sight to see British officers taking orders from Indian Ministers. In

many instances the officers had in earlier years issued orders for the arrest of the same 'seditious' individuals who were now in office as the people's elected representatives. Provincial self-government brought the sensation of at least partial freedom, as a half-way house on the road to independence. In the provinces of U.P. and Bihar, legislation of far-reaching importance was introduced for changing the exploitative system of Zamindari, or landlord intermediaries between the cultivator and the government, though the reform could be completed only in the years following independence.

Muslim League's 'Deliverance Day'

The Congress Ministries resigned in protest against India being dragged unilaterally into hostilities when the Second World War broke out in September 1939. At a valedictory meeting of the Madras Provincial assembly, C. Rajagopalachari made a statement reviewing the pluses and minuses of his government's performance. In the course of this statement he gave detailed figures of the recruitment to the provincial civil services, during its two years in office, of scheduled castes, non-Brahmins and Muslims. The figures, reproduced in Rajmohan Gandhi's biography of Rajaji, show an impressive acceleration in respect of all the three categories.

The Congress Ministry could have reviewed and altered the Justice Party government's decision in 1935 regarding preferential treatment of non-Brahmins in recruitment to the services. Instead, the policy was continued.

The accelerated pace of recruitment of Muslims to the Madras civil services is of special interest in view of the hue and cry made by the All India Muslim League that injustice was done to the Muslims, even that 'atrocities' were committed against them with the acquiescence of the British Governors, doing the rule of the Congress Ministries. The Muslim League went to the extent of appointing a committee which purported to go into the matter and came up with a report making allegations. When the Congress Ministries resigned, the Muslim League observed a 'Deliverance Day'.

Both the Muslim League in Madras and the non-Brahmin (also known as Dravidian) movement in the Tamil region led

by E.V. Ramaswami Naicker were strenously opposed, though for different reason, to the Rajaji Ministry's encouragement of the study of Hindi in schools. The Dravidian movement's objection to Hindi is based on its assertion, in disregard of the racial mixing that has gone on in the sub-continent over the centuries, that Brahmins are Aryans, racially different from the Dravidian Tamils; that the Congress is a Brahmin-dominated party; and that Hindi is an Aryan language which is sought to be imposed on the Dravidians. In consonance with this approach to history, leaders of the Dravidian movement look upon Ravana as the hero of the Ramayana epic and Rama as an Aryan colonialist.

All this is curious since E.V. Ramaswami Naicker, who was to found the non-Brahmin Self-Respect movement, began as an ardent nationalist and Congressman. He participated in and was arrested during the first non-cooperation movement. Like Jinnah, 'E.V.R.' later became a separatist, to the point of the Dravidian movement talking of an independent Dravidastan.

As for the Muslim League, its objection was that Hindi is a language associated with the Hindus. It wanted only Urdu. This was reminiscent of the Hindi-Urdu controversy in the U.P. at the start of the 20th century. It used to be the practice there that petitions to the courts would be written in Urdu. When the government passed an order on 8 April 1900 to the effect that law courts and government offices should also entertain petitions written in Hindi and Devanagari script, many Muslim politicians objected and held protest meetings. They said it would lower the status and prestige of Urdu.

Rajaji tried to point out that the language sought to be promoted was Hindustani, with an admixture of words derived from Sanskrit as well as Persian, rather than Sanskritised Hindi. But the Muslim League of Madras persisted in its opposition. This experience of adamancy might have influenced C. Rajagopalachari, along with other factors, in coming to the conclusion ahead of other national leaders that partition should be conceded if people in the Muslim-majority areas of the country insisted on it.

THE WAR : FOR EMPIRE OR DEMOCRACY ?

Jawaharlal Nehru was largely responsible for the outward-looking, international dimension of India's freedom movement. The Indian National Congress-expressed itself against the policy of appeasement of Nazi-Germany and Fascist Italy which was being pursued during the 'thirties by the major West European countries. Practising democracy at home and imperialism abroad, they were only postponing the day of reckoning.

The Tripuri Congress, Meeting in March 1939—six months before the outbreak of World War II—expressed its "entire disapproval of British foreign policy culminating in the Munich Pact, the Anglo-Italian Agreement and recognition of Rebel Spain. This policy has been one of deliberate betrayal of democracy, repeated breach of pledges, the ending of the system of collective security, and co-operation with governments which are avowed enemies of democracy and freedom "

"The Congress is opposed to Imperialism and Fascism alike, and is convinced that world peace and progress require the ending of both of these. In the opinion of the Congress, it is urgently necessary for India to direct her own foreign policy as an independent nation, thereby keeping aloof from both Imperialism and Fascism and pursuing her path of peace and freedom."

When Britain at last gave up the policy of appeasement and declared war on Germany on 3 September 1939, the Viceroy followed suit and declared that India was at war without even the formality of consulting the Central legislature.

Meeting at Wardha in mid-September 1939, the Congress Working Committee reaffirmed its disapproval of Fascism and Nazism but held that "The issue of war and peace for India must be decided by the Indian people, and no outside authority can impose this decision upon them, nor can the Indian people permit their resources to be exploited for imperialist ends.

"If the war is to defend the *satus quo*, imperialist possessions, colonies, vested interests and privileges, then India can have nothing to do with it. If, however, the issue is democracy

and a world order based on democracy, then India is intensely interested in it. The Committee are convinced that the interests of Indian democracy do not conflict with the interests of British democracy or of World democracy. But there is an inherent and ineradicable conflict between democracy for India or elsewhere and imperialism and fascism."

"If Great Britain fights for the maintenance and extension of democracy then she must necessarily end imperialism in her own possessions, establish full democracy in India, and the Indian people must have the right of self-determination by framing their own constitution through a Constituent Assembly without external interference, and must guide their own policy. A free democratic India will gladly associate herself with other free nations for mutual defence against aggression and for economic co-operation. She will work for the establishment of a real world order based on freedom and democracy, utilising the world's knowledge and resources for the progress and advancement of humanity."

The Congress Working Committee therefore invited the British Government to declare in unequivocal terms what their war aims were, and in particular how those aims were going to apply to India both immediately and after the war. Gandhiji with his total belief in nonviolent resistance to evil, be it British imperialism or Hitlerism or Japanese militarism, was out of tune with most of the senior Congress leaders, including Jawaharlal Nehru, the Congress President Maulana Azad and C. Rajagopalachari. They were in favour of extending not only moral but material support to the Allied powers if India's right to independence was recognised and given immediate practical recognition in a suitable form pending the conclusion of hostilities. Gandhiji did not insist on acceptance of his position with regard to participation in the war.

The Viceroy's response to the Congress Working Committe's Wardha Resolution was infuriating to Indian nationalists. Linlithgow said that, at the end of the war, any necessary changes in the scheme of the Government of India Act of 1935 would be considered "with representatives of the several communities, parties and interests in India, and with the Indian Princes." The Congress Ministeries resigned in protest.

Again, in July 1940, the Congress offered to support the war effort if the British Government agreed to recognise India's independence at the end of the war and to form a provisional national government immediately. This offers was rejected.

Satyagraha was therefore resumed by the Congress, but in order not to embarass the British during 'the perils and dangers of war', it was confined to token civil disobedience by individuals chosen by, or with the prior approval of Gandhiji. It was only in the early part of 1942, when the war was going very badly for the allies, that Sir Stafford Cripps was sent to India on behalf of the British Cabinet to negotiate with Indian leaders.

Cripps Offer : A Post-dated Cheque

Cripps conducted negoitations on the basis of a declaration of policy by the British Cabinet. Its main features were : convening, after the war, a constituent assembly to be formed through elections on a system of a proportional representation ; the right of province that was not prepared to accept the new Dominion constitution to retain its existing arrangenments ; and co-operation by Indian parties in the war effort, with the British government continuing to be fully responsible for the defence of India. As for the Indian states, they would also have the power to opt out, like the provinces. However, Cripps told the representatives of the states that the British Crown would not come to the aid the princes if any of them should aspire for independence.

Here was acceptance of Pakistan in principle within two years of the demand being formulated by the Muslim League. This kind of development had been foreseen and cautioned against by Subhas Bose in his address at the Tripura Congress in February 1938 : "Every imperialism is based on the policy of divide and rule. But I doubt if any imperialism in the world has practised this policy so skilfully, systematically and ruthlessly as Great Britain. In accordance with this policy, before power was handed over to the Irish people. Ulster was separated from the rest of Ireland. Similarly, before any power is handed over to the Palestinians the Jews will be separated from the Arabs". After referring to the Juxtaposition of autocratic princes and democratically elected representative from the

British Indian provinces in the federal scheme of the government of India Act of 1935, Bose went on to say: "If the new constitution (the 1935 Act) is finally rejected, whether owing to the opposition of British India or owing to the refusal to the princes to joint it, I have no doubt that British ingenuity will seek some other constitutional device fortiitioning India and thereby neutralising the transference of power to the Indian people. Therefore, any Constitution for India which emanates from Whitehall must be examined with the utmost care and caution."

However, the negotiations between Cripps and the Congress broke down not on the question of the unity of India but of the arrangements to be made immediately regarding reconstitution of the Viceroy's Executive Council so as to consist of Indian members commanding the confidence and support of the people. There were two issues; whether the Executive council would functice in practice as a cabinet, with the Viceroy as the formal head; and the precise scope of responsibility of the Indian War Member. On the first question Cripps gave a more or less affirmative answer. But on the second there was no agreement. The Viceroy, Lord Linlithgow, and the then Commander-in-Chief of the British Indian Army, Lord Wavell (who was later to become Viceroy) would not allow Cripps to yield any substantial ground.

While Congress leader wanted the Indian War Member to have full responsibility in all matters except decisions on the actual conduct of war operations which would lie with the Commander-in-Chief, the British side was not prepared to go that far. Accordingly the Congress Working Committee passed a Resolution in April 1942 which marked the failure of the Cripps Mission. It noted that the Cripps proposals related principally to the future upon the cessation of hostilities, and "while recognising that self-determination for the people of India is accepted in principle in that uncertain future", said: "The aceeptance beforehand of the novel principle of non-accession for a province is also a severe blow to the conception of Indian unity and an apple of discord likely to generate growing trouble in the provinces, and which may well lead to further difficulties in the way of the Indian States merging

themselves in the Indian Union." The resolution also deplored the treatment of the 90 million people of the Indian states as 'commodities' whom the rulers could take for granted and speak on behalf of. Turning to the proposals relating to the immediate situation, the Working Committee said : "To take away defence from the sphere of responsibility at this stage is to reduce that responsibility to a farce and a nullity", since the enthusiastic response of the people in defence efforts could not be evoked without devolution of responsibility to Indian hands in the matter of defence. It would not do to give the Indian Member responsibility only for the canteen stores department and the like.

Gandhiji had at one stage of the Cripps described the offer as a 'post-dated cheque', to which an imaginative journalist added the words 'on a crashing bank'. This caused misunderstanding of the Mahatma position in some circles outside India. They thought, sepecially after he sponsored the 'Quit India' call in August 1942 and in the context of the poor translation of his active concept of Satyagraha as 'pacifism', that Gandhiji was defeatist if not pro-Axis. It was given to General Smuts, the old adversary-turned-admirer, to tell the international Press in ringing words in London, in November 1942 : "It is sheer non-sense to talk of Mahatma Gandhi as a fifth columnist. He is a great man. He is one of the great men of the world."

INEXORABLE DRIFT TO PARTITION

Muslim Separatism : Iqbal and Jinnah

Badruddin Tyabji and Syed Ahmad Khan, as we saw in Chapter III, represented the two tendencics, nationalist and separatist, which were at work among the Muslim intelligentsia during the 19th century. Mohammad Iqbal (1873-1938) and Mohammad Ali Jinnah (1876-1949) were the two major personalities who articulated, and in turn intensified, Muslim separatism during the 20th century.

Iqbal was a great Urdu poet and philosopher who also took part in public life. He shared Syed Ahmad Khan's distrust of the movement for democratic self-government. In his presidential

address at the Allahabad session of the Muslim League in December 1930, he quoted Renan's statement on what makes nation : A great aggregation of men, sane of mind and warm of heart, creates a moral consciousness which is called a nation.'

Such a national ethos was lacking in India, according to Iqbal. "It might have been a fact in India if the teaching of Kabir and the Divine Faith of Akbar had seized the imagination of the masses of the country. Experience, however, shows that the various caste units and religious units in India have shown no inclination to sink their respective individualities in a larger whole. Part of her people have cultural affinities with nations in the east and part with nations in the middle and west of Asia."

After discussing the demand for the creation of 'a Muslim India within India'. Iqbal said : "Personally I would go further I would like to see the Punjab, North-West Frontier Province, Sind and Baluchistan amalgamated into a single state. Self-government within the British empire or without the British empire, the formation of a consolidated North-West Indian Muslim state appears to me to be the final destiny of the Muslisms, at least of North-West India." The words proved prophetic. Pakistan emerged in 1947 with an eastern wing besides the western : and the Bengali-speaking people of East Pakistan formed the majority of the new states's population. But the denial of democratic rights to the people of the eastern wing led to the break-up of Pakistan in 1971 and the formation of a new and independent state of Bangladesh. Pakistan now consists of precisely those provinces of the north-west which were listed by Iqbal.

It is one of those ironies in which history abounds that Jinnah began as a nationalist Muslim. His father was a merchant in Karachi and sent him to England for training as a barrister. In England he was attracted by Liberalism, and admired the Parsi nationalist, Dadabhai Naoroji, who was elected to the House of Commons from Central Finsbury on the Liberal ticket. On return to India, Jinnah set up practice in Bombay, joined the Indian National Congress, and served his political apprenticeship as honorary secretary to Dadabhai

Naoroji during the latter's term as Congress President in 1906. Jinnah was a friend of Gopal Krishna Gokhale, and continued to work for Hindu-Muslim understanding even after he joined the Muslim League in 1913.

It should be noted here that though the British rulers encouraged the formation of the Muslim League in order to separate the Muslims from the mainstream of Indian nationalism, the League was not always separatist in its approach. Depending on the circumstances and on the party's leadershp at a given time, there were periods when the League and the Congress worked closely together; so much so that, on occasion, the annual sessions of the two organisations would be held side by side. In 1913, the Karachi session of the Congress welcomed a resolution adopted a little earlier by Muslim League which stated that the future development of the country depended on the harmonious co-operation of various communities. Similarly the Hindu Mahasabha (formed in 1906, the same year as the Muslim League) and the Congress did not always work at cross purposes. Indeed, the founder of the Hindu Mahasabha was Pandit Madan Mohan Malaviya who served more than once as Congress president in subsequent years. The Mahasabha's session at Akola in 1931 was presided over by C.Vijayaraghavachariar, lawyer and social reformer from Salem who was a former Congress president.

The nationalism of the early Jinnah led him to say in his address to the Lahore session of the Muslim League in 1924 : "We must not forget that one essential requisite condition to achieve Swaraj is political unity between the Hindus and the Mohammadans. I am almost inclined to say that India will get Dominion Responsible Government the day the Hindus and Muslims are united." Gandhiji endorsed this view : "I agree with Mr. Jinnah that Hindu-Muslim unity means Swaraj." About the outbreaks of Hindu-Muslim conflict from time to time, usually on the occasion of religious festivals and over cow-killing or music before mosques, Jinnah told a joint select committee of the British Parliament : "If you ask me, very often these riots are based on some misunderstanding, and it is because the police have taken one side or the other." As

a rationalist, Jinnah kept away from the pan-Islamic Khilafat movement.

Towards the close of 1939 Jinnah told a delegation of Muslim students from Cambridge, who were advocates of the creation of Pakistan : "I am getting more and more convinced that you are right in spite of myself." Pakistan was an acronym coined in 1930 by Chaudhari Rahmat Ali, a Muslim student at Cambridge, by taking 'P' from Punjab 'A' from Afghania (standing for the North-West Frontier Province), 'K' from Kashmir, 'S' from Sind and 'tan' from Baluchistan. In Urdu it means 'land of the pure'.

Though a late convert to separatism, it was Jinnah who presided over the Lahore Session of the Muslim League in March 1940 which adopted the resolution asking for the partition of India. The resolution said : "No constitutional plan would be workable in this country or acceptable to the Muslim's unless it is designed on the following basic principles, *viz.*, that geographically contiguous units are demarcated into regions which should be so constituted, with such territorial readjustments as may be necessary, that the areas in which the Muslims are numerically in a majority as in the North-Western and Eastern Zones of India should be grouped to constitute Independent States in which the constituent units shall be autonomous and sovereign." The resolution did not spell it out in so many words, but obviously envisaged the inclusion of the whole of Punjab, with its large Hiudu minority, in an independent state in the western zone with autonomy for the constituent units ; and the inclusion of the whole of Bengal. again with a large Hindu minority, in an independent state in the eastern zone which would also include the Muslim majority areas of Assam.

This is of interest because the Pakistan of Jinnah's original conception (he described what he actually got in 1947 as a 'moth-eaten' version) ran flaltly counter to the theory of two nations on the basis of which he asked for partition. These are the words in Jinnah propounded the two-nation theory in his presidential address at the 1940 session of the Muslim League : "The Hindus and Muslims belong to two different religious philosophies, social customs, literatures. To yoke

together two such nations under a single state, one as a numerical minority and the other as a majority, must lead to growing discontent and final destruction of any fabric that may be so built up for the government of such a state. Musalamans are a nation according to any definition of a nation and they must have their homelands, their territory, and their state."

Hindu Advocates of two-Nation Theory

Following the Hindu-Muslim riots which began in the early 'twenties, Lala Lajpatrai proposed a partition on religious lines. He suggested in 1924 that "the Punjab should be partitioned into two provinces, the Western Punjab with a large Muslim majority to be a Muslim-governed province, and the Eastern Punjab with a large Hindu-Sikh majority to be a non-Muslim governed province. Under my scheme the Muslims will have four Muslim states : (i) the Pathan province or the North-West Frontier ; (ii) Western Punjab ; (iii) Sind ; and (iv) Eastern Bengal." This was a pre-vision of the Pakistan of 1947.

Veer Savarkar, presiding over a session of the Hindu Mahasabha in 1937, said : "India cannot be assumed today to be a unitarian a homogeneous nation, but on the contrary there are two nations in the main ; the Hinuds and the Muslims. These two antagonistic nations are living side by side in India."

The Congress had no use for this theory. As Jawaharlal Nehru pointed out. "These two 'nations' existed in varying proportions in most of the villages of India. They were nations which had no boundaries ; they were all over the place."

Congress Secularism ; Losing Battle

The Congress was committed from its inception to the principle that the observance of different religions in personal and social life is compatible with the people working together in a country's public life. This is what has come to be known as secularism.

Pherozeshah Mehta, the distinguished Parsi leader who presided over the Calcutta Congress in 1890, said : "To my

mind a Parsi is a true Parsi, a Mohammadan or a Hindu is a better Mohammadan or Hindu, the more he is attached to the land which gave him birth, the more he is bound in brotherly relations and attached to all the children of the soil."

The creation of separate electorates under the Indian Councils Act was strongly disapproved in a resolution at the Lahore Congress of 1909. Pandit Madan Mohan Malaviya, persiding, referred to the relaxation of franchise qualifications in favour of Muslims and said they were "not out of any love for our Mohammadan brethren but to keep them from standing shoulder to shoulder with their Hindu brothers to agitate for reforms. This policy of partiality will not live, as it does not deserve to live."

The constellation of leaders of the Congress over the six decades from its formation till India's independence included such shining stars as Hakim Ajmal Khan, Dr. M.A. Ansari, Khan Abdul Ghaffar Khan, M. Asaf Ali and Maulana Azad. Communal separatism was foreign to their nature. Asaf Ali, for example, was so deeply interested in the Gita and the Mahabharata that he embarked on their translation; his friends would jestingly refer to him as 'Pandit Asaf Ali'.

Maulana Azad (1888-1958) was born in Mecca but the family soon moved over to Calcutta, where he grew up. Something of a prodigy as a student, he completed by the time he was sixteen the course of traditional education in Persian and Arabic, philosophy and mathematics and theology, which young scholars would ordinarily conclude by the age of twenty-five. Thereafter he learnt English and studied history and modern political thought.

As a young man Azad became acquainted with Shyam Sunder Chakravarty, a revolutionary worker, and was attracted to the cause. This was surprising to the revolutionary group which he joined, because the Muslim elite of Bengal had by and large succumbed to the blandishments of the British at the time of the partition of the province. During a tour that Azad underook in 1908 of Egypt and some countries of West Asia, his talks with Arab and Turk revolutionaries confirmed him in his militant nationalism. On return, he decided to start a

journal for mobilising Indian Muslims for the freedom movement. *Al Hilal*, brought out in June 1912, reached within two years a circulation of 26,000 copies per week, a figure till then unheard of in Urdu journalism. The views propagated in the journal were disapproved by the British government which demanded a security of Rs. 2,000 under the Press Act. Soon this deposit was forfeited and a fresh deposit of Rs. 10,000 was demanded. This was also lost, and the press itself was confiscated in 1915. Azad then brought out another weekly, *Al Balagh*, but this too closed in 1916 when he was interned.

Through these journals and numerous pamphlets, Azad urged that "the seventy million Muslims of India should so combine with their two hundred million Hindu brethren of India that the two together should form one people and one nation." He saw no contradiction between being a good Muslim and a good Indian : "I am a Muslim and I feel proud that I have inherited glorious traditions extending over 1300 years. I am not prepared to allow its least part to be lost. With all these sentiments I possess another sentiment, which has been produced by the realities of my life. The spirit of Islam does not prohibit it. On the other hand, it directs me this way. I feel proud that I am an Indian. I am a part of the indivisibly united nationality of India. I am an important element in this united nationality. Without me the temple of its greatness remains incomplete."

Later, after the Muslim League had formulated the demand for Pakistan, he said : "I must confess that the very term Pakistan goes against my brain. It suggests that some portions of the world are pure while others are impure. Such a division of territories into pure and impure is a repudiation of the very spirit of Islam. The Prophet says, 'God has made the whole world a mosque for me'."

Even in terms of practical advantage, he argued, the creation of Pakistan would hurt the interests of the millions of Muslims who would be left outside it. While the 90 million Muslims of undivided India formed a quarter of the total population, and thus a substantial minority, after partition there would remain 35 million Muslims scattered in small minorities in the Hindustan state : "With 17 per cent in U.P.,

12 per cent in Bihar and nine per cent in Madras, they will be weaker than they are today. They will awaken and discover that they have overnight become aliens and foreigners."

Unexpected Help for Muslim League

Within a couple of years of the Congress relinquishing office in the provinces, the Muslim League received aid and comfort from an unexpected quarter-the Indian Communists. What they had been denouncing as an imperialist war became for them, overnight, a people's war with Hitler's attack on Russia in June 1941. Ruling out any confrontation with the British authorities in India since that would obstruct the war effort, the Communists began to advocate Congress-League understanding on the basis of a new theory of Indian nationalities. The demand for Pakistan, it was explained, was nothing but the desire for self-determination of certain nationalities. The Communist were untroubled by the implications of this rationalisation of the Muslim League's separatism : for example, that the sub-nationalism of the Sindhi Hindu was expressed by the Muslim League which it would be ludicrous for him to try to join.

Also, C. Rajagopalachari had begun to urge that partition should be conceded in principle if, on ascertainment, that turned out to be the wish of the people in certain areas. This was commended as 'the lesser evil' compared to continued British rule, in a resolution sponsored by Rajaji for consideration by the Madras Congress Legislature Party. He resigned from the Congress Working Committee in April 1942 on objection being raised to bringing up such a resolution with his colleagues in the Working Committee. Although Rajaji's motivation was different from that of the Communists, the effect of his campaign was favourable to the Muslim League.

The League had done badly in the 1937 elections, securing only 109 of the 482 seats reserved for Muslims in the various provincial assemblies. By the time elections were held again towards the close of 1945, it had vastly improved its position : it won almost all the reserved seats except in the North West Frontier Province. In the elections to the Central Assembly the League won every Muslim seat. The drift to partition had become inexorable.

REVOLT BY A POLITICALLY AWAKENED PEOPLE

Each reverse suffered by the British in the eastern theatre during World War II was welcomed by a section of politically conscious Indians, for two reasons. One was that the British imperialists, who were refusing to get off India's back were being humbled. The other reason was that the advancing Japanese forces were accompanied by the Indian National Army formed by Subhas Chandra Bose. After effecting a sensational escape in January 1941 from his Calcutta home where he had been interned, Bose had made his way first to Germany (he made a broadcast from Berlin in March 1942) and proceeded from there to Japan. About 20,000 Indian officers and men of the British Indian Army, taken prisoner by the Japanese, joined the force raised by Bose, which was to fight alongside the Japanese to drive the British out of India.

'Quit India' Resolution

The Congress viewed with concern the growing sense of satisfaction at the success of Japanese arms, since it could lead to a passive acceptance of aggression. Following the failure of the Cripps mission the Congress Working Committee adopted on 14 July 1942 at Wardha a resolution calling for "the withdrawal of British rule from India" so that a provisional government, representative of all important sections of the people, could be formed for organising effective resistance to aggression. The withdrawal of British rule was necessary because a solution of the communal tangle had been "made impossible by the presence of the foreign power whose long record has been to pursue relentlessly the policy of divide and rule." The resolution made it clear that the intention was not to jeopardise the defensive capacity of the Allied Powers : "The Congress is therefore agreeable to the stationing of the armed forces of the Allies in India."

The notice to the British power to quit India, embodied in the above document, was reiterated, and the sanctions for enforcing the demand spelt out, in a resolution (see v under Documents) placed before the All India Congress Committee in Bombay on 7 August 1942. The operative portion said : "The

Committee resolves to sanction, for the vindication of India's inalienable right to freedom and independence, the starting of a mass struggle on non-violent lines on the widest possible scale, so that the country might utilise all the non-violent strength it has gathered during the last twenty-two years of peaceful struggle. Such a struggle must inevitably be under the leadership of Gandhiji and the Committee requests him to take the lead and to guide the nation in the steps to be taken.

"The Committee appeals to the people of India to carry out his instructions as disciplined soldiers of Indian freedom. They must remember that non-violence is the basis of this movement. A time may come when it may not be possible to issue instructions or for instructions to reach our people, and when no Congress committees can function. When this happens, every man and woman who is participating in this movement must function for himself or herself within the four corners of the general instructions issued. Every Indian who desires freedom and strives for it must be his own guide urging him on along the hard road where there is no resting place and which leads ultimately to the independence and deliverance of India."

The publication of the September Resolution of the Working Committee, followed by the A.I.C.C. resolution, had an electrifying effect on public opinion. People stood ready to receive and carry out Gandhiji's instructions. But the people were left to their own devices by the British authorities, who arrested Gandhiji and all the Congress leaders in the early hours of 9 August 1942 following the adoption of the Quit India resolution by the A.I.C.C. the previous day. It was a preplanned operation which took everyone including Gandhiji by surprise, and infuriated the people who rose and gave vent to their anger.

Provocative Arrests, People's Anger

The Mahatma said later : "The movement was not started by the resolution of 8 August. Before I could function, they arrested not only me, who was to lead and guide the movement if negotiations failed, but principal Congressmen all over India. Thus Mark the words, 'if negotiations failed'. Gandhiji had

concluded his speech on the Quit India resolution at the A.I.C.C. with these words : "The Congress will do or die. ... I shall make every effort to see the Viceroy or address a letter to him and wait for his reply before starting the struggle. It may take a week or a fortnight or three weeks." And the Congress president announced that he was sending copies of the Resolution to President Roosevelt, to the Chinese government and to the Soviet ambassador in London. Quite clearly they were not expecting to be rounded up in an operation that has been aptly compared with the Japanese attack on Pearl Harbour.

People in their anger tore up railway track, cut telegraph lines, blew up bridges. Students and youth were to the fore in the movement, which resembled nothing so much as the anti-Fascist underground movement in Occupied Europe. There was wide circulation of underground literature, printed and cyclostyled, and even an underground radio transmitter at Bombay. From the moment the national leaders were arrested, India indeed came under Britain's armed occupation.

The following account brings out both the intensity of the spontaneous revolt and the savagery of the government's repressive measures : "The events of 1942 showed the depth of the national will. Communications, particularly in the United Provinces and Bihar, were cut and the war effort seriously impeded. The government struck hard to crush this resistance. In August and September, 57½ battalions were emyloyed in this activity, and there were killings in Bihar and Eastern U.P. on a scale greater than even that in the Punjab in 1919. In other parts of the country also there were instances of military and police savagery. The Whipping Act was revived. Considered as the most serious threat to the *raj* since the revolt of 1857, it was handled with the same severity."

'1857' Re-enacted at a Higher Level

The comparison with the 1857 revolt is appropriate. The two uprisings were similar in the intensity of feeling against the foreign oppressor, in the spontaneity of the revolt and the courage shown by the participants. But 1942 was not a repetition of 1857 but the re-enactment of a patriotic rising at an incomparably higher level of political consciousness. The

intervening 85 years had seen the birth and growth of the world's largest and most sustained freedom struggle. The participanst in the Quit India Movement were looking forward, to the establishment of a democratic and egalitarian order in an independent India, not backward to the restoration of the powers and privileges feudal princes and their emperor.

Like 1857, the 1942 Movement was inspired by heroic personalities round whom legends grew. There was Jaya Prakash Narayan, the Congress socialist leader who was, like his friend Jawaharlal Nehru, strongly artracted to the un-Marxist Mahatma. Narayan made a during escape from custody in the jail at Hazaribagh and led the movement in various parts of the country from underground till his capture in October 1943. And Aruna Asaf Ali, (D, 1909) the Rani of Jhansi of 1942, who had a price on her head but successfully evaded arrest for more than three years and surfaced to the ground only after the cancellation of her arrest warrant. This brings out another difference from the situation in 1857. The administration was now manned to a large extent by Indians, many of whom sympathised with the cause of freedom. Aruna could not have avoided capture for as long as she did without timely tip-offs on intended raids.

A letter to her from Gandhiji brings out in poignant words the Mahatma's adamantine adherence, for himself, to non-violence and open revolt and his admiration at the same time for dedicated patriots following methods other than his : "I have been filled with admiration for your courage and heroism. I have sent you messages that you must not die underground. You are reduced to a skeleton. Do come out and surrender yourself and win the prize offered for your arrest. Reserve the prize for the Harijan cause."

The scale of the sacrifices made be the common people during the Quit India Movement can be gauged from the numbers of those killed and injured in military and police firing, and those arrested or detained under the Defence of India Rules. The figures (doubtless erring on the side of under-estimation) were furnished by the British authorities in the Central Assembly, and they pertain only to about three months till November 1942 :

Number of persons killed in military or police firing	940
Injured in such firing	1,630
Number of persons arrested	60,229
Number of persons detained under Defence of India Rules	18,000

Outside of the urban centres, there was a parallel administration run by nationalist volunteers in some parts of the country for months together. Developments like these were little reported at the time, because of censorship both formal and *de facto*. For the same reason, the country did not know the full extent of the death and misery caused by the famine and epidemics which ravaged Bengal during 1943-44.

I.N.A. Trials and R.I.N. Mutiny

The notice to Quit India, which was formally served by the Congress in 1942 and thunderingly echoed by the people, was reinforced by the popular sympathy for the prisoners in the trial, for treason, of officers and men of the Indian National Army who were captured by the British on their reoccupation of lost territories in the east. The proceedings of the trials received very wide publicity in the Press, with many of the country's most eminent lawyers conducting the defence.

As nationalists saw it, the British government could not reasonably complain of the conduct of the I.N.A. personnel. A part of the British Indian Army had been sent to Burma and Singapore. When Japan occupied these regions, the British government left the Indian Army to its fate. If the Indians had remained supine, as prisoners of war they would still have been compelled to undertake the construction of roads, or other work in factories, which would help the Japanese War effort. Instead, they decided that they would fight for Indian freedom. This was meant to enable the liberation of India by a National Army rather than the occupation of India by the Japanese armies.

At the end of the trials, during which the defence arguments were followed with great interest and enthusiasm by the public, all the I.N.A. officers were released either on the

orders of the court or by the exercise of clemency by the Viceroy.

Soon came another, and strong, signal to the Empire, already enfeebled as it was by World War II, that its days in the sub-continent were numbered. There were mutinies in the Royal Indian Air Force and the Royal Indian Navy. The expression of disaffection in the Air Force was small in its scale, though serious enough, while the mutiny by about 3,000 ratings of the Navy spilled over into the streets of Bombay city. There was exchange of fire between the mutineers and British troops, and Bombay's industrial workers went on a strike to demonstrate their sympathy for the ratings. This was the first rebellion by Britain's Indian forces since 1857, and it was now rebellion by educated young men very different in their political consciousness and knowledge of the world around them from the sepoys of the East India Company's armies.

PARTITION AND INDEPENDENCE

Fruitless Round of Parleys

From 1944, when Gandhiji was released on account of his failing health, there was a dreary round of triangular parleys between the British authorities, Congress and the Muslim League—with the Indian princes hovering on the sideliness. Gandhiji discussed with Jinnah a formula suggested by Rajaji, envisaging the separation of areas with an absolute Muslim majority, but with a limited federal tie-up with the rest of India for safeguarding defence, commerce and communications. Jinnah rejected the formula.

With the release the following year of the other Congress leaders, the new Viceroy, Wavell, held a conference at Simla in the summer of 1945. The Congress went so far in pursuit of a compromise settlement as to agree to parity between 'Caste Hindus' and Muslims in a new Executive Council of the Viceroy. But Jinnah insisted that the Congress should nominate no Muslim, and refused even the Viceroy's proposal to include a Unionist Muslim from Punjab in addition to League Muslims. The Viceroy could have called Jinnah's bluff and cut him down to size. The Viceroy chose to be vetoed by Jinnah.

Then came a parliamentary delegation from Britain, followed by a mission consisting of three Cabinet Ministers of the post-War Labour Government : Lord Pethick-Lawrenee, Sir Stafford Cripps and A.V. Alexander. They suggested a plan, in May 1946, which would preserve the sub-continent's political unity in a three-tier arrangement of provinces, groupings of provinces and a weak federal centre. This was the first time that a British-sponsored scheme did not envisage the break-up of the sub-continent. But it was too late. The Muslim separatism nurtured by British imperialism over a half-century had grown into a Frankenstein's monster whom even its creator could not control. Jinnah was insistent on outright partition, and the sanction he invoked for it was the observance of Direct Action Day on 16 August 1946. On that day the most terrible killings and arson were witnessed in Calcutta, where the provincial government was now the Muslim League's and headed by H.S. Suhrawardy. Massive Hindu—Muslim riots spread from Calcutta to East Bengal, and from there to Bihar and Punjab.

Even the conservative *Daily Telegraph* of London, which was hostile to the cause of Indian freedom and was therefore well disposed towards anti-Congress forces like the Muslim League, strongly criticised the launching of direction action (See facsimile on page) : "In the Corpses that belitter the streets of Calcutta and in crowded hospital wards are seen the first consequences of the 'direct action' resolved on by the Muslim League. An opportunity for the outbreak was provided by the incredible folly of the Muslim government in Bengal in proclaiming the "Direct Action Day" as a public holiday."

On 2 September 1946, the Viceroy formed an 'interim government', as the Congress liked to regard it, by reconstituting his Executive Council Jawaharlal Nehru was its vice-president, and held the portfolios of External Affairs and Commonwealth Relations. Initially the League boycotted the reconstituted Executive Council and it functioned somewhat like a government. But when the League lifted the boycott and entered the Executive Council, it became a house at war. Liaqat Ali, as member holding the finance portfolio, would

veto or delay every proposal that came from any department headed by a Congress member.

On 20 February 1947 the British Prime Minister, Clement Attlee, announced that Britain would withdraw from India by June 1948, and that Lord Mountbatten would succeed Lord Wavell as Viceroy. Mountbatten arrived in March 1947 and soon came to the conclusion that partition was unavoidable. He recalled in the course of a Nehru Memorial Lecture at Cambridge on 14 November 1968 : "I first tried very hard to revive the Cabinet Mission plan with Jinnah in order to retain the unity of India, but he wouldn't hear of it. He insisted on the partition of India into a Muslim State, to be called Pakistan, and the very large non-Muslim residue which he used to refer to as Hindustan. He wished to include not only the provinces, like Sind, which had a very large Muslim majority but also Bengal and the Punjab which had very large non-Muslim minorities. I told him that if he insisted on partitioning India he would have to agree to partition these two provinces and only to include the Muslim majority areas in Pakistan. He objected violently to 'a moth-eaten Pakistan'. He pointed out that it was unreasonable to divide these two great provinces, as their inhabitants were primarily Bengalis or Punjabis, which was more important than whether they were Muslims or Hindus. I then applied the same logic to the whole of India, claiming that a man was an Indian first and foremost before he was a Muslim or a Hindu. Therefore the whole of India should not be partitioned. This annoyed him. I tried to tempt Jinnah by offering him Bengal and the Punjab unpartitioned provided he would agree that though the provinces with Muslim majorities would have self-government they must be within an overall federal government at the centre. However, he said he would sooner have a moth-eaten Pakistan that owed no allegiance to a central government than a larger and more important area which came under it. I then ascertained from the Congress and Sikh leaders that, heart-broken though they were at the very thought of partitioning India, if the Muslim League would not accept a transfer of power on any other basis they would have no option but to accept, if they were not to remain indefinitely under British rule." Assuming the fullest sincerity on the part

of Lord Mountbatten, the last British Viceroy could not obviously control the Frankenstein's monster of separatism which a succession of his predecessors had created and nurtured.

Acceptance of partition by the Congress was hastened by the bitter experience of working with the Muslim League in the Interim Government. Liaqat Ali Khan as Finance Minister presented a Budget for 1947-48 which contained highly irresponsible taxation proposals which were a parody of Jawaharlal Nehru's socialist ideas. Jinnah was saying : "If he (Nehru) can only come down to earth and think coolly and calmly, he must understand that he is neither the Prime Minister nor is it a Nehru Government. He is only the Member for the External Affairs and Commonwealth Department."

With communal disturbances rocking the country, partition now seemed the only alternative to anarchy. The date for the transfer of power, and simultaneously with it the implementation of the Mountbatten plan of partition, was advanced to 15 August 1947.

A Diminished but Strong India

After the experience of the interim government, it seemed to many in retrospect a good thing that the cabinet Mission's Plan had not been put through. India would have had a weak central government. This would have made it impossible to undertake economic planning for the best utilisation of the country's resources. It seemed that, with the amputation of a diseased limb, India could recover political health.

Mercifully the Muslim League did not lift its boycott of the Constituent Assembly which had been inaugurated in 1946. The Assembly was able to proceed with its work of drafting a constitution for independent India on the basis of the principles of democracy, fundamental rights. and an egalitarian social and economic order. The president of the Constituent Assembly was Rajendra Prasad (1884-1963), the gentle Gandhian from Bihar who was to become the first President of the Indian Repulic.

15 August : The Glory and the Burden

The national mood at the moment of long-awaited

independence was a strange mixture of elation and sorrow. Brother was killing or hounding out brother in Punjab, Bengal and elsewhere. It is estimated that about five million Hindus and Sikhs abandoned their homes and lands in West Punjab and other parts of Pakistan and came to India for safety, and a similar number of Muslims moved over to Pakistan from East Punjab, Uttar Pradesh, Bihar and elsewhere. It was the biggest mass migration known in history. The refugees were the victims of the amoral and divisive policy pursued by imperialism and the folly of its Indian dupes, a burden on the resources of the two infant Dominions, and a burden more especially on the soul of every human person on either side of the Indo-Pakistan borders.

Gandhiji had been trudging in the Noakhali district of East Bengal and later in Bihar, persuading people to ignore the incitement by short-sighted politicians and to live in peace with each other. When Independence Day dawned on 15 August 1947, he was not in Delhi with those who celebrated the event, but away in Calcutta, trying to shame Hindus and Muslims into civilised behaviour and accomplishing, in the words of the London *Times*, what several divisions of troops could not have done.

"Long years ago," Jawaharlal Nehru said in an address to the Constituent Assembly as the hour of freedom approached on the night of August 14, "we made a tryst with destiny. Any now the time comes when we shall redeem our pledge, not wholly or in full measure, but very substantially. At the stroke of the midnight hour, when the world sleeps, India will awake to life and freedom. It is fitting that at this solemn moment we take the pledge of dedication to the service of India and her people, and to the still larger cause of humanity."

In a message to the people through the Press (see *VI* under *Select Documents*), Jawaharlal Nehru said : "We rejoice in that freedom even though clouds surround us and many of our people are sorrow-stricken and difficult problems encompass us. But freedom brings responsibilities and burdens and we have to face them in the spirit of a free and disciplined people."

From Dominion to Republic

The status that India attained on 15 August 1947 was that of a self-governing Dominion of the Commonwealth, with the British monarch as the appointing authority of the Governor-General of India (see facsimile in the centre-spread). Complete independence was to come two-and-a-half years later, when the republican Constitution came into force.

The interval was a period of consolidation. The urgent tasks before the Government headed by Jawaharlal Nehru were to organise relief and rehabilitation of the millions of refugees from Pakistan, to restore communal harmony and law and order, to cope with the problem of the princely States and to begin the restructuring of the economy ravaged by war and partition.

Restoration of communal harmony was no easy task. The refugees brought with them heart-rending accounts of loot, rape and murder in the Pakistan areas which inflamed many Hindus into acts of senseless retaliation against Muslim neighbours. Jawaharlal Nehru gave first priority to the restoration of order through firm administrative measures as Prime Minister, as well as through direct intervention in crisis situations even at risk to his personal safety. Gandhiji's martyrdom on 30 January 1948, when a Hindu fanatic shot him dead at a prayer meeting, shocked and chastened the majority community. A dedicated life came to a poetic end. The manner of the Mahatma's death served to hasten the return of sanity and normalcy. The re-assertion of the Indian ethos of tolerance was reflected in the Constitution which was in the process of being framed by the Constituent Assembly.

The British scheme for the transfer of power left wide open the question of the 565 princely States which accounted for a total population of 93 million. They ranged in size from Hyderabad with an area of 82,000 square miles and a population of 16 million to smaller territories, some of them tiny. The British Crown had exercised paramountcy over these States, and paramountcy was to lapse with the withdrawal of British power. In theory, therefore, they could be independent. There was every prospect of the balkanisation of India, which would

have delighted the hearts of the British imperialists who were mourning the loss of the Indian empire.

The only saving grace in the situation was Lord Mountbatten's attitude. He made it clear that the princely States could not become members of the British Commonwealth, that each ruler should accede to either of the two new Dominions, and that the choice had necessarily to be based on considerations of geography. All the princely States which were surrounded by or adjoined Indian territory had acceded to India by 15 August 1947 with the exception of three: Hyderabad in central India; Junagadh in the Kathiawar peninsula (in present Gujarat) on the west coast; and Jammu & Kashmir which was contiguous both to India and to Pakistan. Eventually these States also acceded to India. The Kashmir ruler's decision which came after aggression on the State from Pakistan, had the full support of the leader of the principal political party, Sheikh Abdullah. He said : "Kashmir has linked itself to India because it is at one with her in the Gandhian ideals of justice, equality and humanity. A progressive state could join hands only with another progressive one, and not with a feudal state like Pakistan. India is pledged to the principle of secular democracy and we are in pursuit of the same objective."

Initially the accession of the princely States was limited to the three subjects of defence, foreign relations and communications, Sardar Patel (1875-1950), as Home Minister, handled the problem of the accession of the princely States with great tact and firmness. He persuaded the rulers to merge into larger Unions of States and to integrate fully with India, in respect of all subjects. To him goes the credit for averting the tragedy of a further fragmentation of the country.

The drafting of free India's Constitution was meanwhile proceeding apace. A notable feature of its provisions was the abolition of untouchability, which was made punishable in accordance with law. The Constitution not only granted full citizenship rights to the former untouchables and to the tribal people; it went further and conferred on them what might be described as discrimination-in-reverse so as to make up for the lag of centuries. Thus, in electoral constituencies reserved—on

the basis of concentration of population—for the Scheduled Castes or Scheduled Tribes, only Harijan or tribal candidates may contest. However, such candidates are free to contest for election from the unreserved, or general, constituencies. This ensures that the proportion of seats held by Harijan and tribal representatives in Parliament and the State legislatures is never below, but can exceed, their proportion in the total population.

Similarly, women were fully enfranchised. India was in this respect ahead of some of the older democracies. The woman of Switzerland gained the right to vote only many years later.

The older democracies had inched their way towards equal citizenship rights over a period of two centuries and more, starting from the industrial revolution and the rudiments of parliamentary democracy based on limited suffrage. In contrast, the Indian Constitution conferred on one-seventh of the human race complete equality of citizenship irrespective of economic or educational status, racial origin, religion or sex. (See VII under *Select Documents*). It had not happened earlier in the world's history that a people secured such comprehensive democratic rights at one stroke. The Indian Constitution which came into force on 26 January 1950—exactly twenty years after the people of India took the pledge of complete independence—may therefore rightly be described as a landmark not only in India's regeneration but also in the political evolution of mankind.

SELECT DOCUMENTS

(*i*) BOYCOTT AND SWADESHI

Excerpts from Resolutions passed at the Calcutta Session of the Indian National Congress in 1906, protesting against the partition of Bengal and extending support to the Boycott of British-made goods and encouragement of Swadeshi. i.e. Buying Indian.)

The Partition of Bengal : This Congress again records its emphatic protest against the Partition of Bengal and regrets that the present Government, while admitting that there were errors in the original plan and that it went wholly and decisively against the wishes of the majority of the people of Bengal, is disposed to look upon it as a settled fact.

This Congress, composed of representatives from all the Provinces of this country, desires earnestly the impress upon the British Parliament and the present Liberal Government that it will be not only just, but expedient to reverse or modify the partition in such a manner as to keep the entire Bengali speaking community under one undivided administration and thus restore contentment to so important a province as Bengal.

Boycott Movement : Having regard to the fact that the people of this country have little or no voice in its administration, and that their representations to the Government do not receive due consideration, this Congress is of opinion that the Boycott Movement, inaugurated in Bengal by way of

protest against the partition of the province was, and is, legitimate.

Swadeshi : This Congress accords its most cordial support to the Swadeshi Movement and calls upon the people of the country to labour for its success by making earnest and sustained efforts to promote the growth of indigenous industries and to stimulate the production of indigenous articles by giving them preference, wherever practicable, over imported commodities, even at a sacrifice.

(*ii*) PROGRAMME OF NON-VIOLENT NON-COOPERATION

The eleven-point programme put before the country in January 1921 by Mahatma Gandhi following the unanimous adoption of the policy of non-violent non-cooperation by the Congress at Nagpur in December (1920).

The Congress gave us a new constitution and unanimously passed the resolution advocating non-violent non-cooperation. Such a huge session of the Congress has never been held, and never before has it deliberated with such seriousness of purpose. The resolution on non-violent non-cooperation has confirmed the resolution of the special session of the Congress at Calcutta with certain additions. Those who have accepted that resolution are obliged to do the following :

1. Title-holders to relinquish their titles.
2. Parents to withdraw their children from Government controlled schools and make some arrangements for them in their homes or through a national school.
3. Any student over sixteen years who is convinced that it is a sin to learn under the shadow of a Government which the people have decided either to reform or to end should occupy himself in some other way.
4. Lawyers should give up practice as soon as possible and devote themselves to the service of the people.
5. Businessmen should give up trade in foreign goods, sever foreign connections as soon as possible encourage hand-spinning and hand-weaving.

6. Those members of Councils who got themselves elected despite voters' opposition should resign and those who in defiance of public opinion, refuse to resign should not be approached by the voters for any political work.
7. Policemen and other Government servants should be polite, kind and truthful in their dealings with the people. : they should attend political meetings but should not make any speeches there and should openly contribute money for the freedom movement.
8. Policemen should not regard service as greater than their religion or country and should, their good behaviour, falsify the charge that they are mercenaries with no feeling for their own community.
9. Every man and woman should make as much sacrifice as possible.
10. All should understand that our victory lies in preserving peace, and that not only in dealing with the Government but also amongst ourselves. Preserving peace means not only avoiding physical violence but eschewing abuse as well.
11. All should try to strengthen Hindu-Muslim unity and, likewise, end the bitterness prevailing among the various sections in the country. The quarrels between Brahmins and non-Brahmins should be ended and the sin of untouchability eradicated.

If we can do this in a year, we shall have Swaraj within that period ; and if we delay doing it, then freedom will also be delayed.

(*iii*) FUNDAMENTAL RIGHTS AND SOCIO-ECONOMIC OBJECTIVES

(Text of the resolution adopted at the Karachi Sesssion of the Congress in 1931 setting out the Fundamental Rights and Duties, and the socio-economic objectives, which should be included in any future Constitution).

This Congress is of opinion that to enable the masses to appreciate what 'Swaraj', as conceived by the Congress, will

mean to them, it is desirable to state the position of the Congress in a manner easily understood by them. In order to end the exploitation of the masses, political freedom must include real economic freedom of the starving millions. The Congress therefore declares that any constitution which may be agreed to on its behalf should provide, or enable the Swaraj government to provide, for the following :

FUNDAMENTAL RIGHTS AND DUTIES

1. (i) Eevery citizen of India has the right of free expression and opinion, the right of free association and combination, and the right to assemble peacefully and without arms, for purposes not opposed to law or morality.

(ii) Every citizen shall enjoy freedom of conscience and the right freely to profess and practise his religion, subject to public order and morality.

(iii) The culture, language and script of the minorities and the different linguistic areas shall be protected.

(iv) All citizens are equal before the law irrespective of religion, caste, creed or sex.

(v) No disability attaches to any citizen by reason of his or her religion, creed or sex in regard to public employment, office of power or honour, and in the exercise of any trade or calling.

(vi) All citizens have equal rights and duties in regard to wells, tanks, roads, schools and places of public resort maintained out of State or local funds or dedicated by private persons for the use of the general public.

(vii) Every citizen has the right to keep and bear arms, in accordance with the regulations and reservations made in that behalf.

(viii) No person shall be deprived of his liberty nor shall his dwelling or property be entered, sequestered or confiscated save in accordance with law.

(ix) The State shall observe neutrality in regard to all religions.

(x) The franchise shall be on the basis of universal adult suffrage.

(xi) The State shall provide for free and compulsory primary education,

(xii) The State shall confer no titles.

(xiii) There shall be no capital punishment.

(xiv) Every citizen is free to move throughout India and to stay and settle in any part thereof, to acquire property and to follow any trade or calling, and be treated equally with regard to legal prosecution or protection in all parts of India.

LABOUR

2. (a) The organisation of economic life must conform to the principles of justice, to the end that it may secure a decent standard of living.

(b) The State shall safeguard the interests of industrial workers and shall secure for them, by suitable legislation and in other ways, a living wage, healthy conditions of work, limited hours of labour, suitable machinary for the settlement of disputes between the employers and workmen, and protection against the economic consequences of old age, sickness and unemployment.

3. Labour to be freed from serfdom and conditions bordering on serfdom.
4. Protection of women workers and, specially, adequate provision for leave during maternity period.
5. Children of school-going age shall not be employed in mines and factories.
6. Peasants and workers shall have the right to form unions to protect their interests.

TAXATION AND EXPENDITURE

7. The system of land tenure and revenue and rent shall be reformed and an equitable adjustment made of the

burden on agricultural land, immediately giving relief to the smaller peasantry by a substantial reduction of agricultural rent and revenue now paid by them, and in cases of uneconomic holdings exempting them from rent so long as necessary, with such reilef as may be just and necessary to holders of small estates affected by such exemption or reduction in rent, and, to the same end, imposing a graded tax on net incomes from land above a reasonable minimum.

8. Death duties on a graduated scale shall be levied on property above a fixed minimum.
9. There shall be drastic reduction of military expenditure so as to bring it down to at least one half of the present scale.
10. Expenditure and salaries in civil departments shall be largely reduced. No servant of the State, other than specially employed experts and the like, shall be paid above a certain fixed figure, which should not ordinarily exceed Rs. 500 per month.
11. No duty shall be levied on salt manufactured in India.

ECONOMIC AND SOCIAL PROGRAMME

12. The State shall protect indigenous cloth; and for this purpose pursue the policy of exclusion of foreign cloth and foreign yarn from the country and adopt such other measures as may be found necessary. The State shall also protect indigenous industries, when necessary, against foreign competition.
13. Intoxicating drinks and drugs shall be totally prohibited except for medicinal purposes.
14. Currency and exchange shall be regulated in the national interest.
15. The State shall own or control key industries and services, mineral resources, railways, waterways, shipping and other means of public transport.
16. Relief of agricultural indebtedness and control of usury, direct and indirect.
17. The State shall provide for military training of citizens

so as to organise a means of national defence apart from the regular military force.

(*iv*) INDEPENDENCE PLEDGE

(*Text of the pledge taken by by the people of India at thousands of meetings throughout the country on 26 January 1930.*)

We believe that it is the inalienable right of the Indian people, as of any other people, to have freedom and to enjoy the fruits of their toil and have necessities of life, so that they may have full opportunities of growth. We believe also that if any Government deprives a people of these rights and oppresses them, the people have a further right to alter it or to abolish it. The British Government in India has not only deprived the Indian people of their freedom but has based itself on the exploitation of the masses, and has ruined India economically, politically, culturally and spiritually. We believe, therefore, that India must sever the British conncetion and attain Purna Swaraj or Complete Independence.

India has been ruined economically. The revenue derived from our people is out of all proportion to our income. Our average income is seven pice (less than two pence) per day, and of the heavy taxes we pay 20 per cent are raised from the Land Revenue derived from the peasantry, and 3 per cent from the Salt Tax, which falls most heavily on the poor.

Village industries, such as hand-spinning, have been destroyed, leaving the peasantry idel for at least four months in the year, and dulling their intellect for want of handicrafts, and nothing has been substituted, as in other countries, for the crafts thus destroyed.

Customs and currency have been so manipulated as to heap further burdens on the peasantry. British manufactured goods constitute the bulk of our imports. Customs duties betray clear partiality for British manufactures, and revenue from them is used not to lessen the burden on the masses but for sustaining a highly extravagant administration. Still more arbitrary has been the manipulation of the exchange ratio which has resulted in millions being drained away from the country.

Politically, India's status has never been so reduced as

under the British regime. No reforms have given real political power to the people. The tallest of us have to bend before foreign authority. The rights of free expression on opinion and free association have been denied to us, and many of our countrymen are compelled to live in exile abroad and cannot return to their homes. All administrative talent is killed and the masses have to be satisfied with petty village offices and clerkships.

Culturally, the system of education has torn us from our moorings and our training has made us hug the very chains that bind us.

Spiritually, compulsory disarmament has made us unmanly and the presence of an alien army of occupation, employed with deadly effect to crush in us the spirit of resistance, has made us think that we cannot look after oureselves or put up a defence against foreign aggression, our even defend our homes and families from the attacks of thieves, robbers and miscreants.

We hold it to be a crime against man and God to submit any longer to a rule that has caused this four-fold disaster to our country. We recognies, however, that the most effective way of gaining our freedom is not through violence. We will, therefore, prepare ourselves by withdrawing, so far as we can all voluntary association from the British Government, and will prepare for Civil Disobedience, including non-payment of taxes. We are convinced that if we can but withdraw our voluntary help and stop payment of taxes without doing violence, even under provocation, the end of this inhuman rule is assured. We, therefore, hereby solemnly resolve to carry out the Congress instructions issued from time to time for the purpose of establishing *Purna Swaraj*.

(*v*) 'QUIT INDIA' RESOLUTION

(Excerpts from the resolution adopted by the All India Congress Committee at Bombay on 8 August 1942)

The immediate ending of British rule in India is an urgent necessity, both for the sake of India and for the success of the cause of the United Nations. The continuation of that rule is

degrading and enfeebling India and making her progressively less capable of defending herself and of contributing to the cause of world freedom.

India, the classic land of modern imperialism, has become the crux of the question, for by the freedom of India will Britain and the United Nations be judged, and the people of Asia and Africa be filled with hope and enthusiasm. The ending of British rule in this country is thus a vital and immediate issue on which depends the future of the war and the success of freedom and democracy. A free India will assure the success by throwing all her great resources in the struggle for freedom and against the aggression of Nazism, fascism and imperialism. This will not only affect materially the fortunes of the war, but will bring all subject and oppressed humanity on the side of the United Nations and give these Nations, whose ally India would be, the moral and spiritual leadership of the world. India in bondage will continue to be the symbol of British imperialism and the taint of that imperialism will affect the fortunes of all the United Nations.

The A.I.C.C. therefore repeats with all emphasis the demand for the withdrawal of the British power from India. On the declaration of India's independence, a Provisional Government will be formed and Free India will become an ally of the United Nations, sharing with them in the trials and tribulations of the joint enterprise of the struggle for freedom. The Provisional Government can only be formed by the cooperation of the principal parties and groups in the country.

The freedom of India must be the symbol of and prelude to the freedom of all other Asiatic nations under foreign dominations. Burma, Malaya, Indo-China, the Dutch Indies, Iran, Iraq must also attain their complete freedom. It must be clearly understood that such of these countries as are under Japanese control now must not subsequently be placed under rule or control of any other colonial power.

The reaction of the British Government and the misguided criticisms in the foreign Press also make it clear that even the obvious demand for India's independence is resisted, though this has been made essentially to meet the present peril and to enable India to defence herself and help China

and Russia in their hour of need. The Committee is anxious not to embarrass in any way the defence of China or Russia, whose freedom is precious and must be preserved, or to jeopardise the defensive capacity of the United Nations.

The A.I.C.C. would yet again, at this last moment, in the interest of world freedom, renew this appeal to Britain and the United Nations. But the Committee feels that it is no longer justified in holding the nation back from endeavouring to assert its will against an imperialist and authoritarian government which dominates over it and prevents it from functioning in its own interest and in the interest of humanity. The Committee resolves, therefore, to sanction for the vindication of India's inalienable right to freedom and independence, the starting of mass struggle on non-violent lines on the widest possible scale, so that the country might utilise all the non-violent strength it has gathered during the last 22 years of peaceful struggle. Such a struggle must inevitably be under the leadership of Gandhiji and the Committee requests him to take the lead and guide the nation in the steps to be taken.

The Committee appeals to the people of India to face the dangers and hardships that will fall to their lot with courage and endurance, and to hold together under the leadership of Gandhiji, and carry out his instructions as disciplined soldiers of Indian freedom. They must remember that non-violence is the basis of this movement. A time may come when it may not be possible to issue instructions or for instructions to reach our people, and when no Congress Commitiee can function. When this happens, every man and women who is participating in this movement must function for himself or herself within the four corners of the general instructions issued. Every Indian who desires freedom and strives for it must be his own guide urging him on along the hard road where there is no resting place and which leads ultimately to the independence and deliverance of India.

Lastly, while the A.I.C.C. has stated its own view of the future government under free India, the A.I.C.C. wishes to make it quite clear to all concerned that by embarking on mass struggle it has no intention of gaining power for the Congress. The power, when it comes. will belong to the whole people of India.

(*vi*) THE APPOINTED DAY

(*A message issued through the Press by Jawaharlal Nehru, 15 August 1947.*)

The appointed day has come—the day appointed by destiny—and India stands forth again, after long slumber and struggle, awake, vital, free and independent. The past clings on to us still in some measure and we have to do much before we redeem the pledges we have so often taken. Yet the turning point is past, and history begins anew for us, the history which we shall live and act and others will write about.

It is a fateful moment for us in India, for all-Asia and for the world. A new star rises, the star of freedom in the East, a new hope comes into being, a vision long cherished materializes. May the star never set and that hope never be betrayed !

We rejoice in that freedom, even though clouds surround us, and many of our people are sorrow-stricken and difficult problems encompass us. But freedom brings responsibilities and burdens and we have to face them in the spirit of a free and disciplined people.

On this day our first thoughts go to the architect of this freedom, the Father of our Nation, who, embodying the old spirit of India, held aloft the torch of freedom and lighted up the darkness that surrounded us. We have often been unworthy followers of his and have strayed from his message, but not only we but succeeding generations will remember this message and bear the imprint in their hearts of this great son of India, magnificent in his faith and strength and courage and humility. We shall never allow that torch of freedom to be blown out, however high the wind or stormy the tempest.

Our next thoughts must be of the unknown volunteers and soldiers of freedom who, without praise or reward, have served India even unto death.

We think also of our brothers and sisters who have been cut off from us by political boundaries and who unhappily cannot share at present in the freedom that has come. They are of us and will remain of us whatever may happen, and we shall be sharers in their good and ill fortune alike.

The future beckons to us. Whither do we go and what shall be our endeavour ? To bring freedom and opportunity to the common man, to the peasants and workers of India; to fight and end poverty and ignorance and disease; to build up a prosperous, democratic and progressive nation, and to create social, economic and political institutions which will ensure justice and fullness of life to every man and woman.

We have hard work ahead. There is no resting for any one of us till we redeem our pledge in full, till we make all the people of India what destiny intended them to be. We are citizens of a great country, on the verge of bold advance, and we have to live up to that high standard. All of us, to whatever religion we may belong, are equally the children of India with equal rights, privileges and obligations. We cannot encourage communalism or narrow-mindedness, for no nation can be great whose people are narrow in thought or in action.

To the nations and peoples of the world we send greetings and pledge ourselves to co-operate with them in furthering peace, freedom and democracy.

And to India, our much-loved motherland, the ancient, the eternal and the ever-new, we pay our reverent homage and we bind ourselves to her service. *Jai Hind.*

(*vii*) PREAMBLE TO THE CONSTITUTION OF INDIA

(India ceased to be a Dominion of the British Commonwealth and became a republic on 26 January 1950, when the new Constitution framed by the Constituent Assembly came into force.)

We, the people of India, having solemnly resolved to constitute India into a Sovereign Democratic Republic and to secure to all its citizens :

Justice, social, economic and political;

Liberty of thought, expression, belief, faith and worship;

Equality of status and of opportunity; and to promote among them all ;

Fraternity assuring the dignity of the individual and the unity of the Nation;

In our Constituent Assembly this twenty-sixth day of November, 1949, do Hereby Adopt, Enact and give to Ourselves this Constitution.

BIBLIOGRAPHY

(This Bibliography is limited to a selection from out of books that are likely to be of interest to the general reader in India and outside).

An Autobiography by Jawaharlal Nehru, Jawaharlal Nehru Memorial Fund, 1980.

The Discovery of India by Jawaharlal Nehru, Jawaharlal Nehru Memorial Fund, 1981.

Eighteen Fifty-Seven by S.N. Sen, Publications Division, 1957.

Gandhi : A Pictorial Biography by B.R. Nanda, Publications Division, 1972.

The Great Integrators by V. Raghavan, Publications Division, 1969.

History of the Freedom Movement in India by R.C. Majumdar, Vols. 1 & 2, Firma K.L. Mukhopadhyaya, 1963.

History of the Freedom Movement in India by Tara Chand, Vols. 1-4, Publications Division, 1965-72.

India Wins Freedom by Maulana Abul Kalam Azad, Longmans Green, 1960.

Indian Heritage by Humayun Kabir, Asia Publishing House, 1955.

India's Struggle for Independence : Visuals & Documents, National Council of Educational Research & Training 1985.

Jawaharlal Nehru : A Pictorial Biography by B.R. Nanda, Publications Division, 1980.

Jawaharlal Nehru : A Biography by S. Gopal, in three volumes, O.U.P., 1975-84.

Rammohun Roy by Iqbal Singh, Vol. I, Asia Publishing House, 1983.

Sources of Indian Tradition ed. by Wm. Theodore de Bary, Motilal Banarsidass, 1963.

The Story of My Experiments with Truth : An Autobiography by M.K. Gandhi, Navajivan Publishing House, 1927.

Subhas Chandra Bose : Selected Speeches with an Introduction by S.A. Ayer, Publications Division, 1965.

INDEX

Index

U

V

W